CONTROVERSIES IN PHILOSOPHY

The Is-Ought Question

CONTROVERSIES IN PHILOSOPHY
General Editor A. G. N. Flew

Forthcoming titles in the series

Published

THE IS-OUGHT QUESTION
Edited by W. D. Hudson

In preparation

THE MIND–BRAIN IDENTITY THEORY
Edited by C. V. Borst

PHILOSOPHY AND LINGUISTICS
Edited by Colin Lyas

WEAKNESS OF WILL
Edited by Geoffrey Mortimer

THE PRIVATE LANGUAGE ARGUMENT
Edited by O. R. Jones

The
Is-Ought
Question

A COLLECTION OF PAPERS ON THE CENTRAL PROBLEM IN MORAL PHILOSOPHY

EDITED BY

W. D. Hudson

CONTRIBUTORS
G. E. M. Anscombe, R. F. Atkinson, Max Black, Antony Flew
Philippa Foot, Kenneth Hanly, R. M. Hare, W. D. Hudson
Geoffrey Hunter, B. P. Komisar, J. E. McClellan
A. C. MacIntyre, H. O. Mounce, D. Z. Phillips, J. R. Searle
James Thomson, Judith Thomson, M. Zimmerman

MACMILLAN

First published 1969 *by*
MACMILLAN AND CO LTD
Little Essex Street London WC2
and also at Bombay Calcutta and Madras
Macmillan South Africa (Publishers) Pty Ltd Johannesburg
The Macmillan Company of Australia Pty Ltd Melbourne
The Macmillan Company of Canada Ltd Toronto
Gill and Macmillan Ltd Dublin

Printed in Great Britain by
WESTERN PRINTING SERVICES LTD
Bristol

Foreword by the General Editor

The series of which the present volume is the first member consists largely but not entirely of material already published elsewhere in scattered sources. It is as a series distinguished by two guiding ideas. First, the individual editors of the various constituent volumes select and collect contributions to some important controversy which in recent years has been, and which still remains, alive. The emphasis is thus upon controversy, and upon the presentation of philosophers in controversial action. Second, the individual editors are encouraged to edit extensively and strongly. The idea is that they should act as firm, fair, and constructive chairmen. Such a chairman gives shape to a discussion and ensures that the several contributors are not merely heard, but heard at the moment when their contributions can be most relevant and most effective. With this in mind the contributions as they appear in these volumes are arranged neither in the chronological order of their first publication nor in any other and arbitrary sequence, but in such a way as to provide and to reveal some structure and development in the whole argument. Again, and for similar reasons, the editorial introductions are both substantial and forthcoming.

They can be seen as representing a deliberate rejection, at least within this special limited context, of the 'throw-a-reading-list-at-them, send-them-away, and-see-next-week-whatever-they-have-made-of-it' tutorial traditions of some ancient British universities.

The present first volume, organised and orchestrated by Dr W. D. Hudson, constitutes an excellent paradigm. For the controversy which he presents deals with what can very reasonably be regarded as the central problem in moral philosophy. Dr Hudson himself claims that it is just that. Again, he presents the contributions in a coherent development; and he is not ashamed in his 'Editor's Introduction' to undertake the pedagogic spadework of explaining painstakingly both what this movement is and how each chosen contribution fits into it.

Four other volumes in the present series will be published simultaneously or not long after, and some others are less definitively on the way. As General Editor I shall be glad to consider other possibilities, whether the suggestions come from colleagues who would like to do the editorial work themselves or whether they are made by others who as teachers feel a need which they would like someone else to fill.

ANTONY FLEW

University of Keele,
Staffordshire,
England

Contents

Contents

Acknowledgements

I should like to express my sincere thanks to all the authors who have allowed me to use their papers in this collection. The journals in which the papers first appeared are as follows.

I. The *Philosophical Review*, LXVIII (1959). II. The *Philosophical Review*, LXX (1961). III. *Philosophy*, XXXVII (1962). IV. *Philosophy*, XXXVIII (1963). V. *Philosophy*, XXXVIII (1963). VI. The *Philosophical Quarterly*, 14 (1964). VII. *Mind*, LXXI (1962). VIII. *Mind*, LXXIII (1964). IX. *Mind*, LXXVI (1967). X. The *Philosophical Review*, LXXIII (1964). XI. *Analysis*, 25 (1964). XII. The *Philosophical Review*, LXXIII (1964). XIII. *Analysis*, 25 (1964). XIV. *Revue Internationale de Philosophie*, no. 70 (1964). XV. *Analysis*, 25 (1964). XVI. The *Philosophical Review*, LXXIII (1964). XVII. *Analysis*, 25 (1965). XVIII. *Philosophy*, XXXIII (1958). XIX. *Proceedings of the Aristotelian Society*, LIX (1958). XX. *Proceedings of the Aristotelian Society*, suppl. vol. XXXV (1961). XXI. *Philosophy*, XL (1965). XXII. *Proceedings of the British Academy* (1963).

My thanks are due to the editors and publishers of all these journals for permission to reprint. I am also indebted to our departmental secretary, Mrs A. Smith, and to my wife, for assistance with the correspondence and typing necessarily involved in preparing a collection such as this.

W. D. HUDSON

Department of Philosophy,
University of Exeter

Editor's Introduction:
The 'is-ought' problem

W. D. Hudson

The central problem in moral philosophy is that commonly known as the *is-ought* problem. How is what *is* the case related to what *ought* to be the case – statements of fact to moral judgements?

Shall we say that moral judgements themselves are statements of fact? At first blush, some of them certainly appear to be. The sentence 'This action is right' is very like the sentence 'This apple is red'. The latter simply describes an apple. Does the former simply describe an action? Some philosophers have supposed it to do so. They have recognised, of course, that rightness is a very different sort of property from redness: we see redness in a literal physical sense, but when we speak of 'seeing' the rightness of an action, we are not using the verb in exactly the same sense. Allowing for this by postulating a faculty of moral intuition in men, the philosophers referred to have held that 'This action is right' states a moral fact just as 'This apple is red' states a physical, and that both statements are similarly capable of being either true or false. Moral judgements, they say, are simply a sub-class of statements of fact.[1] But now notice this. Saying 'This apple is red' is perfectly compatible with instructing or advising someone to do or not do practically anything with it. 'Eat it!', 'Don't eat it!' 'Paint it!', 'Don't paint it!', etc. etc. – it would not strike us as odd to utter such imperatives after 'This apple is red'. If, however, someone were to say 'This act is right, but don't do it', or '... but keep it dark!' or '... but try to get other people to stop doing it!' or '... but I'm sorry it has been done', we should be puzzled, should we not? I do not deny that these remarks could make sense in certain contexts; but, to say the least, if we heard any of them in isolation, we should feel that they needed further explanation. When people say 'This action is right', they *normally*

---

[1] On some of the philosophers referred to see my *Ethical Intuitionism* (1967).

want it to be done or are registering satisfaction that it has been done. That is why the remarks which I quoted a moment ago seem odd. So, although 'This apple is red and 'This action is right' are grammatically – syntactically – identical in form, the question arises as to whether or not they have precisely the same kind of *meaning*. There seem to be limits on the kind of thing which it ordinarily makes sense to say when you have uttered a moral judgement, which do not restrict what can come naturally after making a statement of physical fact. Such considerations as these have convinced many modern moral philosophers[2] that it is quite mistaken to suppose that moral judgements are a sub-class of factual statements. The job they do is different. When you say that something is good, or right, or such as ought to be done, you are not describing. You are evaluating, prescribing, advising, registering an attitude to, that to which you apply these moral expressions. Wittgenstein warned against confusing the real and the apparent logical forms of a proposition.[3] And it became fashionable in contemporary moral philosophy to say that there is really a logical divide – a radical difference of meaning – between 'is' and 'ought' however closely the sentences in which such expressions get used may resemble one another in appearance.

Suppose we accept this and refuse to regard what ought to be the case as simply one aspect of what is the case. The question nevertheless remains: how are moral judgements and statements of fact *related* to one another? Whenever people talk or argue about what they choose to regard as a moral issue, it will be found that they use *is* and *ought* in very close conjunction (or expressions logically similar to these respectively). Let us consider this example:

A: 'Religion ought not to be taught in schools.'
B: 'Why?'
A: 'Because the subject is debatable and there is room for doubt about it.'
B: 'But aren't science and history debatable? Would you ban them?'
A: 'Of course not. There is general agreement about them.'
B: 'So you're saying that we ought to teach beliefs provided the majority of people accept them?'
A: 'Not at all. I'm saying that children in school haven't de-

[2] E.g. R. M. Hare, *The Language of Morals* (Oxford 1952) and P. H. Nowell-Smith, *Ethics* (1954).
[3] For a brief discussion of this see my paperback *Ludwig Wittgenstein* (Lutterworth 1968) p. 55.

veloped their intelligence sufficiently to consider religion critically.'

B: 'You don't know much about children. Some of the most penetrating and difficult questions about God are asked by children.'

Any snatch of dialogue such as that illustrates how moral argument veers from ought-judgements to is-statements and back again. Some modern philosophers[4] hold that every step in such an argument involves the application of what may be called the moral, or practical, syllogism. For example, from 'Religion *is* debatable' you can move logically to 'Religion *ought* not to be taught in schools' only by invoking the premise 'Whatever is debatable *ought* not to be taught in schools'. In other words, you cannot derive an 'ought' directly from an 'is'. The syllogism in the above example is:

Major Premise (Universal Ought Principle): Whatever is debatable ought not to be taught in schools.
Minor Premise (Is-Statement): Religion is debatable.
Conclusion (Particular Ought-Judgement): Religion ought not to be taught in schools.

This, the argument runs, is how it always has to be in *valid* moral reasoning. The premises must include an 'ought' if the conclusion is to do so.

The philosophers who consider that there is a logical gulf between 'is' and 'ought' in the two ways which I have been discussing – (i) 'ought' cannot be *reduced* to 'is'; (ii) 'ought' cannot be *derived* from 'is' – are challenged today by what appears to be an ever increasing number of their professional colleagues. Can they legitimately claim, as they do claim, that they are simply saying what the great David Hume said? Are they correct in thinking that the job which *ought* does is logically so unlike that which *is* does? Is there really no way of deriving *ought* logically from *is*? Have they rightly understood the logical character of the factual statements which are made in the course of moral reasoning? These are the questions with which the four sections of this collection are concerned respectively. These questions throw the whole *is-ought* problem wide open and have of late been the subject of lively controversy in the leading philosophical journals. The two sides of the argument – those who say that there is an unbridgeable gap between 'is' and 'ought' and those who say that there is not – are represented in each section. What I hope the reader will find here is a

[4] E.g. Hare, *Language of Morals*.

clear and detailed picture of how the debate has gone and is going.
He will find that these papers shed light on many aspects of moral
philosophy. As a collection, they constitute a paradigm case of
philosophical discussion as it is conducted amongst analytical philosophers at the present day.

It may be of use to some readers, if I offer a brief conspectus of
the discussion so that they can see, before embarking upon the
detail of the papers, what its main lines are. This I will now attempt
to do.

HAS HUME BEEN CORRECTLY INTERPRETED ON IS-OUGHT?

Professor MacIntyre (Paper I) rejects the standard interpretation of
Hume's *is-ought* passage. He recalls that Hume's famous doubts
about induction were based on the assumption that an inference
must be either deductive or defective; and that modern philosophers, not finding that assumption acceptable, have criticised Hume
for harbouring his doubts. Is it not surprising, asks MacIntyre, that
these same philosophers praise Hume for his contention that it is
logically impossible to deduce 'ought' from 'is', a contention which,
on their interpretation of it, carries the implication that any valid
inference from 'is' to 'ought' must be either deductive or defective?
MacIntyre's point, however, is not that Hume should be condemned, rather than praised, for the *is-ought* passage; it is that this
passage has been seriously misinterpreted by contemporary philosophers. They should have seen that Hume was not intent upon
exposing an unbridgeable gap between 'is' and 'ought', but simply
upon showing how an inference from the one to the other could,
and should, be drawn.

MacIntyre attributes to Hume this view:

> 'To say that we ought to do something is to affirm that there
> is a commonly accepted rule; and the existence of such a rule
> presupposes a consensus of opinion as to where our common in-
> terests lie. An obligation is constituted in part by such a consensus
> and the concept of "ought" is logically dependent on the concept
> of a common interest and can only be explained in terms of it.'
> (below, p. 41).

Such a view seems to reduce 'ought' to 'is' and to be plainly
inconsistent with the standard interpretation of Hume's *is-ought*
passage. MacIntyre thinks that this inconsistency should have been
enough to make philosophers question that standard interpretation.
What alternative interpretation, then, does he propose? In the *is-*

ought passage, Hume said that it 'seems altogether inconceivable'
how 'ought' 'can be a deduction from' 'is'. The standard interpretation takes the former phrase to be an example of Hume's famous
irony (what he really meant was that it is beyond dispute inconceivable); and it takes 'deduction' to mean logical entailment. But,
against this, MacIntyre sees no reason to agree that Hume was being
ironical here. And, with regard to Hume's word 'deduction', he
contends that it did not mean in Hume's day what it means in ours;
in eighteenth-century usage it was a synonym for 'inference', not
for 'entailment'. From such considerations, MacIntyre proceeds to
the conclusion that Hume was simply claiming, in the *is-ought* passage, that others had given a mistaken account of what the facts,
from which moral judgements can be inferred, are and that his own
account of them was the correct one. Hume's quarrel, that is to say,
was with what he called 'the vulgar systems of morality', by which
he meant the religious morality of his day. According to the latter,
the judgement that X ought to be done can be inferred from the
belief that God has commanded X to be done. This was the inference which Hume was rejecting, says MacIntyre. He was 'repudiating a religious foundation for morality and putting in its place
a foundation in human needs, interests, desires, and happiness'
(below, p. 46).

How do we know that this is what Hume was doing? MacIntyre's
answer appears to be twofold: (i) We know that Hume had read in
his youth religious writings which offered as the ground for our
obligation to help others such religious beliefs as that it was God's
purpose in giving men the ability to help others that this ability
should be used; and (ii) we find Hume saying, in the section immediately preceding the *is-ought* passage, that no matter of fact can
serve as a reason for acting except those facts which he calls the
passions, i.e. needs, desires, interests, and so on. We are entitled,
then, to conclude, according to MacIntyre, that what Hume intended to say was that religious moralists fail to realise that morality
finds its logical foundation in such facts concerning man, rather
than in the facts of God's law or purpose. From the facts that doing
X is what men want or need, what will serve their common interest
or achieve their health and happiness, it follows that X ought to be
done. These, Hume would have said, according to MacIntyre, are
the 'bridge notions' of moral reasoning, rather than those universal
moral principles which enable us to derive particular moral judgements from statements of fact in the practical syllogisms invented by
philosophers such as Hare. In this, MacIntyre contends, Hume was

at one with the inventor of the practical syllogism, for in Aristotle's examples of the latter we usually have a premise which includes some such term as 'suits' or 'pleases'.

Professor Atkinson (Paper II) challenges MacIntyre's interpretation of Hume at a number of points. He takes Hume's 'seems altogether inconceivable' as a typical example of the latter's irony, though he concedes that this is a matter of opinion. Against MacIntyre's account of what 'deduction' meant in Hume's day, he calls Reid, Hume's contemporary, to witness. Reid took Hume's 'deduction' in the *is-ought* passage to mean entailment. MacIntyre argues that the 'vulgar' systems of morality, which Hume was intent upon subverting, were those of popular religion and he explicitly contrasts these with systems such as that of the philosopher, Wollaston. But Atkinson points to a passage in Hume where the disagreement *amongst philosophers* about the respective degrees of self-love and benevolence in human nature is described as a 'vulgar' dispute. And he notes that, at the beginning of the *is-ought* passage itself, Hume calls in question 'every system' of morality. These references suggest that Hume's adjective 'vulgar' may be pejorative rather than classificatory; and if so, there is no ground for MacIntyre's assurance that Hume's quarry in the *is-ought* passage was simply popular religious morality – or, at least, for the view that this conclusion can be deduced merely from Hume's use of 'vulgar'.

To take another point in Atkinson's reply, there is the question: How in fact did Hume dispose of Wollaston's system? Wollaston believed that all immoral behaviour is, in the last analysis, lying. If, for instance, I steal someone's property, I implicitly deny that it is his property. My action contradicts how things are – is an untruth – and this constitutes its wrongness. Similarly, if I fail to show a benefactor gratitude, I deny that he is my benefactor. And so on. All immorality is falsehood. Hume pointed out that this 'whimsical system' leaves us with the question unanswered: Why is falsehood wrong? It fails, according to Hume, because the facts – how things are – cannot provide a logical basis for morality apart from some principle to the effect that these facts ought not to be denied. In other words, 'ought' cannot be deduced from 'is'.[5] This argument of Hume's is entirely in line with the standard interpretation of the *is-ought* passage and reinforces the opinion that the latter is correct.

Mr Hunter's attack (Paper III) on the standard interpretation is less subtle and involved than MacIntyre's. He cites these words of Hume from the passage immediately preceding that on *is-ought*:

[5] See my *Ethical Intuitionism*, pp. 38–41, on Wollaston.

'when you pronounce any action or character to be vicious, *you mean nothing but* that from the constitution of your nature you have a feeling or sentiment of blame from the contemplation of it' (below, p. 59; italics mine). Hunter takes this to imply that Hume's central point was that moral judgements simply *are* statements of fact to the effect that there is a causal relationship between the speaker's contemplation of some actual or imagined state of affairs and having certain feelings about it. On this view, Hume took ought-propositions to be logically equivalent to certain is-propositions, which is plainly at variance with the standard interpretation of the *is-ought* passage. What then was Hume doing in that passage? According to Hunter, he was simply summing up his moral philosophy to the effect that what has seemed inconceivable to others has been shown by him to be perfectly conceivable. It is perfectly possible to deduce 'ought' from 'is' because ought-propositions are simply disguised is-propositions. Hunter adds that he thinks this view of Hume's is mistaken because there follows from it the conclusion that if I say that X ought to be done and you say that it ought not, we are not necessarily contradicting one another. All I may mean is that X causes me to feel praise, and all you may mean is that X causes you to feel blame – both of which may be true. This is surely at variance with the facts of moral argument; disputes about what ought to be done are real disagreements. However, in his second contribution (Paper V) Hunter goes back on this criticism of Hume.

Professor Flew (Paper IV) takes Hunter to task on two main grounds. First, he points out that, even if the standard interpretation of the *is-ought* passage renders it inconsistent with certain views of Hume's, it does not follow that therefore the standard interpretation is wrong. Hume may simply have been contradicting himself. We certainly need good reason for such an accusation where philosophers of Hume's stature are concerned, but Hunter begs the question by his presumption that the charge could not conceivably be made to stick. However, Flew goes on to say that he does not think Hume was inconsistent, only that Hunter is mistaken in his interpretation of the passage which he (Hunter) has quoted (see above). The burden of Hume's argument in that passage was, according to Flew, *not* that moral judgements are logically equivalent to statements of fact about human feelings, though Hume's words may appear to bear that meaning on their face. Says Flew (p. 66): 'It would be so much better to say that Hume's central insight was: that moral judgements are *not* statements of *either* logically necessary truths *or* facts about the natural (or supernatural) universe around us; *and, hence,* that "All morality depends upon our sentiments" (*Treatise* III. ii. 5)' (p. 66). The crux of the matter is what 'depends' means here. One view could be that moral judgements *report* the fact that those who utter them have certain feelings; another, that they *express* the feelings of those who utter them.

Flew's second ground for rejecting Hunter's case is his conviction that the words which Hunter quotes and much else in Hume's moral philosophy will bear the latter meaning. In support of this, he cites, among other passages, Hume's words from the first appendix to his second *Inquiry*: 'when we *express* that detestation against him [Nero] ...we *feel* sentiments...' (p. 68 – Flew's italics). This seems to say that moral judgements are expressions, not statements, of feeling. If this is what Hume thought, then he was, as Flew maintains, the precursor of modern subjectivists or emotivists, such as Stevenson, and indeed of all philosophers who consider moral discourse to be fundamentally not descriptive but expressive or evaluative. As such, Hume would have held that 'ought' cannot be deduced from 'is'. If Flew's account of Hume's ethical theory is correct, then the standard interpretation of the *is-ought* passage is, if somewhat less than incontrovertible, at any rate plausible.

In my own contribution (Paper VI) to this discussion of Hume, I try to draw its main threads together and to bring out what appear to me to be salient points for a correct understanding of the *is-ought* passage. I emphasise the importance of setting Hume's remark in the context of the eighteenth-century debate about the nature of moral judgements to which it purported to contribute. His real quarry was the rational intuitionism of writers such as Cudworth, Clarke and Price. They thought that moral judgements attribute objective properties to actions or states of affairs, these being self-evident to reason. In other words, moral judgements describe matters of fact, though of special 'non-natural' (to use the word favoured by later intuitionists) fact. The section in which the *is-ought* passage occurs is headed 'Moral distinctions not derived from reason'; and there is good ground for believing that it was this prevalent rational intuitionism which Hume was mainly out to subvert.

In the *is-ought* passage, Hume says that he has been listening to the uses made of 'is' and 'ought' and has been surprised by them. I ask: what surprised him? Simply that some managed to hold religious beliefs concerning God's law or purpose? No: he says explicitly enough that his surprise has to do with 'every system' of morality, not just the 'vulgar' ones. It is surely incorrect to interpret his surprise in such a way that the simple substitution of factual

statements about human feelings for those about God would suffice
to dispose of it. I air a number of doubts about the quotation from
MacIntyre, given above on page 14, which purports to give Hume's
view of what we are saying when we say that we ought to do something. To say this is to say, according to those words of MacIntyre's,
that there is a commonly accepted rule based upon a consensus of
opinion as to where our interests lie. Without, of course, denying
that Hume finds a very close connexion between the notions of
obligation and common interest, I give reasons for thinking that
he did not wish to reduce the one to the other. I try to draw what I
consider to be a vital distinction between what logically constitutes
morality and the circumstances in which it occurs; and I contend
that Hume was alive to this. It is undoubtedly true that moral
judgements occur where men have feelings, interests, needs, desires,
etc. – what MacIntyre calls 'bridge notions' (cf. above, p. 15) – but
it does not follow that such notions provide the whole logical framework of morality any more than it follows that the circumstances in
which the game of football normally takes place (e.g. in winter, for
pleasure or profit, before spectators, etc.) constitute rules of the
game. I allow that Hume may well have been opposed to religious
morality and desirous of substituting for it some form of humanism,
but I try to show that this provides no good reason for saying that
the *is-ought* passage amounts to nothing more than the recommendation of such a change. MacIntyre expressed surprise that
philosophers who decry Hume's doubts about induction because
they rest on the false assumption that reasoning is deductive or
defective should praise him for exposing a putative gap between 'is'
and 'ought' which only exists on the same assumption; but I point
out that it would surely be even *more* surprising if Hume had been
uneasy about induction because he made the assumption just referred to, but at the same time perfectly content to recommend a
move from 'is' to 'ought' which runs counter to that assumption.

Can 'Ought' be Reduced to 'Is'?

Professor Zimmerman (Paper VII) seeks to solve the *is-ought* problem by dispensing altogether with the use of 'ought'. He contends
that everything which can be achieved by ought-statements can be
achieved equally well by is-statements; and that once we see that
this is so, we are released from pointless worries about how to infer
the one from the other. Part of the time he seems to be arguing for
the psychological thesis that is-talk can be as effective in getting

people to do what we want them to do as ought-talk. We can do that, he says, by pointing out to them that if they do not do what we want them to do, things will happen to them which they do not want to happen. Again, is-discoveries, i.e. those of the psychologists, economists and sociologists, can often be used far more effectively than moral persuasion to manipulate other people for our purposes. All this may well be true, but, of course, it has no bearing on the question of how 'is' and 'ought' stand to one another logically.

However, Zimmerman does concern himself with specifically logical considerations. He asks, for example, whether it is possible to resolve disagreements between men, when they are discussing what they 'ought' to do, as it is not, when they are speaking simply of what they 'want'. If one of them says 'I want this' and another, 'I don't', that, it would seem, is that. But if one says 'I ought to do this' and another, 'You ought not', are there not ethical or moral standards to which they can appeal in order to settle the argument? There are, says Zimmerman. But then what can they appeal to if they disagree as to standards? 'Is it not [then] merely a matter of some saying we ought because we ought and others saying we ought not because we ought not?' (below, p. 85).

Another logical question which he raises is this: is it true that we can give reasons for ought-statements as we cannot for state-ments of want? Zimmerman thinks not. Suppose we are discussing a man who has committed murder whilst insane.

> What are we aiming for here in getting people to say that an insane man ought not to be punished, if other than that we do not want to and will not punish an insane man? Would it be any different if we had said that since he could not help doing what he did, we have an acceptable reason for saying that we do not want, we do not want others to want, we will not and will try to persuade others not to, punish him? Do we really think that any-body who accepts the above 'is-ought' argument as reasonable, will not do the same for the above 'is-is' argument? And if there are a few people who do not find the 'is-is' argument reasonable, do we really believe they will find the 'is-ought' argument reason-able? (below, p. 88).

Reason-giving is usually offered as one of the defining characteris-tics of moral discourse. Zimmerman is maintaining that if reason-giving is appropriate in the discussion of what ought to be done, it is equally in place in the discussion of what we want to do. Thus he seeks not so much to solve the is-ought problem as to deliver us from any concern with it by taking 'ought' out of our language.

Everything we say in terms of it, he thinks, could be said as signifi-cantly without it.

Mr Hanly's reply to all this (Paper VIII) is that even if we drop 'ought' from our language, we are still left with the problem of how two uses of is-statements are related to one another, namely the descriptive and the evaluative uses. Take the statement 'I want to do X'. This may simply say that I have a strong desire or inclination to do X. But then, whilst it makes sense to look for a *cause* of this desire, it will make no sense to demand a reason for it. On the other hand, 'I want to do X' may be used evaluatively, i.e. to select doing X from all the alternative courses of action open to the speaker. When so used, it makes perfectly good sense to ask a *reason* why I want it, i.e. why I make this particular selection. As soon as we offer a reason, we indicate implicitly standards or rules in accord-ance with which we have made the selection and anyone who agrees with us does so, not because he just happens to have the same desire as we do, but because he subscribes to the same standards or rules. It would, therefore, make perfectly good sense for someone to say 'I want to do X (i.e. in the sense that I have a desire or inclination to do it) but I do not want to do X (in the sense that it is contrary to the standards or rules of behaviour to which I subscribe)'. Reasons for what is wanted in this latter sense are logically the same kind of thing as reasons why such-and-such *ought* to be done.

Zimmerman replies very briefly to Hanly (Paper IX). He gives as the advantage in his own view the fact that, once it is accepted, we are not faced with the problem of justifying ought-statements. It seems to me that here he somewhat misses Hanly's main point – that we have the problem of justifying, i.e. giving reasons for, our evaluative judgements whether they are expressed in terms of 'ought' or 'is'. But the reader will be able to judge for himself whether or not this is fair to Zimmerman.

Can 'Ought' be Derived from 'Is'?

Professor Black (Paper X) starts his attempt to show how 'ought' – or rather 'should' in his case, though he uses this word as synony-mous with 'ought' – can be derived from 'is' by a reference to Hume's *is-ought* dichotomy, describing the latter as 'Hume's Guillo-tine'. He thinks modern philosophers have been disposed to endorse Hume's Guillotine as the result of making either or both of two mistakes: (i) they have presumed uncritically that no term (in this case 'ought') may occur in the conclusion of a valid argument which does not occur in the premises; (ii) they have taken it that ought-statements make no truth claims and presumed falsely that they are therefore not qualified to serve as either the premises or the conclusions of valid arguments. These mistakes Black attempts to expose and correct before proceeding to his positive argument. Coming to the latter, he offers this counter-example to Hume's Guillotine to begin with:

> Fischer wants to mate Botwinnik.
> The one and only way to mate Botwinnik is for Fischer to move the Queen.
> Therefore, Fischer should move the Queen.

The premises are factual; the conclusion non-factual. Black defends this counter-example against various possible lines of criticism. For example, he will not have it that the conclusion is simply a disguised factual statement to the effect that the one and only way for Fischer to win is by moving the Queen. Against this he insists on what J. L. Austin called the 'performative'[6] aspect of the above conclusion, 'Fischer should move the Queen' – in saying this 'a speaker . . . [is] doing something more than, or something other than, saying something having truth value' (below, p. 104). Precisely what more or other he is doing, as Black recognises, is a complicated question, but he contends that it is something with an evaluative and imperative force. Against another possible criticism, Black is just as unwilling to concede that the conclusion of his example, 'Fischer should move the Queen' is elliptical for some such hypothetical as 'If Fischer wants to win the game, he should move the Queen'. It is a presupposition of the argument, which does not need to be built into it, he says, that what is in question is what should be done in the game of chess. 'Given that my interlocutor is playing chess and solicits advice about the game, the fact, if it is a fact, that he can mate the opponent only by moving the Queen provides me with a *conclusive* reason for urging him to do that rather than anything else' (below, p. 109). If now we take a case where the interlocutor is seeking *moral* advice, much the same considerations apply, according to Black. He recognises that it is not possible to opt in or out of morality as it is of chess. And he argues that the main difference between the should-conclusion, which follows from exclusively is-premises, and the conclusion 'Q' in the argument, if P then Q, and that P therefore Q, is as follows. If a man refused to draw the conclusion 'Q' in the above case, we could accuse him of ignorance or stupidity; but a man could

---

[6] Cf. his *How To Do Things With Words* (Oxford 1962).

refuse to draw a moral conclusion even though he had asserted the relevant factual premises without being guilty of either. Black thinks that this possibility of refusing to give moral advice may help to explain the common assumption that moral conclusions do not follow from factual premises. But what he does insist upon is that, given the willingness to draw such a conclusion, there is only 'a single possibility' of moral advice (below, p. 111). This parallels theoretical argument. In both cases, given the relevant premises, only one conclusion follows. As an example of a valid argument from factual premises to a moral conclusion, Black offers this:

> Doing A will produce pain.
> Apart from producing the pain resulting from A, doing A will have the same consequences that not doing A would have had.
> Therefore, A ought not to be done (below, p. 113).

He challenges anyone to show 'that a person ready to make a moral judgement and accepting the premises could decline to make the moral judgement expressed by the conclusion, without thereby convicting himself of failure to understand the terms used, or some other cognitive defect' (below, p. 113).

Mr Phillips (Paper XI) challenges Black at, I think, three main points. (i) He disputes that in many typical cases where a moral conclusion follows, or appears to follow, from factual premises there is only 'a single possibility' as to what this conclusion should be. Developing Black's own example of a request for moral advice by a chess-player, A, who can win the game in circumstances where his opponent, B, is in precarious health and may be killed by the shock of defeat, Phillips adds the suppositions that B would also be upset to know that he had been 'given' a game, loves chess so much that he insists on playing it despite his doctor's advice, and so on. Is there only 'a single possibility' of moral advice in such a situation? asks Phillips. He thinks not and offers what seem to him to be a number of alternative possibilities. (ii) He concedes that '*within* a given moral viewpoint' the facts may well bind those who share it to draw the same conclusion; but he contends that there is no straightforward move from the facts to a should-conclusion. It is the moral beliefs men hold which give the facts their relevance, where moral advice is sought. It is these which limit advice to 'a single possibility' where it is so limited, not the facts as such. (iii) Phillips takes up Black's challenge to show how the conclusion of his final example could be rejected. He suggests the case of a man convinced that he ought to die for a cause, although he knows that the cause is lost; or of a soldier refusing to divulge plans to an enemy under torture, although he knows that the plans have already been discovered. If Black's reply is that the agent's regard for his moral convictions must be included in the 'consequences' referred to in his second premise, then that second premise can be reworded: 'Apart from producing the pain resulting from A, doing A will have the same *point* (not consequences) that not doing A would have had' (below, pp. 118–19, my italics). Point for the agent, that is. Then Black's challenge becomes: show that pointless pain has a point. He may certainly feel confident, says Phillips, that no one can do that, but his confidence is bought at the cost of triviality. The whole moral issue is what is to count as *pointless* pain and the facts do not tell us this.

Professor Searle's paper (Paper XII) has been the subject of much discussion. It is interesting and important, I think, for two main and closely related reasons: (i) for the detailed attempt to derive 'ought' from 'is' which the author makes; and (ii) for his discussion, in his third section, of the notion of an 'institutional fact'. From the is-statement 'Jones uttered the words 'I hereby promise to pay you, Smith, five dollars' Searle derives the ought-conclusion 'Jones ought to pay Smith five dollars' by the following steps:

(1) Jones uttered the words 'I hereby promise to pay you, Smith, five dollars'.
(2) Jones promised to pay Smith five dollars.
(3) Jones placed himself under (undertook) an obligation to pay Smith five dollars.
(4) Jones is under an obligation to pay Smith five dollars.
(5) Jones ought to pay Smith five dollars.

Says Searle: 'I shall argue concerning this list that the relation between any statement and its successor, while not in every case one of "entailment", is none the less not just a contingent relation; and the additional statements necessary to make the relationship one of entailment do not need to involve any evaluative statements, moral principles, or anything of the sort' (below, p. 121). The additional statements referred to here are as follows (below, pp. 121–4):

Between (1) and (2):
    (1a) Under certain conditions C anyone who utters the words (sentence) 'I hereby promise to pay you, Smith, five dollars' promises to pay Smith five dollars.
    (1b) Conditions C obtain.
Between (2) and (3):
    (2a) The tautological premise: All promises are acts of placing oneself under (undertaking) an obligation to do the thing promised.

Between (3) and (4):

(3a) Other things are equal.

(3b) The tautological premise: All those who place themselves under an obligation are, other things being equal, under an obligation.

Between (4) and (5):

(4a) Other things are equal.

(4b) The tautological premise: Other things being equal, one ought to do what one is under an obligation to do.

The crux of the matter is whether or not Searle is right in his contention that these extra premises are 'in no case moral or evaluative in nature', but simply 'empirical assumptions, tautologies, and descriptions of word usage' (below, p. 125).

The criticism of Searle in the papers which follow his, is addressed to that crucial question. The argument of those which precede my own is very skilful and detailed; it requires close and careful attention if it is to be followed. No brief summary could do justice to it and so I shall not attempt one. I can do no more than indicate in very general terms the main lines of the criticism.

Professors Flew (Paper XIII) and Hare (Paper XIV) concentrate their attack upon Searle's moves from (1) to (2) and (2) to (3) and concern themselves particularly with his extra premise (1a). Flew considers 'necessary and decisive' the distinction between using the word 'promise' as a detached reporter of verbal usage and as an engaged participant. If we change from being the former to being the latter, this can only be by that 'commitment to the incapsulated values which alone warrants us to draw the normative conclusions' (below, p. 30). In other words, by jumping the *is-ought* gap. Hare's argument is to similar effect. He considers in detail what Searle's premise (1a) could conceivably be. Against what he takes to be Searle's view that it is a synthetic empirical statement about English word-usage, he argues that it is, or implicitly contains, a synthetic evaluation or prescription, not merely about word-usage. To commit oneself to the institution of promising is, says Hare, to commit oneself not just verbally but morally. He relates this to the notion of an 'institutional fact'.

It may seem as if the 'brute fact' that a person has uttered a certain phonetic sequence entails the 'institutional fact' that he has promised, and that this in turn entails that he ought to do a certain thing. But this conclusion can be drawn only by one who accepts, in addition, the non-tautologous principle that one ought to keep one's promises. For unless one accepts this principle, one is not a subscribing member of the institution which it constitutes, and therefore cannot be compelled logically to accept the institutional facts which it generates in such a sense that they entail the conclusion, . . .' (below, p. 155).

Professors McClellan and Komisar (Paper XV) and Professor and Mrs Thomson (Paper XVI) direct their criticism mainly at Searle's use of *ceteris paribus* premises between (3) and (4) and (4) and (5) respectively. Searle has it that other things are equal when 'no reason . . . can in fact be given' for thinking that the obligation [at (4)] is void or the agent ought not to keep the promise [at (5)]. Where this is the case, he contends that no evaluation is involved; though if reason can be given, an evaluation will no doubt be needed. Against this McClellan and Komisar insist that 'no reason can be given' must either state a fact or register a judgement. If it simply means that at this moment someone cannot in fact give a reason why he does not have an obligation – possibly because his mouth is full of potatoes – it is surely absurd to suppose that this can make an action obligatory which would otherwise not be. Searle cannot have meant that. But if 'no reason can be given' registers a judgement, is not this necessarily evaluative? In that case, Searle has not carried through his programme of getting from 'is' to 'ought' without any premise 'evaluative in nature'. Again, Searle has it that even if his claim that the *ceteris paribus* clauses need not be evaluative is rejected, he can still rewrite his example in such a way that this clause is included in (5) and so get from 'is' to 'ought'. But the Thomsons point out that Searle says that (5) is categorical; and this is inconsistent with his present point which renders (5) hypothetical – *If* other things are equal, then Jones ought to pay Smith five dollars.

In my own contribution to this debate (Paper XVII) I endeavour to defend Searle's claim against some of Flew's criticism and, whilst conceding the validity of the criticisms offered by McClellan and Komisar and the Thomsons about Searle's use of *ceteris paribus*, I hazard the opinion that Searle could have got on very well without it in deriving (4) from (3) and (5) from (4).

ARE MORAL JUDGEMENTS DESCRIPTIVE OR EVALUATIVE?

Miss Anscombe's interesting paper (Paper XVIII) serves somewhat the function of a watershed in this collection. She touches on some of the matters discussed by previous authors in a characteristically original way. She argues, for instance, that Hume's famous *is-ought* passage reflects a situation in which the word 'ought' survives 'outside the framework of thought that made it a really intelligible one' (below, p. 181). This framework was the law-conception of ethics, the concept of 'being bound or required as by a law' (below, p. 181); which concept is only significant if you believe in God as a law-giver, like the Stoics, Jews and Christians but not Hume and his followers. Detach the term 'ought' from that background and it becomes meaningless and the problems which its continued use engenders, bogus ones. Miss Anscombe also differentiates between institutional facts (e.g. I owe the grocer £1) and relevant 'brute relative' facts (e.g. The grocer delivered the goods which I ordered). She seeks to show that some of the problems about *is-ought* may well arise from failure to recognise the logical distinction between those two types of fact. Searle (above, p. 130n.) acknowledges his indebtedness to her.

Miss Anscombe's paper also prepares the way for the others which follow. She goes so far as to say that moral philosophy 'should be laid aside . . . until we have an adequate philosophy of psychology' (below, p. 175); and she makes a beginning towards providing this. Her discussion of notions such as 'wanting', 'needing', and 'flourishing' is full of interest. Are these notions factual or non-factual? Have we already made a value judgement when we say that some state of affairs or course of action constitutes what men want or need, or what will cause them to flourish? Even if we have, are there not limitations in the facts of human existence itself upon what can intelligibly or rationally be thought of as wants or needs or flourishing? We find that Miss Anscombe sets the scene for these questions which have become of late, as they were of old, central in moral philosophy.

Mrs Foot's two papers (Papers XIX and XX) have also been very influential. In the first, 'Moral Beliefs', she challenges the assumptions commonly made about evaluation (ought) by those who differentiate it sharply from description (is): namely, that (i) a man can (logically) propose his own criteria of evaluation, even though no one else would recognise them as evidence of (positive or negative) value, and (ii) can (logically) reject any criteria of evaluation proposed by anyone else. Note that what she is questioning is that it would *make sense* to do either of these things in *any circumstances whatever*. She claims that, in evaluating intelligibly, some account must be taken of the object being evaluated. Suppose someone said that A was a good man and, asked 'Why?', replied, 'Because he clasps his hands three times an hour'. Now, given a certain 'background', this could make sense, e.g. to keep the illustration fantastic, if he thereby distracted the attention of a violent man who was plotting murder. But without this background what sense could there be in the opinion that clasping one's hands three times in an hour was a criterion of goodness in men? Again, suppose that we are told that we ought not to do such and such an action because it will injure our physical health. Here, likewise, a special background might render refusal to accept this, as a reason for not doing the action, intelligible, e.g. a missionary doctor going to some disease-ridden part of the earth knowing it to be inevitable that he will contract the disease. But without this sort of background such a refusal would not make sense. We do not, she claims, need a reason why we should consider the fact that an act will cause us physical injury a reason for not doing it. We cannot intelligibly reject this reason – special backgrounds apart – as a criterion of what ought or ought not to be done.

In her second paper, 'Goodness and Choice', Mrs Foot continues her attack on the view that, in evaluating, a speaker cannot only make up his own mind but also, without any restriction, his own evidence.[7] She argues that a connexion with the speaker's choices is neither a necessary nor a sufficient condition for using 'good'. She concludes: 'If a man who calls an *A* a good *A* has reason, other things being equal, to prefer it to other *A*'s, this is because of the kind of thing that an *A* is, and its connexion with his wants and needs' (below, p. 227). Mrs Foot takes the view that there are wants which all men have and that is where moral 'oughts' find their logical grounding.

Messrs Phillips and Mounce (Paper XXI) will not have this. They contend that (i) there are no wants which all men have; (ii) moral beliefs are often not derived from wants, but wants from moral beliefs. I think that they are right on these two counts. In their example, a Roman Catholic mother and a scientific rationalist, who disagree about birth control, are agreed 'about providing the good things of life for children' (below, p. 238), the difference between them being as to what these good things are. But is it simply that the mother subscribes to the moral principles 'Obey the will of God!', 'Create new life!', or whatever, and the rationalist does not, as these authors appear to suggest? Or does the root difference lie in belief, not about what is good for man, but about what man *is*? The mother believes him a child of God destined for eternal life, the rationalist takes an entirely material and terrestrial view of man's

[7] Cf. G. J. Warnock to the same effect, *Contemporary Moral Philosophy* (1967) p. 47.

existence. This raises the question: Can we say that there is a logical connexion between what any man finds it intelligible to regard as a *good* man and what he believes man to *be*? If so, there would be that much connexion between fact and value at least. And should we not be entitled to go on to say that, if we could settle what man is, we could demonstrate what he ought to do? At the very least, the connection between what we take man to be and what we find it intelligible to consider morally good or bad, obligatory or disobligatory, seems to me to call for closer consideration.

The final paper in this collection (Paper XXII) is a British Academy lecture by Professor Hare which, curiously, does not seem to be so widely known as his other publications. Hare is the main target of recent writers, such as Miss Anscombe and Mrs Foot, who attack the view that there is an unbridgeable gulf between 'is' and 'ought'. He calls them descriptivists; others have called them neo-naturalists. In this paper Hare very skilfully defends himself against some of their criticisms and launches his own counter-offensive. He thinks them guilty of all the philosophical mistakes which 'the old fork invented by Hume' was designed to weed out. First he defends the logical distinction between description and evaluation. We must recognise, he says, that the fundamental distinction which has to be drawn is not that between descriptive and evaluative *terms*, but between the descriptive and evaluative *meaning* which a single term, e.g. 'generous', may have. The case which he takes it that he has to answer is: there are contexts in which these meanings *cannot* be separated. He tries to show how they can be separated even in cases where we may not have an expression for those factual properties of an object (e.g. wine) in virtue of which we call it good. As long as we can *coin* a word for them (e.g. ϕ), we can make it clear that in saying that, to use our example, wine is ϕ, we are doing something different from commending wine. The logical distinction between description and evaluation is thus preserved. Similarly, thinks Hare, it is always logically possible – and is indeed the only way of improving one's aesthetic appreciation – to spell out in non-evaluative terms the features of a work of art in virtue of which we call it good or bad. Coming to specifically moral examples, the same is true where terms such as 'generous' or 'courageous' are concerned. 'Citations for medals do not simply say that the recipient behaved courageously; they give descriptive details; and though these, for reasons of brevity, often themselves contain evaluative terms, this need not be the case, and in a good citation it is the neutral descriptions which impress' (below, p. 246).

Hare proceeds to deal with particular descriptivist arguments against his own position.

1. It is held by some that not just anything can (logically) be called good because we can (logically) think good only such things as possess, or are the means to ends which possess, 'desirability characterisations'. Hare differentiates two meanings which this expression may have. (i) One is: 'a description of that about the object which makes it an object of desire' (below, p. 247), e.g. that wine is φ. The point being made is, then, that whenever we think something good we do so because of something about it. With this Hare has no quarrel at all. (ii) The other meaning is: 'we give a "desirability characterisation" of an object if we say something about it which is logically tied in some way (weak or strong) to desiring' (below, p. 248), e.g. saying that something is pleasant, or fun, or delightful. Hare now points out that 'a careless descriptivist' might think that his viewpoint can be established by the following argument, which confuses these two senses of 'desirability characterisation': (a) Anything that is thought good must also be thought to be the subject of some desirability characterisation (in either sense). (b) Only some *words* can be desirability characterisations in sense ii. (c) Therefore only some *things* can be the subjects of desirability characterisations in sense i. This conclusion is only reached by equivocation on the phrase 'desirability characterisation' and by fallaciously assuming that because there are logical restrictions on the use to which certain *words* can be put there are limitations upon what *things* can be thought good. It is always possible to think good new sorts of thing, Hare insists.

2. He next turns to Mrs Foot's contention that a connection with the speaker's choices is never a sufficient condition for the use of the word 'good' (cf. above, p. 215). We must guard, he says, against ambiguity in the expression 'conditions for the use of a word'. It may mean: (i) 'conditions for a word being said to be used correctly to express what the speaker who calls a thing "good" (for example) is wishing to convey'; or (ii) 'conditions for a thing's being said to be good' (below, p. 252). In the latter sense, Hare thinks it quite clear that a connection with the speaker's choices is not a sufficient condition; and claims that he has never maintained this. So, if Mrs Foot is maintaining that in this sense a connexion with the speaker's choices is not a sufficient condition for the use of 'good', Hare has no quarrel with her. If, however, as he gives reasons for supposing, she is talking about conditions for the use of the word 'good' in the other sense [(i) above], then Hare considers her opinion unplausible.

The word 'good' is used correctly to express what the speaker who uses it of something is wishing to convey, if its use is connected with his choices.

3. Hare next turns to the point, which seems to support descriptivism, that there are some things (e.g. food, warmth) which, if wanted or thought good, seem not to call for explanation, and other things which do. Does this mean that there are some things which it would make no sense at all to deny were good, as descriptivists appear to think? Hare finds here a confusion between logical absurdity and contingent improbability. It would indeed be highly improbable that anyone should commend a man for clasping his hands three times an hour. It may well be that this is improbable because the action has nothing to do with human survival, growth, procreation. These latter are objects which we normally desire. We call them needs because we do so desire them. Once we have called anything a need it would be logically odd to deny that it is good. But because the *word* 'good' is thus logically tied in certain contexts, to the *word* 'needs', 'good', says Hare, is not, as descriptivists have mistakenly supposed, therefore logically tied to certain concrete *things* which are generally thought to be needs.

PART ONE

The Interpretation of Hume on Is-Ought

I Hume on 'is' and 'ought'

A. C. MacIntyre

I

Sometimes in the history of philosophy the defence of a particular philosophical position and the interpretation of a particular philosopher become closely identified. This has notoriously happened more than once in the case of Plato, and lately in moral philosophy it seems to me to have happened in the case of Hume. At the centre of recent ethical discussion the question of the relationship between factual assertions and moral judgements has continually recurred, and the nature of that relationship has usually been discussed in terms of an unequivocally sharp distinction between them. In the course of the posing of this question the last paragraph of book III, part i, section i, of Hume's *Treatise* has been cited over and over again. This passage is either quoted in full or at least referred to – and with approval – by R. M. Hare,[1] Professor A. N. Prior,[2] Professor P. H. Nowell-Smith,[3] and a number of other writers. Not all contemporary writers, of course, treat Hume in the same way; a footnote to Stuart Hampshire's paper, 'Some Fallacies in Moral Philosophy',[4] provides an important exception to the general rule. But very often indeed Hume's contribution to ethics is treated as if it depended largely on this one passage, and this passage is accorded an interpretation which has acquired almost the status of an orthodoxy. Hare has even spoken of 'Hume's Law'.[5]

What Hume says is:

> In every system of morality which I have hitherto met with, I have always remark'd, that the author proceeds for some time in the ordinary way of reasoning, and establishes the being of a God, or makes observations concerning human affairs; when of a sudden I am surpriz'd to find, that instead of the usual copulations

[1] *Language of Morals* (Oxford 1952) pp. 29 and 44.
[2] *Logic and the Basis of Ethics* (Oxford 1949) pp. 32–3.
[3] *Ethics* (1954) pp. 36–8.
[4] *Mind*, LVIII (1949) p. 466.
[5] *Proceedings of the Aristotelian Society*, LV (1954–5) p. 303.

of propositions, *is*, and *is not*, I meet with no proposition that is not connected with an *ought*, or an *ought not*. This change is imperceptible; but is, however, of the last consequence. For as this *ought* or *ought not*, expresses some new relation or affirmation, 'tis necessary that it should be observ'd and explain'd; and at the same time that a reason should be given, for what seems altogether inconceivable, how this new relation can be a deduction from others, which are entirely different from it. But as authors do not commonly use this precaution, I shall presume to recommend it to the readers; and am persuaded that this small attention wou'd subvert all the vulgar systems of morality, and let us see, that the distinction of vice and virtue is not founded merely on the relations of objects, nor is perceiv'd by reason.[6]

The standard interpretation of this passage takes Hume to be asserting here that no set of non-moral premises can entail a moral conclusion. It is further concluded that Hume therefore is a prime opponent of what Prior has called 'the attempt to find a "foundation" for morality that is not already moral'. Hume becomes in this light an exponent of the autonomy of morality and in this at least akin to Kant. In this paper I want to show that this interpretation is inadequate and misleading. But I am not concerned with this only as a matter of historical interpretation. The thread of argument which I shall try to pursue will be as follows. First, I shall argue that the immense respect accorded to Hume thus interpreted is puzzling, since it is radically inconsistent with the disapproval with which contemporary logicians are apt to view certain of Hume's arguments about induction. Second, I shall try to show that if the current interpretation of Hume's views on 'is' and 'ought' is correct, then the first breach of Hume's law was committed by Hume; that is, the development of Hume's own moral theory does not square with what he is taken to assert about 'is' and 'ought'. Third, I shall offer evidence that the current interpretation of Hume is incorrect. Finally, I shall try to indicate what light the reinterpretation of Hume can throw upon current controversies in moral philosophy.

II

To approach the matter obliquely, how can we pass from 'is' to 'ought'? In Chapter iv of *The Language of Morals*, Hare asserts that a practical conclusion and *a fortiori* a moral conclusion is

[6] L. A. Selby-Bigge's edition, p. 469.

reached syllogistically, the minor premise stating 'what we should in fact be doing if we did one or other of the alternatives open to us' and the major premise stating a principle of conduct. This suggests an answer to our question. If you wish to pass from a factual statement to a moral statement, treat the moral statement as the conclusion to a syllogism and the factual statement as a minor premise. Then to make the transition all that is needed is to supply another moral statement as a major premise. And in a footnote to chapter iii of *Ethics* we find Nowell-Smith doing just this. He quotes from Bishop R. C. Mortimer the following passage: 'The first foundation is the doctrine of God the Creator. God made us and all the world. Because of that He has an absolute claim on our obedience. We do not exist in our own right, but only as His creatures, who ought therefore to do and be what He desires.'[7] On this Nowell-Smith comments: 'This argument requires the premise that a creature ought to obey his creator, which is itself a moral judgement. So that Christian ethics is not founded solely on the doctrine that God created us.'[8] That is, he argues that the inference, 'God created us, therefore we ought to obey him', is defective unless and until it is supplied with a major premise, 'We ought to obey our creator.'

I can only make sense of this position by supposing that underlying it there is an assumption that arguments must be either deductive or defective. But this is the very assumption which underlies Hume's scepticism about induction. And this scepticism is commonly treated as resting upon, and certainly does rest upon, a misconceived demand, a demand which P. F. Strawson has called 'the demand that induction shall be shown to be really a kind of deduction.'[9] This is certainly an accurate way of characterising Hume's transition from the premise that 'there can be no *demonstrative* arguments to prove, that those instances of which we have had no experience resemble those of which we have had experience' to the conclusion that 'it is impossible for us to satisfy ourselves by our reason, why we should extend that experience beyond those particular instances which have fallen under our observation.'[10] Part of Hume's own point is that to render inductive arguments deductive is a useless procedure. We can pass from 'The kettle has been on the fire for ten minutes' to 'So it will be boiling by now' (Strawson's example) by way of writing in some such major premise as 'Whenever kettles

[7] *Christian Ethics* (1950) p. 7.
[8] *Ethics*, p. 51.
[9] *Introduction to Logical Theory* (1952) p. 250.
[10] *Treatise*, I. iii. 6; Selby-Bigge, pp. 89, 91.

have been on the fire for ten minutes, they boil.' But if our problem
is that of justifying induction, then this major premise itself embodies
an inductive assertion that stands in need of justification. For the
transition which constitutes the problem has been justified in the
passage from minor premise to conclusion only at the cost of re-
appearing, as question-beggingly as ever, within the major premise.
To fall back on some yet more general assertion as a premise from
which 'Whenever kettles have been on the fire for ten minutes they
boil' could be derived would merely remove the problem one stage
farther and would be to embark on a regress, possibly infinite and
certainly pointless.

If then it is pointless to present inductive arguments as deductive
what special reason is there in the case of moral arguments for
attempting to present them as deductive? If men arguing about
morality, as Bishop Mortimer is arguing, pass from 'God made us'
to 'We ought to obey God', why should we assume that the transition
must be an entailment? I suspect that our inclination to do this may
be that we fear the alternative. Hare suggests that the alternative
to his view is 'that although, in the strict sense of the word, I have
indeed shown that moral judgements and imperatives cannot be
entailed by factual premises, yet there is some looser relation than
entailment which holds between them.' I agree with Hare in finding
the doctrine of what he calls 'loose' forms of inference objection-
able; although I cannot indeed find this doctrine present in, for
example, Professor S. E. Toulmin's *The Place of Reason in Ethics*
which Hare purports to be criticising. And certainly entailment
relations must have a place in moral argument, as they do in scientific argument. But since there are important steps in scientific argument which are not entailments, it might be thought that to insist
that the relation between factual statements and moral conclusions
be deductive or non-existent would be likely to hinder us in elucidating the character of moral arguments.

How does this bear on the interpretation of Hume? It might be
held that, since Hume holds in some passages on induction at least
that arguments are deductive or defective, we could reasonably
expect him to maintain that since factual premises cannot entail
moral conclusions – as they certainly cannot – there can be no
connections between factual statements and moral judgements (other
perhaps than psychological connections). But at this point all I am
suggesting is that our contemporary disapproval of Hume on induction makes our contemporary disapproval of what we take to be
Hume on facts and norms seem odd. It is only now that I want to

ask whether – just as Hume's attitude to induction is much more complex than appears in his more sceptical moments and is therefore liable to misinterpretation – his remarks on 'is' and 'ought' are not only liable to receive but have actually received a wrong interpretation.

III

The approach will still be oblique. What I want to suggest next is that if Hume does affirm the impossibility of deriving an 'ought' from an 'is' then he is the first to perform this particular impossibility. But before I proceed to do this, one general remark is worth making. It would be very odd if Hume did affirm the logical irrelevance of facts to moral judgements, for the whole difference in atmosphere – and it is very marked – between his discussion of morality and those of, for example, Hare and Nowell-Smith springs from his interest in the facts of morality. His work is full of anthropological and sociological remarks, remarks sometimes ascribed by commentators to the confusion between logic and psychology with which Hume is so often credited. Whether Hume is in general guilty of this confusion is outside the scope of this paper to discuss. But so far as his moral theory is concerned, the sociological comments have a necessary place in the whole structure of argument.

Consider, for example, Hume's account of justice. To call an act 'just' or 'unjust' is to say that it falls under a rule. A single act of justice may well be contrary to either private or public interest or both.

> But however single acts of justice may be contrary, either to public or to private interest, 'tis certain, that the whole plan or scheme is highly conducive, or indeed absolutely requisite both to the support of society, and the well-being of every individual. 'Tis impossible to separate the good from the ill. Property must be stable, and must be fix'd by general rules. Tho' in one instance the public be a sufferer, this momentary ill is amply compensated by the steady prosecution of the rule, and by the peace and order, which it establishes in society.[11]

Is Hume making a moral point or is he asserting a casual sociological connection or is he making a logical point? Is he saying that it is logically appropriate to justify the rules of justice in terms of

[11] *Treatise*, III. ii. 2; Selby-Bigge, p. 497.

interest or that to observe such rules does as a matter of fact conduce
to public interest or that such rules are in fact justified because they
conduce to public interest? All three. For Hume is asserting both
that the logically appropriate way of justifying the rules of justice
is an appeal to public interest and that in fact public interest is
served by them so that the rules are justified. And that Hume is
clearly both justifying the rules and affirming the validity of this
type of justification cannot be doubted in the light of the passage
which follows.

> And even every individual person must find himself a gainer on
> balancing the account; since, without justice, society must imme-
> diately dissolve, and everyone must fall into that savage and
> solitary condition, which is infinitely worse than the worst situa-
> tion that can possibly be suppos'd in society.

Moreover, this type of argument is not confined to the *Treatise;*
elsewhere also Hume makes it clear that he believes that factual
considerations can justify or fail to justify moral rules. Such considerations are largely appealed to by Hume in his arguments in the
'Essay On Suicide' that suicide is morally permissible.

To return to the justification of justice: Hume clearly affirms that
the justification of the rules of justice lies in the fact that their
observance is to everyone's long-term interest; that we ought to obey
the rules because there is no one who does not gain more than he
loses by such obedience. But this is to derive an 'ought' from an
'is'. If Hare, Nowell-Smith, and Prior have interpreted Hume correctly, Hume is contravening his own prohibition. Someone might
argue, however, that Hume only appears to contravene it. For, if
we ignore the suggestion made earlier in this paper that the attempt
to present moral arguments as entailments may be misconceived, we
may suppose that Hume's argument is defective in the way that
Bishop Mortimer's is and attempt to repair it in the way Nowell-
Smith repairs the other. Then the transition from the minor premise,
'Obedience to this rule would be to everyone's long-term interest',
to the conclusion 'We ought to obey this rule' would be made by
means of the major premise 'We ought to do whatever is to everyone's long-term interest.' But if this is the defence of Hume, if Hume
needs defence at this point, then he is indefensible. For the locution
offered as a candidate for a major premise, 'We ought to do what
is to everyone's long-term interest', cannot function as such a
premise for Hume since in his terms it could not be a moral principle at all, but at best a kind of compressed definition. That is, the
notion of 'ought' is for Hume only explicable in terms of the notion

of a consensus of interest. To say that we ought to do something is to affirm that there is a commonly accepted rule; and the existence of such a rule presupposes a consensus of opinion as to where our common interests lie. An obligation is constituted in part by such a consensus and the concept of 'ought' is logically dependent on the concept of a common interest and can only be explained in terms of it. To say that we ought to do what is to the common interest would therefore be either to utter an aphoristic and misleading truism or else to use the term 'ought' in a sense quite other than that understood by Hume. Thus the locution 'We ought to do what is to everyone's long-term interest' could not lay down a moral principle which might figure as a major premise in the type of syllogism which Hare describes.

The view which Hume is propounding can perhaps be illuminated by a comparison with the position of J. S. Mill. On the interpretation of Mill's ethics for which Professor J. O. Urmson has convincingly argued,[12] Mill did not commit the naturalistic fallacy of deriving the principle that 'We ought to pursue the greatest happiness of the greatest number' from some statement about what we ourselves or all men desire. He did not commit this fallacy for he did not derive his principle at all. For Mill 'We ought to pursue the greatest happiness of the greatest number' is the supreme moral principle. The difference between Mill's utilitarianism and Hume's lies in this: that if we take some such statement as 'We ought to do whatever is to the advantage of most people', this for Mill would be a moral principle which it would be morally wrong to deny, but which it would make sense to deny. Whereas for Hume to deny this statement would be senseless, for it would detach 'ought' from the notion of a consensus of interest and so evacuate it of meaning. Roughly speaking, for Mill such a principle would be a contingent moral truth; for Hume it would be a necessary truth underlying morality.

Moreover, Hume and Mill can be usefully contrasted in another respect. Mill's basic principle is a moral affirmation independent of the facts: so long as some course of action will produce more happiness for more people than alternative courses will, it provides at least some sort of effective moral criterion. But at any rate, so far as that part of his doctrine which refers to justice is concerned, it is quite otherwise with Hume. We have moral rules because we have common interests. Should someone succeed in showing us that the facts are different from what we conceive them to be so that we have no

[12] *Philosophical Quarterly*, 3 (1953) p. 33.

common interests, then our moral rules would lose their justification. Indeed the initial move of Marx's moral theory can perhaps be best understood as a denial of the facts which Hume holds to constitute the justification for social morality. Marx's denial that there are common interests shared by the whole of society in respect of, for instance, the distribution of property meets Hume on his own ground. (We may note in passing that the change from Hume's characterisation of morality in terms of content, with its explicit reference to the facts about society, to the attempt by later writers to characterise morality purely in terms of the form of moral judgements is what Marxists would see as the significant change in philosophical ethics. Since I would agree with Marxists in thinking this change a change for the worse – for reasons which I shall indicate later in the argument – I have been tempted to retitle this paper 'Against Bourgeois Formalism in Ethics'.

One last point on the contrast between Hume and Mill: since Mill's basic principle in ethics is a moral principle, but Hume's is a definition of morality, they demand different types of defence. How does Hume defend this view of the derivation of morality from interest? By appeal to the facts. How do we in fact induce someone to do what is just? How do we in fact justify just actions on our own part? In observing what answers we have to give to questions like these, Hume believes that his analysis is justified.[13]

IV

What I have so far argued is that Hume himself derives 'ought' from 'is' in his account of justice. Is he then inconsistent with his own doctrine in that famous passage? Someone might try to save Hume's consistency by pointing out that the derivation of 'ought' from 'is' in the section on justice is not an entailment and that all Hume is denying is that 'is' statements can entail 'ought' statements, and that this is quite correct. But to say this would be to misunderstand the passage. For I now want to argue that in fact Hume's positive suggestions on moral theory are actually an answer to a question posed in the 'is' and 'ought' passage, and that that passage has nothing to do with the point about entailment at all. The arguments here are twofold.

First, Hume does not actually say that one cannot pass from an

13 *Treatise*, Selby-Bigge, p. 498.

'is' to an 'ought' but only that it 'seems altogether inconceivable' how this can be done. We have all been brought up to believe in Hume's irony so thoroughly that it may occasionally be necessary to remind ourselves that Hume need not necesssarily mean more or other than he says. Indeed the rhetorical and slightly ironical tone of the passage renders it all the more ambiguous. When Hume asks how what seems altogether inconceivable may be brought about, he may be taken to be suggesting either that it simply cannot be brought about or that it cannot be brought about in the way in which 'every system of morality which I have hitherto met with' has brought it about. In any case it would be odd if Hume thought that 'observations concerning human affairs' necessarily could not lead on to moral judgements since such observations are constantly so used by Hume himself.

Second, the force of the passage as it is commonly taken depends on what seems to be its manifest truth: 'is' cannot entail 'ought'. But the notion of entailment is read into the passage. The word Hume uses is 'deduction'. *We* might well use this word as a synonym for entailment, and even as early as Richard Price's moral writings it is certainly so used. But is it used thus by Hume? The first interesting feature of Hume's use of the word is its extreme rarity in his writings. When he speaks of what we should call 'deductive arguments' he always uses the term 'demonstrative arguments'. The word 'deduction' and its cognates have no entry in Selby-Bigge's indexes at all, so that its isolated occurrence in this passage at least stands in need of interpretation. The entries under 'deduction' and 'deduce' in the Oxford English Dictionary make it quite clear that in ordinary eighteenth-century use these were likely to be synonyms rather for 'inference' and 'infer' than for 'entailment' and 'entail'. Was this Hume's usage? In the essay entitled 'That Politics may be Reduced to a Science', Hume writes, 'So great is the force of laws, and of particular forms of government, and so little dependence have they on the humours and tempers of men, that consequences almost as general and certain may sometimes be deduced from them as any which the mathematical sciences afford us.'[14] Clearly, to read 'be entailed by' for 'deduced from' in this passage would be very odd. The reference to mathematics might indeed mislead us momentarily into supposing Hume to be speaking of 'entailment'. But the very first example in which Hume draws a deduction makes it clear how he is using the term. From the example of the Roman republic which gave the whole legislative power to the people without allow-

[14] Essay iii, in Hume, *Theory of Politics*, ed. F. Watkins (1951) p. 136.

ing a negative voice either to the nobility or the consuls and so ended
up in anarchy, Hume concludes in general terms that 'Such are the
effects of democracy without a representative.' That is, Hume uses
past political instances to support political generalisations in an
ordinary inductive argument, and he uses the term 'deduce' in
speaking of this type of argument. 'Deduction' therefore must mean
'inference' and cannot mean 'entailment'.

Hume, then, in the celebrated passage does not mention entailment. What he does is to ask how and if moral rules may be inferred
from factual statements, and in the rest of book III of the *Treatise* he
provides an answer to his own question.

V

There are, of course, two distinct issues raised by this paper so far.
There is the historical question of what Hume is actually asserting
in the passage under discussion, and there is the philosophical
question of whether what he does assert is true and important. I do
not want to entangle these two issues overmuch, but it may at this
point actually assist in elucidating what Hume means to consider
briefly the philosophical issues raised by the difference between
what he actually does say and what he is customarily alleged to say.
Hume is customarily alleged to be making a purely formal point
about 'ought' and 'is', and the kind of approach to ethics which
makes such formal analyses central tends to lead to one disconcert-
ing result. The connection between morality and happiness is made
to appear purely contingent and accidental. 'One ought to . . .' is
treated as a formula where the blank space might be filled in by
almost any verb which would make grammatical sense. 'One ought
occasionally to kill someone' or 'One ought to say what is not true'
are not examples, of moral precepts for more than the reason that
they are at odds with the precepts by which most of us have decided
to abide. Yet if ethics is a purely formal study any example ought
to serve. If a philosopher feels that the connection between morality
and happiness is somehow a necessary one, he is likely to commit, or
at least be accused of, the naturalistic fallacy of defining moral
words in factual terms. It is obvious why philosophers should seem
to be faced with this alternative of committing the naturalistic fallacy or else making the connection between morality and happiness
contingent and accidental. This alternative is rooted in the belief

that the connections between moral utterances and factual statements must be entailments or nothing. And this belief arises out of
accepting formal calculi as models of argument and then looking
for entailment relations in non-formal discourse.

To assert that it is of the first importance for ethics to see that
the question of the connection between morality and happiness is a
crucial one is not, of course, to allow that Hume's treatment of it is
satisfactory. But at least Hume did see the need to make the connection, whereas the 'is' and 'ought' passage has been interpreted
in such a way as to obscure this need.

Second, the reinterpretation of this passage of Hume allows us to
take up the whole question of practical reasoning in a more fruitful
way than the formalist tradition in ethics allows. If anyone says
that we cannot make valid inferences from an 'is' to an 'ought', I
should be disposed to offer him the following counter-example: 'If
I stick a knife in Smith, they will send me to jail; but I do not want
to go to jail; so I ought not to (had better not) stick a knife in him.'
The reply to this may be that there is no doubt that this is a valid
inference (I do no see how this could be denied) but that it is a perfectly ordinary entailment relying upon the suppressed major
premise 'If it is both the case that if I do x, the outcome will be y,
then if I don't want y to happen, I ought not to do x.' This will
certainly make the argument in question an entailment; but there
seem to me three good reasons for not treating the argument in this
way. First, inductive arguments could be rendered deductive in this
way but, as we have already noted, only a superstitious devotee of
entailment could possibly want to present them as such. What additional reason could there be in the case of moral arguments that is
lacking in the case of inductive arguments? Moreover, a reason akin
to that which we have for not proceeding in this way with inductive
arguments can be adduced in this use also, namely, that we may
have made our argument into an entailment by adding a major
premise; but we have reproduced the argument in its non-entailment
form as that premise, and anything questionable in the original
argument remains just as questionable inside the major premise.
That premise itself is an argument and one that is not an entailment;
to make it an entailment will be to add a further premise which will
reproduce the same difficulty. So whether my inference stands or
falls, it does not stand or fall as an entailment with a suppressed
premise. But there is a third and even more important reason for
not treating the transition made in such an inference as an entailment. To do so is to obscure the way in which the transition within

the argument is in fact made. For the transition from 'is' to 'ought'
is made in this inference by the notion of 'wanting'. And this is no
accident. Aristotle's examples of practical syllogisms typically have
a premise which includes some such terms as 'suits' or 'pleases'. We
could give a long list of the concepts which can form such bridge
notions between 'is' and 'ought': wanting, needing, desiring,
pleasure, happiness, health – and these are only a few. I think there
is a strong case for saying that moral notions are unintelligible apart
from concepts such as these. The philosopher who has obscured the
issue here is Kant whose classification of imperatives into categorical
and hypothetical removes any link between what is good and right
and what we need and desire at one blow. Here it is outside my
scope to argue against Kant; all I want to do is to prevent Hume
from being classified with him on this issue.

For we are now in a position to clarify what Hume is actually
saying in the 'is' and 'ought' passage. He is first urging us to take
note of the key point where we do pass from 'is' to 'ought' and
arguing that this is a difficult transition. In the next part of the
Treatise he shows us how it can be made; clearly in the passage itself
he is concerned to warn us against those who make this transition in
an illegitimate way. Against whom is Hume warning us?

Hume himself identifies the position he is criticising by saying that
attention to the point he is making 'wou'd subvert all the vulgar systems of morality.' To what does he refer by using this phrase? The
ordinary eighteenth-century use of 'vulgar' rules out any reference
to other philosophers and more particularly to Wollaston. Hume
must be referring to the commonly accepted systems of morality.
Nor is there any ground for supposing Hume to depart from ordinary eighteenth-century usage on this point. Elsewhere in the
Treatise[15] there is a passage in which he uses interchangeably the
expressions 'the vulgar' and 'the generality of mankind'. So it is
against ordinary morality that Hume is crusading. And for the
eighteenth century ordinary morality is religious morality. Hume is
in fact repudiating a religious foundation for morality and putting
in its place a foundation in human needs, interests, desires, and
happiness. Can this interpretation be further supported?

The only way of supporting it would be to show that there were
specific religious moral views against which Hume had reason to
write and which contain arguments answering to the description he
gives in the 'is' and 'ought' passage. Now this can be shown. Hume
was brought up in a Presbyterian household and himself suffered a

[15] *Treatise*, I. iv. 2.

Presbyterian upbringing. Boswell records Hume as follows: 'I asked him if he was not religious when he was young. He said he was, and he used to read the *Whole Duty of Man*; that he made an abstract from the Catalogue of vices at the end of it, and examined himself by this, leaving out Murder and Theft and such vices as he had no chance of committing, having no inclination to commit them.'[16] *The Whole Duty of Man* was probably written by Richard Allestree, and it was at once a typical and a popular work of Protestant piety, and it abounds in arguments of the type under discussion. Consider, for example, the following: 'whoever is in distress for any thing, where-with I can supply him, that distress of his makes it a duty on me so to supply him and this in all kinds of events. Now the ground of its being a duty is that God hath given Men abilities not only for their own use, but for the advantage and benefit of others, and there-fore what is thus given for their use, becomes a debt to them when-ever their need requires it...'[17] This is precisely an argument which runs from 'the being of a God' or 'observations concerning human affairs' into affirmations of duty. And it runs into the difficulty which Hume discusses in the section preceding the 'is' and 'ought' passage, that what is merely matter of fact cannot provide us with a reason for acting – unless it be a matter of those facts which Hume calls the passions, that is, of our needs, desires, and the like. Interest-ingly enough, there are other passages where Allestree provides his arguments with a backing which refers to just this kind of matter. 'A second Motive to our care of any thing is the USEFULNESS of it to us, or the great Mischief we shall have by the loss of it... 'Tis true we cannot lose our Souls, in one sense, that is so lose them that they cease to Be; but we may lose them in another... In a word, we may lose them in Hell...'[18] That is, we pass from what God commands to what we ought to do by means of the fear of Hell. That this can provide a motive Hume denies in the essay 'Of Suicide': obviously in fact, though he does not say so very straight-forwardly, because he believes that there is no such place.

The interpretation of the 'is' and 'ought' passage which I am offering can now be stated compendiously. Hume is not in this passage asserting the autonomy of morals – for he did not believe in it; and he is not making a point about entailment – for he does

---

[16] Boswell, 'An Account of My Last Interview with David Hume, Esq.', reprinted in *Dialogues Concerning Natural Religion*, ed. Kemp Smith (2nd ed. New York 1948).

[17] Sunday XIII: sec. 30.

[18] Preface.

not mention it. He is asserting that the question of how the factual basis of morality is related to morality is a crucial logical issue, reflection on which will enable one to realise how there are ways in which this transition can be made and ways in which it cannot. One has to go beyond the passage itself to see what these are; but if one does so it is plain that we can connect the facts of the situation with what we ought to do only by means of one of those concepts which Hume treats under the heading of the passions and which I have indicated by examples such as wanting, needing, and the like. Hume is not, as Prior seems to indicate, trying to say that morality lacks a basis; he is trying to point out the nature of that basis.

VI

The argument of this paper is incomplete in three different ways. First, it is of a certain interest to relate Hume's argument to contemporary controversies. On this I will note only as a matter of academic interest that there is at least one recent argument in which Hume has been recruited on the wrong side. In the discussion on moral argument between Hare and Toulmin,[19] Hare has invoked the name of Hume on the side of his contention that factual statements can appear in moral arguments only as minor premises under the aegis of major premises which are statements of moral principle and against Toulmin's contention that moral arguments are non-deductive. But if I have re-read Hume on 'is' and 'ought' correctly, then the difference between what Hume has been thought to assert and what Hume really asserted is very much the difference between Hare and Toulmin. And Hume is in fact as decisively on Toulmin's side as he has been supposed to be on Hare's.

Second, the proper elucidation of this passage would require that its interpretation be linked to an interpretation of Hume's moral philosophy as a whole. Here I will only say that such a thesis of Hume's as that if all factual disagreement were resolved, no moral disagreements would remain, falls into place in the general structure of Hume's ethics if this interpretation of the 'is' and 'ought' passage is accepted; but on the standard interpretation it remains an odd and inexplicable belief of Hume's. But to pursue this and a

[19] *Language of Morals*, p. 45; *Philosophical Quarterly*, I (1950–1) p. 372 and *Philosophy*, xxxi (1956) p. 65.

large variety of related topics would be to pass beyond the scope
of this paper.

Finally, however, I want to suggest that part of the importance
of the interpretation of Hume which I have offered in this paper
lies in the way that it enables us to place Hume's ethics in general
and the 'is' and 'ought' passage in particular in the far wider context of the history of ethics. For I think that Hume stands at a
turning point in that history and that the accepted interpretation of
the 'is' and 'ought' passage has obscured his role. What I mean by
this I can indicate only in a highly schematic and speculative way.
Any attempt to write the history of ethics in a paragraph is bound
to have a '1066 and All That' quality about it. But even if the paragraph that follows is a caricature it may assist in an understanding
of that which it caricatures.

One way of seeing the history of ethics is this. The Greek moral
tradition asserted – no doubt with many reservations at times – an
essential connection between 'good' and 'good for', between virtue
and desire. One cannot, for Aristotle, do ethics without doing moral
psychology; one cannot understand what a virtue is without understanding it as something a man could possess and as something related to human happiness. Morality, to be intelligible, must be
understood as grounded in human nature. The Middle Ages pre-
serves this way of looking at ethics. Certainly there is a new element
of divine commandment to be reckoned with. But the God who
commands you also created you and His commandments are such
as it befits your nature to obey. So an Aristotelian moral psychology and a Christian view of the moral law are synthesised even if
somewhat unsatisfactorily in Thomist ethics. But the Protestant
Reformation changes this. First, because human beings are totally
corrupt their nature cannot be a foundation for true morality. And
next because men cannot judge God, we obey God's commandments not because God is good but simply because He is God. So
the moral law is a collection of arbitrary fiats unconnected with anything we may want or desire. Miss G. E. M. Anscombe has recently
suggested that the notion of a morality of law was effectively dropped
by the Reformers;[20] I should have thought that there were good
grounds for asserting that a morality of law-and-nothing-else was
introduced by them. Against the Protestants Hume reasserted the
founding of morality on human nature. The attempt to make Hume
a defender of the autonomy of ethics is likely to conceal his difference from Kant, whose moral philosophy is, from one point of view,

[20] Paper XVIII.

the natural outcome of the Protestant position. And the virtue of Hume's ethics, like that of Aristotle and unlike that of Kant, is that it seeks to preserve morality as something psychologically intelligible. For the tradition which upholds the autonomy of ethics from Kant to Moore to Hare moral principles are somehow self-explicable; they are logically independent of any assertions about human nature. Hume has been too often presented recently as an adherent of this tradition. Whether we see him as such or whether we see him as the last representative of another and older tradition hinges largely on how we take what he says about 'is' and 'ought'.

II Hume on 'is' and 'ought': A reply to Mr MacIntyre

R. F. Atkinson

I

In a recent paper in the *Philosophical Review*,[1] Mr A. C. MacIntyre criticises what he takes to be the current interpretation of a celebrated passage in Hume's *Treatise*[2] and suggests an alternative for which he claims the important merit that it makes Hume's ethical views self-consistent. The main point that I wish to make in this discussion is the general one that MacIntyre's treatment of the question whether Hume did or did not affirm the 'autonomy of morality' is vitiated by a failure to make clear what he understands by that phrase; but I shall also contend more particularly that MacIntyre's arguments against the received interpretation are less than conclusive, and suggest that even on MacIntyre's interpretation Hume's views are by no means wholly consistent with themselves.

II

According to MacIntyre, the 'standard' interpretation of this passage[2] is that Hume is asserting that no set of non-moral premises can entail a moral conclusion, from which it is held to follow that Hume is opposed to any attempt to supply a non-moral 'foundation' for morality and accordingly that he is an exponent of 'the autonomy of morality'.

It is important to get clear what we are to understand by the phrase 'autonomy of morality'. It is by no means self-explanatory, nor unfortunately is it used with much precision, and it would perhaps be conducive to clarity if its application could be confined to

[1] Paper I.
[2] i.e. the one quoted by MacIntyre above, pp. 35–6.

a thesis of Kant's. Nevertheless the phrase is, I believe, nowadays
quite frequently used as a convenient label for the view that moral
conclusions cannot be entailed by non-moral premises. I shall call
this Autonomy$_1$. This view itself is often confused with or unclearly
related to the view that *evaluative* conclusions cannot be deduced
from non-evaluative (by which is usually intended factual) premises
– no doubt because it is often held that moral judgements are a
species of value judgements and hence that if value judgements are
not, then neither can moral judgements be deducible from non-
evaluative premises. There is a real need for a thorough attempt to
disentangle the various views that have been or could be maintained
in this field, but it could hardly be started within the scope of the
present discussion. For the present purpose it is enough to remark
that MacIntyre cannot, or cannot consistently, be using 'autonomy
of morality' in the sense I have distinguished as Autonomy$_1$, for
while he makes it very clear that he is opposed to Autonomy, he
nevertheless writes that factual statements 'certainly cannot' entail
moral conclusions.[3] In fact, the version of autonomism MacIntyre
rejects – call it Autonomy$_2$ – seems to be the view that factual statements are logically irrelevant to (in a sense stronger than that of 'do
not entail') moral judgements. The two versions of autonomism are
clearly different and are related in the following way: Autonomy$_2$
entails Autonomy$_1$, but not conversely. Autonomy$_2$ is, however,
deducible from Autonomy$_1$ *together with* the additional and independent thesis that, as MacIntyre succinctly expresses it, arguments are 'either deductive or defective'.

If we are concerned to deny that Hume, either generally or in the
particular passage under discussion, was an autonomist, it is obviously essential to make clear whether we are denying that he was an
autonomist in sense$_1$ or in sense $_2$. It is clear that MacIntyre denies
that he was an autonomist$_2$, but somewhat unclear whether he also
denies that he was an autonomist$_1$; my impression, for what it is worth,
is that he does not. But if this is the case, then it would seem very hard
for him to maintain that Hume was a *consistent* repudiator of
Autonomy$_2$. For MacIntyre admits that in his treatment of induction, Hume does assume that arguments are either deductive or
defective – and we shall see in Section III below that he also does
so in at least one place in his ethical writings.

These general remarks have a bearing on the interpretation of the

[3] Above, p. 38. Somebody might, but so far as I can see MacIntyre does
not, hold that while factual premises cannot, some other sort of non-moral
premises can entail moral conclusions.

'ought/is' passage in particular. For if, as I suggest, Hume else-where maintains Autonomy$_1$ or $_2$, there is so much the less reason for denying in order to save his consistency that he maintained either or both of these views in the passage in question. Because of this there seems to me to be comparatively little force in two of the general points MacIntyre makes against the standard interpretation of the passage.

The first of these is his 'general remark' (p. 39) to the effect that it would be very odd indeed if Hume did affirm the logical irrelevance of facts to moral judgements, that is, Autonomy$_2$ – odd because his work is full of anthropological and sociological re-marks which have a necessary place in the whole structure of his argument, for instance in his treatment of justice. The second point, which partly overlaps with the first, is MacIntyre's observation (p. 42) that Hume in his justification of justice clearly does derive an 'ought' from an 'is' – 'derive' apparently here being used in such a way that one can consistently say both that an 'ought' can be derived from an 'is' and that an 'ought' is never entailed by an 'is'.[4]

It is, moreover, only in the light of MacIntyre's apparent assump-tion that the standard interpretation of the 'ought/is' passage is that Hume is there maintaining Autonomy$_2$ – an assumption partly determined no doubt by his unclear or ambiguous use of the phrase 'autonomy of morality' – that these points seem to have any force at all. For if Hume were maintaining Autonomy$_1$ only – and this I am sure is the standard interpretation, if there is one – he could quite consistently allow that 'ought's' can, in some sense, be derived from 'is's', that facts are logically relevant to moral judgements. MacIntyre, at any rate, is in no position to deny the consistency of this since he holds such a view himself.

There is a further general point made by MacIntyre (p. 48) against the received interpretation, namely, that it fails to accom-modate Hume's thesis that if all factual disagreements were resolved no moral disagreements would remain. I am not sure whether MacIntyre means to suggest that this thesis is actually incompatible with autonomism in either sense, or merely that it is a rather uncon-genial associate for these views. I am, however, quite sure that the thesis is not incompatible with autonomism. An autonomist (sense$_1$ or sense$_2$) certainly can *consistently* maintain that people fully in-formed on all factual matters will agree in their moral judgements with regard to a given situation. They will so agree if they make the same fundamental moral judgements or accept the same ultimate

[4] Cf. Paper I, p. 42.

moral principles. Whether people do so or not is, of course, a question of fact, but an open question so far as the autonomist is concerned. In the particular case of Hume, I think that Stevenson's exegesis is highly plausible, namely that Hume holds that there will be no moral disagreement between factually fully informed people because he assumes, in Stevenson's view falsely or rashly, that all people are inclined to approve the same sorts of thing.[5] For Hume morality is indeed founded on sentiment, but he also holds that the sentiments of mankind are uniform to a high degree.[6]

III

So much in general terms. Consider now MacIntyre's more particular objections to the received interpretation of the passage in question. (a) The first of these is that Hume does not assert that we *cannot* pass from 'is' to 'ought' but only that it is very difficult to see how we can (pp. 42–3). We are informed that 'We have all been brought up to believe in Hume's irony so thoroughly that it may occasionally be necessary to remind ourselves that Hume need not necessarily mean more or other than he says' (p. 43). 'Pass from' is perhaps ambiguous as between 'deduce' in the modern narrow sense which is tied to entailment and the more general 'infer' or 'derive'. MacIntyre, however, clearly intends it to be used in the latter, wider sense, for he goes on to observe that (b) Hume is not even asserting that 'is' cannot entail 'ought'. Entailment is read into the passage. Hume's word is 'deduce', which in his day and in his writings had the meaning of the modern 'infer' (pp. 43–4).

In other words, MacIntyre is denying that Hume in the passage in question is maintaining either Autonomy$_2$–objection (a) or Autonomy$_1$–objection (b). Before going on to consider what MacIntyre thinks Hume *is* maintaining, it is perhaps worth observing that neither of his objections is wholly convincing. With regard to (a), while it is clearly true that there are many places where Hume is not

[5] *Ethics and Language* (New Haven, Conn. 1944) ch. xii, sec. 5. Stevenson perhaps slightly over-states Hume's claim. It might be nearer the mark to say that Hume held that *most* people approve *very much the same* sorts of thing. Cf. A. Stroll, *The Emotive Theory of Ethics* (Berkeley 1954) p. 77.

[6] See *Treatise*, p. 547n; *Enquiry concerning the Principles of Morals* (Selby-Bigge edition) p. 272. The most useful source for Hume's views on this topic is the *Dialogue* printed at the end of the Selby-Bigge edition of the *Enquiries*.

writing ironically, I cannot think that this is one of them, though I grant that opinions are likely to differ on points of this nature. Further, on the suggestion that entailment is read into the passage from which objection (*b*) derives, it seems to me that even if it be true it does not, without the at best dubious support of objection (*a*), do much to help MacIntyre's case. Certainly if Hume was not talking about entailment because he had not got the concept of entailment as we now understand it, he cannot have been maintaining Autonomy$_1$ explicitly and in contradistinction from Autonomy$_2$. But this does not exclude the possibility, indeed it rather suggests, that he was maintaining Autonomy$_2$. All this apart, I am not sure that it is really plausible to suggest that entailment is simply read into the passage. For, as Professor Flew[7] has pointed out to me, Hume thinks it worthy of remark that the relations expressed by 'ought' and 'ought not' are 'entirely different' from those expressed by 'is' and 'is not'. And this, so far as it goes, suggests that it is something akin to entailment or deduction (narrow sense) that Hume has in mind rather than inference in the wide sense – the crucial difference between entailment and inference being just this, that we may speak of *inferring* conclusions differing from or going beyond, and hence not *entailed by*, the premises. Moreover Reid, a contemporary of Hume and one very much on the lookout for any departure from the common usage of his day, interprets the 'ought/is' passage as if it concerned the entailment or deduction (narrow sense) of moral conclusions.[8] He does not deny that 'ought' expresses a different relation (though he will not have it that there is anything unfamiliar or unintelligible about it), nor does he suggest that this relation can be deduced or in some other sense derived or inferred from other relations entirely different from it. He is content to insist that the first principles of morals are not deductions at all but like axioms in other fields self-evident truths, and that moral truths which are not self-evident are deduced from the first principles of morals and not from relations entirely different from them.

We have seen what, in MacIntyre's opinion, Hume is *not* trying to show in the 'ought/is' passage. What, then, is he supposed to be doing? The suggestion is that he is first urging us to take note of the key point where we pass from 'is' to 'ought' and arguing that

[7] To whom, and to my colleague Mr Montefiore, I am indebted for a number of valuable comments.

[8] *Essays on the Active Powers*, ch. vii (pp. 577–9 of vol. III of the Edinburgh edition of 1819). Cf. Prior, *Logic and the Basis of Ethics* (Oxford 1949) p. 33.

it is a difficult transition. He is not arguing that it cannot be made, only that it can be made legitimately or illegitimately. And in the next part of the *Treatise*, he shows how it can legitimately be done. In fact what Hume is warning us against is not the attempt to provide a basis for morality – he himself goes on to supply one – but against those who try to supply a particular sort of basis, namely, a religious one. Given the ordinary eighteenth-century use of the term 'vulgar' the 'vulgar systems' he expects to subvert cannot be philosophical systems (for example Wollaston's), but they very well could be religious systems (pp. 46–7).

I do not think very much weight can be attached to the ordinary eighteenth-century use of the term 'vulgar' for in the *Enquiry concerning the Principles of Morals* Hume refers to the 'vulgar dispute' concerning the respective degrees of benevolence and self-love in human nature and this surely was a dispute which figures in philosophical writings.[9] And, incidentally, the 'ought/is' passage itself opens with a reference to *every* system of morality, which surely suggests that the term 'vulgar' when it is introduced later on is being used in a pejorative rather than a purely classificatory sense. But even if Hume did not have *philosophical* systems in mind when he wrote the passage it does not follow that he was not there maintaining Autonomy$_1$ or Autonomy$_2$. The most natural approach is, it seems to me, to take the passage in the context of the section of which it forms the last paragraph – the section headed 'Moral Distinctions not deriv'd from reason'. Viewed in this light, Hume's position would seem to have been this: that he thought that he had disposed of the philosophical systems in the earlier part of the section by showing that virtue and vice consist neither in 'relations of ideas' nor in 'matters of fact'. (This surely amounts to Autonomy$_1$ at least, even though it may be anachronistic to suppose that Hume's distinction exactly coincides with the analytic *a priori* synthetic *a posteriori* distinction as it is commonly drawn today, and even though Hume tends to write as if he – inconsistently – regarded moral judgements not as expressing approval, but rather as statements to the effect that the speaker or others approve certain things.) And then, thinking very reasonably that what has upset the philosophical systems will upset the vulgar too, Hume in the concluding paragraph of the section in effect summarises his arguments and directs them at the vulgar. The last few lines of the paragraph seem to me very clearly to support this interpretation. The 'small attention' recommended is held not merely to 'subvert all the vulgar systems of

[9] Selby-Bigge edition, p. 270.

morality', but also to make clear to us – what Hume has laboured to show in the preceding parts of the section – 'that the distinction of vice and virtue is not founded merely on the relations of objects, nor is perceiv'd by reason.'

Be all this as it may, it is instructive to refer to Hume's discussion of Wollaston, whom he takes to have maintained that an action's tendency to cause a false judgement in others is 'the first spring or original source of all immorality.'[10] Against this he argues that such an attempt to supply a non-moral foundation for morality is either circular or invalid. The point that it is, on one interpretation, circular is made in paragraphs 6 and 7 of the footnote:

> Besides, we may easily observe, that in all those arguments there is an evident reasoning in a circle. A person who takes possession of *another's* goods, and uses them as his *own*, in a manner declares them to be his own; and this falsehood is the source of the immorality of injustice. But is property, or right, or obligation, intelligible, without an antecedent morality?
>
> A man that is ungrateful to his benefactor, in a manner affirms that he never received any favours from him. But in what manner? Is it because 'tis his duty to be grateful? But this supposes, that there is some antecedent rule of duty and morals. . . .

The alternative charge of invalidity is made in paragraph 8:

> But what may suffice entirely to destroy this whimsical system is, that it leaves us under the same difficulty to give a reason why truth is virtuous and falsehood vicious, as to account for the merit or turpitude of any other action. I shall allow, if you please, that all immorality is derived from this supposed falsehood in action, provided you can give me any plausible reason, why such a falsehood is immoral. If you consider rightly of the matter, you will find yourself in the same difficulty as at the beginning.

Hume has, of course, a variety of arguments against Wollaston, but one of them, which I have tried to illustrate by the above quotation, is that Wollaston's arguments either lack a moral premise and hence are defective, *or*, if they have a moral premise and so are deductive, that they are circular and fail to supply a (non-moral) foundation for morality. Hume, in fact, commits himself to the view I have labelled Autonomy$_2$. It is no doubt partly for this reason that MacIntyre takes the trouble to remark (p. 46) that Hume would not have counted Wollaston's 'whimsical system' among the vulgar. But even so there is surely little reason to suppose that Hume

[10] *Treatise*, p. 461 and n.

intended to retract what he had said against Wollaston when criticising the vulgar in the 'ought/is' passage. Nor, clearly, could he
have consistently done so. At the very best, MacIntyre's Hume
would not appear to be markedly more consistent than the Hume of
the so-called standard interpretation.

To conclude: I do not want to be taken as suggesting that Mac-
Intyre's points are unworthy of serious consideration, but only that
they are not conclusive against the received interpretation whether
that be that Hume is maintaining Autonomy$_1$ or Autonomy$_2$. I think
further that proponents of one or other version of the received interpretation ought to be grateful to MacIntyre for arousing it from 'the
deep slumber of a decided opinion'? So much on the interpretation
of the 'ought/is' passage in particular. On the topic of Hume's
ethical views as a whole, I quite agree with MacIntyre that it would
be grossly misleading to represent him as taking a view of the same
general type as, say, Hare's, and I do not doubt that a Toulmin-type
view can fairly readily be constructed out of Humean materials –
but so can a Stevenson-type view for that matter. On no such interpretation or re-interpretation, it seems to me, can Hume be made
wholly consistent. This is no doubt to a large extent due to his
immense subtlety, insight, and open-mindedness. As for Hume's
place in the history of ethics, I agree that he belongs to the Aristotelian rather than the Kantian camp, though I find a thought
extravagant the suggestion that Hume was the *last* representative of
the Aristotelian tradition.

III Hume on *is* and *ought*

Geoffrey Hunter

Was Hume here[1] claiming or implying that propositions about what men ought to do are radically different from purely factual propositions, and that they cannot ever be entailed by any purely factual propositions? No, despite Mr Hare, Professor Nowell-Smith, Professor Ayer, Miss Murdoch, Professor Flew, Mr Basson, and the *Observer*'s Brief Guide to philosophy.

Mr A. C. MacIntyre has argued at length (Paper I) against what I shall call the 'Brief Guide interpretation' of Hume; and my aim here is only to show more shortly and more simply than he does that the Brief Guide interpretation is wrong.

In the paragraph *immediately before* the one quoted above Hume writes:

> when you pronounce any action or character to be vicious, you mean nothing, but that from the constitution of your nature you have a feeling or sentiment of blame from the contemplation of it.

This is no casual statement: Hume thought the passage important enough to ask Hutcheson's advice about it before publication (in a letter dated 16 March 1740). And what Hume is saying here is that 'This action is vicious' *just means* 'Contemplation of this action causes a feeling or sentiment of blame in me'. Now the statement 'Contemplation of this action causes a feeling or sentiment of blame in me' *is a statement of fact*, in the Brief Guide's sense of 'statement of fact'. And Hume obviously thinks that a similar sort of analysis holds good for all moral judgements, including statements of moral obligation. Cp. *Treatise*, III. ii. 2 (Selby-Bigge ed. p. 498):

> the *moral* obligation, or the sentiment of right and wrong. . . .

and III. ii. 5 (S.-B. p. 517):

> All morality depends upon our sentiments; . . . and when the neglect, or non-performance of [an action], displeases us *after a* [certain] manner, we say that we lie under an obligation to perform it.

[1] i.e. in the passage quoted by MacIntyre above, pp. 35–6.

Cp. also *Treatise* III. ii. 8 (S.-B. pp. 546–7):

> The distinction of moral good and evil is founded on the pleasure
> or pain, which results from the view of any sentiment, or charac-
> ter; and as that pleasure or pain cannot be unknown to the per-
> son who feels is, it follows, that there is just so much vice or virtue
> in any character, as every one places in it, and that 'tis impossible
> in this particular we can ever be mistaken.

and III. ii. 2 (S.-B. p. 471):

> We do not infer a character to be virtuous, because it pleases: But
> in feeling that it pleases after such a particular manner, we in
> effect feel that it is virtuous.

In short, it is a central part of Hume's moral theory that moral
judgements *are* statements of fact[2] (in the Brief Guide's sense of
'statement of fact'), namely statements to the effect that there is a
causal relation between the speaker's contemplation of some actual
or imagined state of affairs and his feeling certain 'peculiar' (S.-B.
p. 472) 'feelings' or 'sentiments'. Hume makes *ought*-propositions a
sub-class of *is*-propositions, namely *is*-propositions about the causa-
tion of certain sorts of feelings. Since he thinks that *ought*-proposi-
tions are logically equivalent to certain *is*-propositions, it is absurd
to attribute to him the view that no *is*-proposition can by itself entail
an *ought*-proposition, or that no statement of fact can by itself entail
a moral judgement.

Thus the celebrated passage about *is* and *ought* must be interpreted very differently from the way it has often been taken during
the last ten years. There seem to be at least two possible interpretations:

(1) 'It *seems* inconceivable that *ought*-propositions should be
deducible from *is*-propositions, but it *is not in fact* inconceivable'
(Hume writes 'seems inconceivable', not 'is inconceivable').

On this interpretation, what Hume is objecting to in the work
of earlier writers is their *failure to explain* (failure to give an
analysis of) the relation expressed by 'ought'. He is not saying
that 'ought' cannot be deduced from 'is', only that earlier writers
have failed to explain how this deduction is possible. He himself
sets out to explain how it is possible. On this interpretation Hume

[2] Cp. *Enquiry concerning the Principles of Morals*, Selby-Bigge ed.
p. 289: 'The hypothesis which we embrace is plain. It maintains that
morality is determined by sentiment. It defines virtue to be *whatever
mental action or quality gives to a spectator the pleasing sentiment of
approbation*; and vice the contrary. We then proceed to examine a plain
matter of fact, to wit, what actions have this influence.'

is certainly not rejecting all theories in which 'ought' is deducible from 'is'; for his own theory would be one such theory.

(2)[3] '*Ought*-propositions cannot ever be deduced from *is*-propositions. But the reason for this is that sentences expressing *ought*-propositions are paraphrases of certain sentences expressing *is*-propositions, and paraphrasing is not deducing. To give a paraphrase is not to make any deductive move or inference, but only to say the same thing over again.'

This interpretation of Hume finds some support in a passage already quoted: 'We do not *infer* a character to be virtuous because it pleases: But in feeling that it pleases after such a particular manner, we in effect feel that it is virtuous' (my italics). If this is how Hume should be interpreted, then his reason for saying that 'ought' cannot be deduced from 'is' is not, as the Brief Guide interpretation has it, that there is a great gulf fixed between *is*-propositions and *ought*-propositions, but rather that since *ought*-propositions are *identical* with certain *is*-propositions, it is absurd to talk of any sort of inferential *move* from one to the other. What rules out the inference of 'ought' from 'is' is not that 'ought' is too far from 'is', but that it is *too close*.

I think that the first of these interpretations is the right one. There may be other possible readings of the passage. But interpretations that make Hume say that moral judgements are not statements of fact, or that there is a logical gulf between a moral judgement and *any* statement of fact, seem to me to be altogether impossible.

James Ward Smith, in an article in the *Philosophical Review* for January 1960, claims that Hume persistently differentiates moral judgements from casual judgements, and he refers to sections II. iii. 3 and III. i. 1 of the *Treatise* in support of his claim. I cannot find anything in section II. iii. 3 that proves Smith's case, and the words he quotes from section III. i. 1 admit of a different interpretation from the one that Smith puts on them. They are:

Nor does this reasoning only prove, that morality consists not in any relations, that are the objects of science; but if examin'd, will prove with equal certainty, that it consists not in any *matter of fact*, which can be discover'd by the understanding (S.-B. p. 468: from the same paragraph as the words 'when you pronounce any action ... to be vicious, you mean nothing, but ...', etc.).

Against Smith, I interpret Hume as saying, in the first part of this passage, that morality consists not in any relations that are the objects of *science in that Hume-ian sense of 'science' in which*

[3] The possibility of this interpretation was suggested to me by Professor Ryle.

science has to do only with relations of ideas (cp. S.-B. p. 466: 'Reason or science is nothing but the comparing of ideas, and the discovery of their relations'). Hume's thought here is only that moral judgements are *not analytic*. In the second part of the passage I take Hume to be saying that the truth of a moral judgement cannot be discovered by the understanding *alone* (cp. S.-B. p. 463: 'If the thought and understanding were alone capable of fixing the boundaries of right and wrong...'). According to Hume, in order for a moral judgement to be true, there must be a causal connection between something and a sentiment; *this sentiment is not discoverable by the understanding*, since ' 'tis the object of feeling, not of reason' (S.-B. p. 469); hence the truth of a moral judgement is not discoverable by the understanding, that is, by the understanding alone. So what Hume is doing in the second part of the passage is differentiating moral judgements, not from causal judgements, but from truths of fact, whether causal or not, *that can be discovered by the understanding alone*.

The last words of the famous paragraph should be understood in a similar way. They are:

> the distinction of vice and virtue is not founded merely on the relations of objects, nor is perceiv'd by reason.

The distinction of vice and virtue is not founded *merely* on the relations of *objects*, because it is founded on the *sentiments* felt by *people contemplating* relations of objects. It is not perceived by reason alone, because these sentiments themselves are the objects not of reason but of feeling. There is nothing here that is incompatible with the view I am attributing to Hume, namely that a moral judgement states that there is a causal relation between the contemplation by the speaker of some actual or imagined state of affairs and a certain sort of feeling or sentiment that he has when he does the contemplating.

Hume's analysis of moral judgements is mistaken. For, among other things, it has the consequence that if one person says of an action that it is wholly virtuous and another person says of the same action that it is wholly vicious, these two people would not be contradicting each other, since one is saying the logical equivalent of 'I [Smith] feel a peculiar sort of pleasure, and I do not feel a peculiar sort of pain, on contemplating this action', while the other is saying the equivalent of 'I [Jones] feel a peculiar sort of pain, and I do not feel a peculiar sort of pleasure, on contemplating this action', and both these statements could be true. If they were both true, and Hume's analysis were correct, then one and the same action would *be* both wholly virtuous and wholly vicious, which, in the ordinary senses of the words used, is absurd.

I leave undiscussed the question whether or not purely factual premises can ever by themselves entail conclusions about what people morally ought to do.

IV On the interpretation of Hume

Antony Flew

(1) In his 'Hume on *Is* and *Ought*' ... Mr Geoffrey Hunter discusses the now famous passage on *is* and *ought* (Treatise, III. i. 1). (It is perhaps worth underlining, parenthetically, that *now*. For in *Principia Ethica* Moore did not even mention the passage; indeed, there is no reference at all to Hume in the Index.) Hunter challenges what he calls 'the Brief Guide interpretation' (BGI). This consists in asserting that Hume here was 'claiming or implying that propositions about what men ought to do are radically different from purely factual propositions, and that they cannot ever be entailed by any purely factual propositions'.

Hunter begins by referring to an article by his former colleague Mr A. C. MacIntyre (see Paper I); and he explains, 'my aim here is only to show more shortly and more simply than he does that the Brief Guide's interpretation is wrong'. Since I believe that my former colleague Professor R. F. Atkinson dealt very faithfully with MacIntyre's arguments in his own reply (see Paper II), I shall follow Hunter in making no further reference to MacIntyre.

Hunter's basic idea is that the BGI cannot be correct; because Hume himself elsewhere offers analyses of moral utterances which construe these as being themselves statements of fact. Hunter, for instance, points out that, in the equally famous paragraph which precedes the one under discussion, Hume insists: 'So that when you pronounce any action or character to be vicious, you mean nothing but that, from the constitution of your nature, you have a feeling or sentiment of blame from the contemplation of it'. Hunter's conclusion runs: 'Since he thinks that *ought*-propositions are logically equivalent to certain *is*-propositions, it is absurd to attribute to him the view that no *is*-proposition can by itself entail an *ought*-proposition, or that no statement of fact can by itself entail a moral judgement. Thus, the celebrated passage about *is* and *ought* must be interpreted very differently from the way in which it has often been taken during the last ten years.'

I want here to do two things. First, in section 2, to argue: both, particularly, that Hunter has given us no good reason for abandoning the BGI; and, generally, that his fundamental principle of interpretation is illegitimate. Second, in sections 3 and 4, to try to show: both, more particularly, how we can come to terms with the apparent contradiction which so disturbs Hunter; and, more generally, how the sorts of misinterpretation to which he and others are here and elsewhere inclined may in part result from a common contemporary failure to take account of Hume's own main stated interests.

(2) The principle which Hunter is following is one which is often, but tacitly, employed by the more devout sort of Kant or Plato scholar, unwilling ever to allow that his hero actually made mistakes. It is also favoured by those philosophers of religion – not by any means always themselves believers – who assume that the philosophical analyst is professionally committed: not just to producing analyses which are in fact correct; but to assuming that no analysis can possibly be correct unless it will allow the belief so analysed to count as rational, or at least as not positively irrational. It is unusual, and in a way refreshing, to find this unsound principle being employed in the defence of Hume; a philosopher who has very rarely been accorded such privileged treatment. Nevertheless, as a principle, it is unsound. It consists simply in insisting that where two passages in an author appear to be inconsistent, one of these passages has to be so interpreted that the apparent inconsistency is resolved. Let us label this, rudely, the Infallibility Assumption.

Now this Infallibility Assumption is quite different from the entirely sound and proper rule that we should always employ all the resources of scholarship in the attempt to show, what may of course turn out not to be true, that any apparent absurdities or apparent inconsistencies in our author are when properly understood neither absurdities nor inconsistencies. The temptation, to which Hunter seems to have succumbed, is to confuse these two principles; and to replace the second, which really is a fudamental rule of sympathetic scholarship, by the first, which has only to be formulated to be seen to be preposterous. This aetiological suggestion is, of course, speculative. But that Hunter's whole argument for forcing some fresh interpretation on to the famous *ought/is* paragraph depends upon the Infallibility Assumption is, surely, certain. Consider again the presuppositions and implications of the sentences already quoted. 'Since he [Hume] thinks that ought-propositions are logically equivalent to certain is-propositions, *it is absurd* to attribute to him

the view that no is-proposition can by itself entail an ought-proposi-
tion, or that no statement of fact can by itself entail a moral judgement. Thus, the celebrated passage about is and ought *must* be
interpreted very differently from the way it has often been taken
during the last ten years.' (The italicising is, this time, mine.)

(3) But, though we may dismiss this insistence that *it is absurd* to
hold that Hume contradicted himself as being itself absurd; and
though we may reject as preposterous the Infallibility Assumption,
which alone could justify the conclusion that this passage *must* be
reinterpreted; still there remains the question of what is to be said
about the apparent contradiction to which Hunter is pointing. The
answer, I think, is: not that we ought to be surprised if we find
Hume being slightly, or even very seriously, inconsistent here; but
that it would be perfectly extraordinary had he contrived not to be
inconsistent at all.

Hunter maintains that 'it is a central part of Hume's moral
theory that moral judgements *are* statements of fact . . . namely statements to the effect that there is a causal relation between the
speaker's contemplation of some actual or imagined state of affairs
and his feeling certain "peculiar" . . . "feelings" or "sentiments".'
Now – waiving the point that in the second *Inquiry* 'a spectator'
replaces 'the speaker' – it may possibly have to be allowed that this
is perhaps strictly correct. But it quite certainly gets the emphasis
wrong. It would be so much better to say that Hume's central insight was: that moral judgements are *not* statements of *either* logically necessary truths *or* facts about the natural (or supernatural)
universe around us; *and, hence,* that 'All morality depends upon our
sentiments' (*Treatise*, III. ii. 5).

It is the disturbing implications of this fundamental anthropo-
centricity which raised the questions about which Hume was consulting Hutcheson in that letter of 1740 to which Hunter refers: 'I
wish from my heart I could avoid concluding that since morality,
according to your opinion as well as mine, is determined merely by
sentiment, it regards only human nature and human life. This has
often been urged against you, and the consequences are very
momentous' (*Letters*, edited by J. Y. T. Greig: vol. I, no. xvi, p. 40).
The point is that Hume's first concern was: not with the idea that
moral judgements report some sort of fact about us; but rather with
the contention that they cannot be analysed in terms simply of any
sort of statement about some objective reality entirely independent
of human sentiments and human desires.

Now if this is right, as surely it is, then Hume is to be regarded as the first parent of all those tough-minded and this-worldly moralists who are characterised by their opponents as, in an admittedly very broad sense, subjectivists, and who might, in America at any rate, label themselves as, in an equally broad and quite unMoorean sense, naturalists: such writers as F. P. Ramsey, Ayer, Stevenson, Hare, Nowell-Smith, Edwards, *et hoc genus omne*. Once we have seen Hume in this perspective we no longer have any business to be surprised if we should find that he fails perfectly and systematically to reconcile what he has to say about *ought* and *is* with either of his two positive accounts of the nature of moral judgement. It is, nevertheless, worth underlining that Hume's 'observation . . . of some importance' about *ought* and *is* meshes in perfectly with his primary rejection of the idea that such judgements are reducible to assertions *either* of logical necessities *or* of facts about the natural (or supernatural) world quite independent of all human interest. No doubt he ought to have said, boldly and consistently, something like: that when we say *This is wrong* we are not stating anything, not even that we have certain feelings, but rather we are giving vent to our feelings; or that when we say *He ought to resign* we are again not stating anything, but instead uttering some rather devious sort of crypto-command. But years of labour and ingenuity have been needed fully to develop such fashionable and sophisticated moves.

What is remarkable is that he should ever have got as near to this as he sometimes did. Take, for instance, the penultimate paragraph of the first *Inquiry*, the paragraph which serves as a 'trailer' for the second *Inquiry*; the work which he described in his autobiography as 'of all my writings, historical, philosophical, or literary, incomparably the best'. This reads: 'Morals and criticism are not so properly objects of the understanding as of taste and sentiment. Beauty, whether moral or natural, is felt more properly than perceived. Or if we reason concerning it, and endeavour to fix the standard, we regard a new fact, to wit, the general taste of mankind, or some such fact which may be the object of reasoning and inquiry.'

(4) One final point, with implications extending over the whole field of Hume interpretation. The *Treatise* and the two *Inquiries* seem often to be read as if they had been written for submission to the journal *Analysis*. But to understand Hume it is necessary always to remember that he thought of himself as contributing in these works to a would-be Newtonian science of man; or, failing that, to some sort of mental geography. (See, for instance, both the subtitle and the whole 'Introduction' of the *Treatise*; and compare section I of the first *Inquiry*. Compare too J. A. Passmore *Hume's Intentions*,

especially chapter III.) In Hume's view the second *Inquiry* is thus a
sort of *Prolegomena to the Mechanics of Morals*: and hence it is
entirely appropriate that most of what it contains in the way of philosophy, in the narrowest modern sense, is stowed away in the
appendices.

The present implication of this is that we need to be much more
cautious in construing Hume's famous definitions of the meaning of
prescriptive moral utterances than Hunter, and many others, have
been. Thus, in the first appendix to the second *Inquiry*, Hume
writes: 'The hypothesis which we embrace is plain. It maintains that
morality is determined by sentiment. It defines virtue to be *whatever
mental action or quality gives to a spectator the pleasing sentiment
of approbation*; and vice the contrary. We then proceed to a plain
matter of fact – to wit, what actions have this influence.' Even from
the rather limited context which we are able to quote it must surely
be clear that Hume's main concern here is not with a question of
logical analysis but with issues of psycho-social fact. Consider too,
from the same appendix: 'But after every circumstance, every relation, is known the understanding has no further room to operate, nor
any object on which it could employ itself. The approbation or
blame which then ensues cannot be the work of the judgement but of
the heart; and it is not a speculative proposition or affirmation, but
an active feeling or sentiment.' Or again, and perhaps still more
striking, consider, from later in the same paragraph: 'And when
we *express* that detestation against him [Nero] ... it is not that we
see any relations of which he was ignorant, but that, ... we *feel*
sentiments against which he was hardened' (italics supplied). These
passages are all no doubt wearisomely familiar. But they are not
being adequately appreciated when Hunter can bluntly assert: 'In
short, it is a central part of Hume's moral theory that moral judgements *are* statements of fact' (italics original).

The other famous 'definition' is that of the *Treatise*: 'So that,
when you pronounce any action or character to be vicious, you
mean nothing but that, from the constitution of your nature, you
have a feeling or sentiment of blame from the contemplation of it.
Vice and virtue, therefore, may be compared to sounds, colours,
heat and cold, which ... are not qualities in objects, but perceptions
in the mind. And this discovery in morals, like that other in physics,
is to be regarded as a considerable advancement of the speculative
sciences ...'. Once again this 'definition' too, when taken in context,
does not seem to be intended by Hume in quite the way in which a
contemporary philosophical moralist might offer a definition epito-

mising his analytical investigations. The emphasis is all on the alleged psychological and other non-linguistic facts rather than on what the words, as currently used, actually mean. The young Hume's choice of phrase is also, surely, significant. These are the phrases of the harsh debunker: 'You pronounce . . .' but 'you mean nothing but that . . .'. When phrases of this sort are employed the point usually is: not that this is what your actual words do actually mean; but rather that this is what, if you would only face the facts and be entirely honest, you would have to admit. It is this sort of brilliant harshness which sometimes makes one want to describe the *Treatise* as Hume's *Language, Truth, and Logic.*

V A reply to Professor Flew

Geoffrey Hunter

In my original note I did not present the case against the BGI as
as well as it could have been presented. Let me try again, this time
profiting from the criticisms of Professor Flew and others, and
especially from the comments of Mr Bernard Williams.

1. The Brief Guide interpretation of the remarks about *is* and
ought in the last paragraph of *Treatise*, III. i. 1 is logically incompatible with what Hume says about moral judgements elsewhere, and
in particular with what he says in the paragraph immediately before,
in which he makes it clear that for him moral judgements are statements of fact, in the Brief Guide's sense of 'statements of fact' (the
whole of that preceding paragraph supports my case, and not just
the few words I quoted from it in my original note).

2. The case for the BGI rests solely on the last paragraph of
Treatise, III. i. 1.

3. In the last paragraph of *Treatise*, III. i. 1 Hume does not say
that no *ought*-proposition can be validly deduced from any set of *is*-
propositions. Taken in conjunction with 2, this means that there is
no sure textual foundation for the BGI.

4. The BGI is a quite recent and parochial interpretation of the
passage, perhaps only to be found among some British philosophers
and only during the last fifteen years: these philosophers have themselves been much concerned with 'the logical gulf between *is* and
ought'. Take this in conjunction with 3, and it begins to look as
though the BGI has its source as much in present-day concern with
the gulf between *is* and *ought* as in the careful reading of Hume.

5. 'But if the BGI is wrong, what does the famous paragraph
mean?' Here my original note was inadequate: I had all the pieces
in my hands but I did not fit them together properly. In that note
I said that what Hume was objecting to in earlier writers was their
failure to explain how *ought* can be deduced from *is*, and that Hume
himself set out to repair this deficiency. But, as Bernard Williams
pointed out to me, to draw attention to earlier writers' failure to
explain something that could be explained would scarcely 'subvert

all the vulgar systems of morality': at most it would show them to be incomplete. If Hare's interpretation ('Earlier writers deduced *ought* from *is*, and this is never legitimate') is too strong, mine ('Earlier writers failed to explain how *ought* can be deduced from *is*') is too weak. Hume must have meant something more than I attributed to him.

6. For what seems to me obviously the right answer I am indebted to Williams. What Hume is objecting to in this passage is, not the deduction-in-general of *ought*-propositions from *is*-propositions, and not the mere failure to explain how such deductions are possible, but the unjustified and unjustifiable deduction of *ought*-propositions from *is*-propositions that refer merely to relations of reason or of external objects and say nothing about human sentiments. Hume is saying: '*Ought*-propositions involve essentially reference to human sentiments or feelings, and sentiments are the objects of feeling, not of reason or the understanding. *Ought*-propositions cannot therefore be validly deduced from propositions that refer merely to objects of reason or the understanding. The vulgar systems of morality fail to take account of this. They all involve a move from propositions that according to them refer merely to objects of reason, such as eternal fitnesses and unfitnesses of things, or else from propositions that refer merely to relations between external objects, i.e. that refer merely to objects of the understanding, to propositions about how men ought to live. But propositions about how men ought to live refer to human sentiments and cannot be deduced from propositions that are merely about the relations of objects or are merely about what can be perceived by reason, i.e. from propositions that do not refer to human sentiments [Cf. the last words of the famous paragraph: '. . . this small attention wou'd subvert all the vulgar systems of morality, and let us see, that the distinction of vice and virtue is not founded merely on the relations of objects, nor is perceiv'd by reason']. So all these systems involve an unjustified and unjustifiable move from some set of *is*-propositions in which no reference is made to human sentiments to *ought*-propositions, which by their very nature do refer to human sentiments.' 'Earlier writers have failed to explain how the deduction of *ought* from *is* is possible': so far my earlier interpretation was right. But I should have added: 'and if you think about what I [Hume] have shown about *ought*-propositions, and if you consider also the nature of those earlier writers' premises, you will see that in their case the deduction is not legitimate'.

It seems to me that there was a good deal of agreement between

Flew's reply to my original note and the note itself (see especially pp. 61–2), and I wonder now whether there is anything in this new and improved version that he really wants to quarrel with. What I was, and am, attacking is the BGI, i.e. the claim that in the last paragraph of *Treatise*, III. i. 1 Hume said that no *ought*-proposition can be validly deduced from any set of *is*-propositions. Hume did not say this. Does Flew think he did?

My colleague Peter Long has found at least one bad mistake in my note. I claimed that if Hume's analysis were correct, then one and the same action might in certain circumstances be both wholly virtuous and wholly vicious (see p. 63 above, last sentence but one). In fact Professor Stevenson has shown, in a careful discussion of a similar claim made by Moore in his *Ethics*, that it does not follow from a Hume-ian analysis of moral judgements that one and the same action might be both right and wrong (in P. A. Schilpp (ed.), *The Philosophy of G. E. Moore*, pp. 74–7). Moore agreed with Stevenson's criticism (op. cit. pp. 547–51). This is a point of philosophical, and not merely historical, importance.

VI Hume on *is* and *ought*

W. D. Hudson

Hume's famous passage[1] has recently come in for some re-interpretation. Contemporary philosophers were accustomed to interpret Hume as condemning any attempt to deduce *ought* from *is*. But Mr A. C. MacIntyre (Paper I) and Mr Geoffrey Hunter (Paper III), amongst others, have assured us that he was doing no such thing. So far from condemning this move, he was in fact intent upon making it himself. In the famous passage he was simply complaining 'that earlier writers have failed to explain how this deduction is possible' (Hunter's interpretation), or rejecting the way in which religious moralists make the move, that is, 'repudiating a religious foundation for morality and putting in its place a foundation in human needs, interests, desires, and happiness' (MacIntyre's interpretation). MacIntyre thinks that Hume's attempt to make the move 'shows us how it can be made' (p. 46); Hunter, on the other hand, says that Hume was 'mistaken' (p. 62). But, in the view that he was attempting to make it, they are at one. I do not think that they have proved their point. Two issues are involved here, of course: (i) what was Hume's opinion in this matter of *is* and *ought*?, and (ii) what is the correct view? I shall try not to confuse them.

I

Hunter calls attention to a paragraph, immediately before the famous one referred to, in which Hume says:

> when you pronounce any action or character to be vicious, you mean nothing, but that from the constitution of your nature you have a feeling or sentiment of blame from the contemplation of it.

The crucial word here is 'mean'. Hunter's interpretation of this passage runs as follows: 'This is no casual statement ... what Hume is saying here is that "This action is vicious" *just means*

[1] I.e. the one quoted by MacIntyre above, pp. 35–6.

"Contemplation of this action causes a feeling or sentiment of blame in me". Now the statement "Contemplation of this action causes a feeling or sentiment of blame in me" *is a statement of fact*. . . . And Hume obviously thinks that a similar sort of analysis holds good for all moral judgements . . .'. Hunter brings out explicitly what he takes the force of Hume's 'mean' to be: 'In short, it is a central part of Hume's moral theory that moral judgements *are* statements of fact' (pp. 59–60). But was it Hume's concern here to maintain that moral judgements are statements of fact? He was certainly intent upon maintaining that they are not matters of fact 'which can be discover'd by the understanding' (*Treatise*, III. i. 1). If his moral philosophy is set in its historical context, it will be seen that its purport was to rebut the doctrine of rational intuitionists, such as Cudworth, Clarke or Richard Price, that moral attributes are non-natural, objective properties, apprehended by reason. The only matters of fact involved, when moral judgements are made, Hume asserts, are 'certain passions, motives, volitions and thoughts' (ibid.). 'You never can find it (*sc.* the viciousness of wilful murder) till you turn your reflexion into your own breast, and find a sentiment of disapprobation, which arises in you, towards this action' (ibid.). It is now that Hume makes his remark that, when we pronounce an act to be vicious, we 'mean nothing but' that we have a sentiment of blame towards it. What shall we take his point to be: (*a*) the positive one that 'X is vicious' is equivalent to 'I have a sentiment of blame towards X', or (*b*) the negative one that 'X is vicious' is not equivalent to 'X has a non-natural, objective property of viciousness, apprehended by reason'? In support of taking it to be the latter, the fact may be adduced that Hume's whole section is headed 'Moral distinctions not deriv'd from reason'.

Professor A. Flew argues that Hume's contention in his 'mean nothing but' is not that the words 'X is vicious' do actually mean 'I have a sentiment of blame towards X', but rather that this is what 'if you would only face the facts and be entirely honest, you would have to admit' (p. 69). But just why did Hume want his readers to admit this? There are two conceivable answers.

(i) He might conceivably have wished to establish the psychological thesis that, when we say 'X is vicious', we are experiencing, or have experienced in the past, a particular sort of feeling about X. The purport of the word 'mean' is not infrequently that some such inference can be drawn. For instance, 'He said that he was going home; that meant he was bored'. Whether, when we say 'X is vicious', we mean that we have a sentiment of blame towards X in this sense is not a logical, but an empirical question, to be answered, not by analysis, but observation. But is it really credible that Hume's contention was simply that certain psychological inferences can be drawn from the fact that we make the moral judgements which we do? If it was simply this, then it was irrelevant to the debate in which it was a contribution, for any of the rationalists would have conceded that investigation might conceivably show that moral judgements were always accompanied by certain feelings. This, however, was entirely beside the point, which was that moral judgements have a certain logical character, namely that of being statements of objective, non-natural fact.

(ii) This brings us to the second conceivable answer to our question. Hume may have wished us to admit that moral judgements are subjective, i.e. that, when we say 'X is vicious', we are voicing our own reaction to it, not stating some fact about it, as the proponents of moral objectivism maintained. Hume writes: 'To have the sense of virtue, is nothing but to *feel* a satisfaction of a particular kind from the contemplation of a character' (*Treatise*, III. i. 2). Now feeling, or rather giving vent to feeling, is not the same logical or linguistic activity as saying that you are having a feeling. Hume, it is true, did not draw this distinction as sharply as a contemporary philosopher would; but it cannot be doubted that, however confused he was about it, it was his concern to make a logical point about moral judgements against the rationalists, rather than to advance a thesis in psychology. It is with this in mind that his 'mean nothing but' should be interpreted. His contention, to use contemporary terms, was that moral judgements are emotive or subjective. But moral judgements even if emotive – one might say particularly if emotive – are logically distinct from statements of psychological fact, and I do not think that it can be shown to follow, from the indisputable fact that Hume made much of the feeling element in moral judgement, that he intended to equate 'X is vicious' with 'I have such-and-such a feeling for X'. He tells us that he has been listening carefully to the uses made of *is* and *ought* (see the passage quoted by MacIntyre, above, pp. 35–6) and has been puzzled as to how men get from one to the other. But what was he puzzled about? If one could take the view that he was intent solely upon subverting religious morality, or some other particular system, then one could perhaps assume that his puzzlement had to do with how men could credit the particular set of is-statements concerned, e.g. 'God gave ten commandments', etc. But against this, notice that he speaks of 'every system of morality', of moralists whose is-statements make 'observations concerning human affairs' as well as of those who speak of the being of a God. It is difficult to see what could have been puzzling Hume, if he had not been of the opinion that, when people pass moral judgements, they are doing something logically different from stating psychological or sociological facts.

II

Some contemporary writers, notably Sir David Ross (see *The Right and the Good*, p. 121) have spoken of the logical relationship between is-statements and ought-statements in terms of constitutive attributes, which are empirical, and consequential ones, which are moral. Act X, for instance, has the constitutive characteristic of being wilful murder, and, because of this, the consequential characteristic of being wrong. Without of course endorsing Ross's intuitionism, Mr R. M. Hare [see *The Language of Morals* (Oxford 1952), pp. 8of., 153, et al.] has the same sort of distinction in mind when he speaks of the 'supervenient' character of moral terms. Is there any indication of such a view in Hume? In the following passage, notice the distinction which is drawn between *observing that* something *is* the case and *justice taking place*:

> When therefore men have had experience enough to observe, that whatever may be the consequence of any single act of justice, perform'd by a single person, yet the whole system of actions, concurr'd in by the whole society, is infinitely advantageous to the whole, and to every part; it is not long before justice and property take place (*Treatise*, III. ii. 2).

According to Hume here, when we observe that X serves the common interest, then 'not long' afterwards, the judgement 'X is just' takes place. Whether this can be substantiated or not, as an empirical claim, is not the point. What matters is that observing that something is the case is differentiated from, yet connected with, pronouncing the moral judgement that it is just. Hume certainly does not make the distinction between constitutive and consequential characteristics explicitly. Nor would one claim that he was as clear about it as modern writers. But that nothing of this kind is in his mind is hard to credit. Here, as elsewhere in Hume, adumbrations of modern theory are distorted by his failure to differentiate clearly and explicitly logical from psychological or sociological issues.

The interpretation which MacIntyre puts on such a passage in Hume as that just quoted is as follows: '... the notion of "ought" is for Hume only explicable in terms of the notion of a consensus of interest. To say that we ought to do something is to affirm that there is a commonly accepted rule; and the existence of such a rule presupposes a consensus of opinion as to where our common interests lie. An obligation is constituted in part by such a consensus and the concept of "ought" is logically dependent on the concept of a common interest and can only be explained in terms of it' (pp. 40–1). A number of doubts arise about all this. (i) I do not think there is anything in Hume which demands the interpretation that 'to say we ought to do something is to affirm that there is a commonly accepted rule'. Hume, of course, makes much of commonly accepted rules in connection with obligation; and to say that one ought to do something is undoubtedly to *use* or *apply* a rule. But that is not logically identical with saying that there is one. (ii) Does Hume say that the *existence* of a commonly accepted rule presupposes a consensus of opinion as to where our interests lie? He makes much of the fact (if indeed it is a fact) that when we see that a rule is in our interest we are ready to *accept* it; but again that is a different matter. (iii) In what way is obligation taken by Hume to be 'logically dependent' on the concept of a common interest? Does he take 'X is in the common interest' by itself to entail 'X is obligatory'? The close connection which he undoubtedly draws between the notions of obligation and common interest need not be interpreted in this way. Mr R. F. Atkinson (above, p. 53) suggests that MacIntyre is not denying that Hume would have objected to this way of interpreting it. Be that as it may, there is an alternative open. 'X is obligatory' can be taken to be entailed *in part* by 'X is in the common interest'. If whatever is in the common interest is obligatory, and X is in the common interest, then X is obligatory. It is true that, where there is a consensus of opinion that X is in the common interest, there is likely to be agreement that it is obligatory. If Hume maintains that this is more than likely, then that, Atkinson suggests, following Stevenson (p. 54), is 'because he assumes... that all people are inclined to approve the same sorts of thing'. The important point here is that the particular moral judgement, 'X is obligatory', is, on this interpretation, logically dependent on a statement of fact in conjunction with a general moral principle. There is, therefore, an 'ought' in the premises as well as in the conclusion. But this can hardly be the logical dependence which MacIntyre has in mind, or takes Hume to have had in mind, because it is perfectly compatible with the customary interpretations of Hume on *is-ought*, in Hare, Nowell-Smith, etc., which MacIntyre claims to be refuting. But I do not see why Hume should not be taken to have had this, however vaguely, in mind, especially in the light of his criticism of Wollaston. Against the latter, he points out (*Treatise*, III. i. 1, note) that, from the fact that X is, in a given sense, a lie, it does not follow that X ought not to be done, unless there is 'some antecedent rule of duty and morals' to the effect that acts, which are in the given sense lies, ought not to be done.

MacIntyre contrasts Hume and Mill, claiming that Mill's greatest-happiness principle is a moral principle which stands 'independent of the facts', whereas Hume's rules of justice would lose their justification 'should someone succeed in showing us that the facts are different from what we conceive them to be so that we have no common interests' (pp. 41–2). But is there really any difference here between Mill and Hume? Not if we have been correct in claiming that Hume does not identify saying that something is in the common interest with judging it morally to be just. Mill's principle is 'Seek the greatest happiness', Hume's is 'Seek the common interest'. Both would lose their justification if the facts were different: if, that is, there were no such thing as that which they commend. If there were no such thing as the greatest happiness, this would certainly 'evacuate . . . of meaning' Mill's principle, just as MacIntyre says that it would 'evacuate . . . of meaning' Hume's, if there were no consensus of interest.

III

Hume writes:

> And thus justice establishes itself by a kind of convention or agreement; that is, by a sense of interest, suppos'd to be common to all, and where every single act is perform'd in expectation that others are to perform the like. Without such a convention, no one wou'd ever have dream'd, that there was such a virtue as justice, or have been induc'd to conform his actions to it . . . 'tis only upon the supposition, that others are to imitate my example, that I can be induc'd to embrace that virtue; since nothing but this combination can render justice advantageous, or afford me any motives to conform my self to its rules (*Treatise*, III. ii. 2).

The thing to notice here is the distinction which is drawn between a convention or agreement and the circumstances in which it is made.

Hume's point is that the convention or agreement by which justice 'establishes itself' is made by those who expect others to do the same. But notice that he writes of 'motives to conform . . . to its rules': he differentiates inducements to enter an agreement from the agreement itself. To enter an agreement, for Hume as much as anyone, it would appear, is to do something which can be distinguished from expecting other people to enter it. It is to commit oneself: in this case to 'such a virtue as justice'. Hume is quite right: apart from this agreement or commitment, justice cannot be dreamed of. It is logically and empirically possible that no one would commit himself, unless he expected others to do so too or unless they had already done so. But the circumstances which attend a commitment are logically distinct from the commitment itself. Surely it is doing less than justice to Hume to suggest that he did not realise this. And if he did realise it, then there are no grounds for supposing that he identified saying that we ought to do something with saying that there is a commonly accepted rule.

In support of this theory that the inference from *is* to *ought* is 'in fact made' by Hume, and legitimately made, MacIntyre speaks of 'bridge notions between 'is' and 'ought': wanting, needing, desiring, pleasure, happiness, health – and these are only a few' (p. 46). He goes on: 'I think there is a strong case for saying that moral notions are unintelligible apart from concepts such as these'. It is undoubtedly the case that moral judgements are made in situations where we want, need, etc., and Hume is aware of this; but it does not follow that he was, or thought he was, deducing *ought* from *is*. To say that a game is played in certain circumstances is not to say that the circumstances are part of the game; football is played in winter, entertains great crowds, gives many people their living, but these are not rules of the game. If you score, you may win a bonus at football, and your motive in trying so hard may be desire, or need, for the extra money; but what 'scoring' means in this game is logically distinct from the motives which induce men to try to do it or the profits they reap by doing it. If, by 'moral notions are unintelligible' apart from wanting, needing, etc., MacIntyre means that we find it hard to believe that men without passions would play the moral language-game, then perhaps he is right. Similarly, one might say that football would not go on unless men got some pleasure or other reward from the game. But this does not mean that, apart from pleasure or reward, the rules of the game do not make sense.

IV

MacIntyre says that in the famous *is-ought* passage Hume is 'assert-ing that the question of how the factual basis of morality is related to morality is a crucial logical issue, reflection on which will enable one to realise how there are ways in which this transition can be made and ways in which it cannot' (p. 48). Hume's main point, he tells us, was that notions such as the will of God will not bridge the gap, but passions, such as wanting, needing, etc., will. Well, the gap is certainly bridged. But it is bridged by what those philosophers whom MacIntyre purports to refute would call 'reason-giving sen-tences' which 'turn out to be practical from the start' (P. H. Nowell-Smith, *Ethics*, p. 82). Hume no doubt believed that 'It satis-fies the desire for happiness' was a better such reason-giving sentence than 'It is the will of God'. But this does not mean that he was, or thought he was, bridging the gap between *is* and *ought* in the way which he is generally believed to have condemned.

What Hume says concerning common interests or passions can be subsumed under two heads, viz. (i) that moral judgements are made only in situations where there are common interests or where pas-sions are felt; (ii) that the satisfaction of certain passions, say for security or happiness, is the highest good.

MacIntyre, at the beginning of his article, finds it remarkable that modern philosophers have (*a*) rejected Hume's doubts about in-duction because they are based on the belief that arguments must be either deductive or defective, and (*b*) at the same time accepted his putative view that *ought* cannot be deduced from *is*, which has the same mistaken basis. But would it not be even more remarkable if, as MacIntyre seems to think, *Hume himself* had (*a*) suspected induction because he thought that arguments must be deductive or defective, and (*b*) at the same time been content to make the move from *is* to *ought*, even though that move is clearly *not* deductive? We might have to conclude that, though remarkable, such was the case, if it were impossible to harmonise what Hume says about interests and passions in their relation to moral judgements with the customary interpretation given to his famous *is-ought* passage. But I have tried to show that this is not impossible.

PART TWO

An Attempt to Reduce
Ought *to* Is

VII The 'is-ought': An unnecessary dualism

M. Zimmerman

Suppose we never break through the 'is-ought' barrier, what then? Let us speculate. Then we can never justify ethics and morality. Well, perhaps this would only be true for naturalists, empiricists, emotivists, i.e. for those who believe that statements are justified only if supported by 'is' statements. Hold on. How could they talk about statements being 'justified' only if supported by 'is' statements, if by 'justified' they mean 'ought to be believed'? Would not this be one case of an 'ought' statement in the need of being justified by being supported by 'is' statements, one alleged break through the 'is-ought' barrier?

Well, let us go on. Suppose everybody took this position, i.e. nobody ever believes anything not supported by 'is' statements. Also, suppose by 'ethics' and 'morality' we mean 'ought' statements. Then it would follow that we could never justify ethics and morality. Remember, nobody believes anything not supported by 'is' statements, we can never get 'ought' statements from 'is' statements (we cannot break through the 'is-ought' barrier), and ethics and morality consist of 'ought' statements.

Disaster! We can never justify ethics and morality? What have they done to us? Well, let us continue speculating.

Suppose a prisoner, who recently killed his wife and three children admittedly to collect their life insurance, and is found sane, is before a judge about to sentence him. Ought the judge to sentence him? Remember, neither we nor the judge believe we 'ought' to do anything since we cannot get an 'ought' from an 'is' and we only believe statements supported by 'is' statements. Well, the judge wants to sentence him. We want the judge to sentence him. We believe the judge will sentence him because we believe the judge wants to remain a judge and will not remain a judge if he does not sentence him. These statements can be supported by 'is' statements, so we *can* believe them. Well, 'ought' the judge to want to sentence

him, 'ought' we to want him to sentence him? Of course not, since
we do not believe 'ought' statements. Does that mean the judge will
not want to sentence him, that we will not want the judge to sentence him? Of course not, since these are all 'is supportable' statements. Well, how do we know the judge wants to and will sentence
him, that we want the judge to sentence him? Well, these are 'is
supportable' statements and we may know them from what we
know about judges who want to remain judges, about people, psychology, law, government, crimes, punishment, etc. These are all
'is supportable' statements.

Well, let us revise our story. Suppose the prisoner turns out to be
insane, completely insane, has been for a long time. Then we ought
not to punish him; confine him, institutionalise him, treat him, yes,
but ought we to punish him? No. But hold on, we cannot say we
'ought' not to, remember? Well, will we refrain from punishing
him, will the judge refrain from sentencing him, knowing that he
is insane? That depends.

Let us digress for a moment. What would happen in a society of
'ought' believers, would they punish the insane man? Well, that
depends. Some people would believe we 'ought' to, and some we
'ought' not to.

Let us return to the society of 'is' believers. Would they punish
the insane man, would the judge sentence him? Well, some of us
would want to punish him even if he is insane. Some of us, however,
would not want to punish him, would feel nothing is to be gained by
it, that more is to be gained by institutionalising him, treating him,
etc. Remember, these are all 'is supportable' statements, and we can
believe them and know them the way we know any kind of an 'is
supportable' statement.

True, but can we show the people who want to punish the insane
man that they 'ought' not to punish an insane man? Of course not.
'Ought' statements, *verboten*, remember? Well, can we show them
that nothing is to be gained by punishing him, that institutionalising
him, etc., will prevent him from committing similar crimes? Surely
we can the way we can for any 'is supportable' statement.

Yes, but will we show them that nothing is to be gained from
punishing him, etc., will we want to do this? Well, some of us will,
some of us will feel sorry for the insane man, will sympathise with
him, because he could not help doing what he did. Hold on. How is
it that because he could not help doing what he did, we will want
him not to be punished, we will want to persuade others not to want
him to be punished, etc.? After all, we cannot say that because he

could not help doing what he did, he ought not to be punished, that we ought not to want him to be punished, can we?

Surely, but it is a fact that some of us will not want him to be punished for something he could not help doing, this is an 'is supportable' statement. It is also a fact that some of us will want to and try to persuade others to feel and want and act in the same way. These are all 'is supportable' statements.

Well, but this is all pretty arbitrary, is it not? After all, people's feelings are pretty fickle, liable to change from one moment to the next. Thus, as originally supposed, if the prisoner were sane, his being punished would depend on how the judge, on how we, happened to feel at the time. Likewise, if the prisoner happened to be insane, his fate would be subjected to the same sort of arbitrariness would it not? Well what do you expect in a society without 'ethics' and 'morality'? It would be no surprise if a sane man got away with murder and an insane man were to be 'murdered'.

Let us digress again. Would it be any different in a society of 'ought' believers? Would not there be some who felt we 'ought' to punish a man even if he were insane? Would anything be gained by saying that something ought to be done or not done merely because it just ought to be done or not done? Would any more be gained in such a society by trying to support 'ought' statements with 'is' statements than in the society we have imagined in which 'ought' statements were dispensed with and only 'is' statements were used?

But still, in a society of 'ought' believers we have 'ethical' and 'moral' standards to appeal to, whereas in a society of 'is' believers there are no ethical and moral standards as guides, so does not this make a big difference?

Well, but in a society of 'ought' believers, where there are disagreements in ethical and moral standards what is there to appeal to? Is it not merely a matter of some saying we ought because we ought and others saying we ought not because we ought not? Is not this arbitrary? And if we appeal to 'is' statements in support of 'ought' statements, are we any better off than a society of 'is' believers, with the added disadvantage of trying to break through the 'is-ought' barrier? How frustrating!

But look here, what about the areas of agreement in ethical and moral standards, not only among different cultures and societies, but even where they disagree, within different cultures and societies? Do not ethical and moral standards serve a useful and essential function here? For example, should not we be thankful that in Western

cultures there is fairly universal agreement (even where we sometimes pay mere lip-service to it) that we 'ought' not to punish an
innocent person and we ought not to punish even a 'guilty' but
insane man?

However, is not the point not that we generally agree that we
ought not to do these things, but rather that we do not do these
things, we do not want to do these things, we want to try to persuade others not to want or do these things, and we set up laws and
courts to prevent these things from occurring? Are not these all 'is'
and 'is supportable' statements which would be just as true and to
the same extent believed in a society of 'is' believers? Do not people
generally try to do or prevent what they want very much to do or
prevent, and would not a society of 'is' believers want and try to do
or prevent what a society of 'ought' believers believe they ought to
do or prevent?

Have we not overlooked an important function of 'ought' statements which is brought out by the fact that we do not normally, it
would be odd to, tell people that they 'ought' to do something they
want to do? Is it not the getting people to do what they do not want
to do or refrain from doing what they want to do, by telling them
they ought or ought not to respectively, precisely what would be
lacking in a society of 'is' believers?

Yes, but can you think of any case where we get people to do what
they ought to though they do not want to, merely because we tell
them they ought to, where we could not have found a better way,
without use of 'ought' statements, to achieve the same end? Let us
look at this more closely.

If a man wants to break promises, tell lies, rape or kill, which
is better, merely telling him he ought not to, even if it succeeds in
restraining him, or telling him that if he does what he wants, he
will be disliked, ostracised, punished or killed? This is not all. We
can not only tell him these things, we can do some or all of these
things. But there is even more, much more and even more important. We can use all our resources of knowledge, in the sciences, in
psychology, economics, sociology, etc., and the further acquisition of
knowledge to get him and others to do the things we want him and
others to do. Note that these are all 'is' or 'is supportable' statements. Incidentally, is not this part of what Socrates was getting at
when he said that evil is a result of ignorance?

Well, but have not we completely disregarded those who believe
we can begin with 'ought' statements, that we do not have to get
them logically, deductively or inductively, from 'is' statements, that

by 'intuition' or 'insight' or non-natural qualities, we can know
what ought or ought not to be? Furthermore, even if we cannot get
from an 'is' to an 'ought' surely this is not a symmetrical relation,
surely we can get from an 'ought' to an 'is'; so if those who believe
we can begin with 'ought' statements are correct, would not dispensing with ought statements be doing away with an important body of
ethical and moral truths? If we can know and let others know, we
ought to tell the truth, to keep promises, to preserve life, not to commit adultery, not to inflict needless pain, and knowing this we can
infer that we are more or less likely to *do* what we ought or ought
not to, would not discarding 'ought' statements be sheer folly, even
madness?

Yes, but even if those who believe we can begin with 'ought'
statements were correct, even if we could know these things, is not
the important thing not that we could know these things, but what
we would do and refrain from doing? Is it really the case that if we
could really 'know' that we ought to do something, that if we were
to nevertheless dispense with believing 'ought' statements, that we
are less likely to do it? Even if we dispensed with 'ought' statements,
is it not true that we would tend to want to do what we happen to
believe we ought to even if we also had 'is' reasons for not wanting
to do it? Even in those cases where we have an overwhelming desire
not to do what we believe we ought to, either the use of 'ought'
statements will be ineffective, or, as already indicated, use of or
appeal to other means (punishment, education, etc.) will be as likely
(if not more) to accomplish the end.

More important than this, it is as difficult, if not more, to show
that we can begin with 'ought' statements as it is to break through
the is-ought barrier. Worse, those who believe we can, have continually disagreed over what ought statements to begin with. If we
are told by some that it is self-evident that we ought to preserve our
own life, and by others that it is self-evident that we ought to sacrifice
our lives for our country, what then? If two incompatible statements
are said to be self-evident and it is really the case that one of them
is self-evident, then it follows that the other one cannot be, but has
been mistakenly taken to be self-evident. It does not even make sense
to ask, how do we decide, for deciding implies looking for evidence
which implies that they are not self-evident to begin with. And even
if we look for evidence, i.e. evidence consisting of 'is supportable'
statements, we are back to the 'is-ought' impasse.

But you know, we have been supposing all along that we cannot
break through the is-ought barrier. Suppose we can, suppose those

who believe we can are correct? Now, I do not have in mind those who believe we can because they believe 'ought' statements are translatable into 'is' statements; in the last analysis, this comes to dispensing with 'ought' statements anyway for it amounts to believing 'is' or 'is supportable' statments only, whether in 'disguised' form or otherwise. I am referring to those who believe that, just as 'is' statements have a 'logic of their own', inductive or deductive, which enables us to give acceptable 'is' reasons in support of them, 'ought' statements have their own kind of logic which permits us to give acceptable 'is' reasons in support of them.

For example, it seems reasonable to accept as an 'is' reason for saying we ought not to punish an insane man, that he could not help doing what he did, does it not? Suppose this were true for other 'ought' statements as well, suppose that, at least in many other cases, we could break through the is-ought barrier, would not dispensing with 'ought' statements be like dispensing with inductive arguments because it has a 'different kind of logic' from that of deductive arguments?

Well, suppose in the case of some 'ought' statements we can break through the is-ought barrier, suppose, for example, that most people find the 'is' statement that a man could not help doing what he did, an acceptable 'is' reason for saying that he 'ought' not to be punished? What are we aiming for here in getting people to say that an insane man ought not to be punished, if other than that we do not want to and will not punish an insane man? Would it be any different if we had said that since he could not help doing what he did, we have an acceptable reason for saying that we do not want, we do not want others to want, we will not and will try to persuade others not to, punish him? Do we really think that anybody who accepts the above 'is-ought' argument as reasonable, will not do the same for the above 'is-is' argument? And if there are a few people who do not find the 'is-is' argument reasonable, do we really believe they will find the 'is-ought' argument reasonable? And even if a person were to accept the 'is-ought' argument and nevertheless reject the 'is-is' argument, would not this amount to his saying that what is an acceptable reason for saying that we ought not to punish an insane man, is *not* an acceptable reason for saying we do not want, we do not want others to want, we will not and will try to persuade others not to, punish him? And would not this defeat the purpose of getting him to say that we ought not to punish an insane man, of getting him to accept the 'is-ought' argument, of not dispensing with 'ought' statements?

Furthermore, in having supposed all along that we could not break through the is-ought barrier, we may have failed to realise that this is much more than a mere supposition. It is a real impasse. Not only is there disagreement about whether we *can* break through the is-ought barrier, and here I suspect that there are more who believe we cannot than there are who believe we can, but even among those who believe we can there is disagreement about which 'is' statements are to be considered acceptable or even relevant reasons in support of 'ought' statements. Even the few who believe that ethical and moral statements have a logic of their own, seem to end up with logics of their own for ethical and moral statements.

Oh well, but we have taken a relatively trivial example of a man having committed a few murders, an example which can hardly serve as a model case of important ethical and moral conflict. When you consider something like contemporary totalitarianism, involving persecution, concentration camps, secret police, executions, destruction of freedom, denial of life, liberty, the pursuit of happiness, and all the other things in life we hold to be of greatest value, then we can see more clearly the importance, indeed the necessity of 'ethics' and 'morality'. What could be a better example of 'is' believers than a society ruled by dictators, tyrants, men who have dispensed with 'ethics' and 'morality' who are not in the least concerned with what 'ought' to be done, only concerned with doing what they want, with what *is*.

Look here. It is not really fair to suggest that Hitler did not believe and say that we 'ought' to persecute Jews, that Stalin did not believe and say that we 'ought' to destroy bourgeois democracy, etc., but let that pass. It is hardly necessary to point out that some of the foulest deeds in history, the present-day brutalities of totalitarianism, have been committed in the name of 'ought' statements.

But to get to the real point. Do we think that in a society of 'is' believers, people are less likely to want and fight for life, liberty, and the pursuit of happiness, that they will want and accept concentration camps, persecution, secret police, etc.? Do we honestly believe that a person does not want to be put in a concentration camp or be executed because he believes that he ought not to be? Do we really believe that the development of democracy, the desire for freedom, etc., is a result of a series of 'ought' beliefs, or do we believe that it is connected with what we know and could know about the kind of animal man happens to be and the world he lives in, which we can describe in terms of 'is supportable' statements? It is true, of course, that some people want to and try to persecute others, destroy freedom, etc., but it is also true that some people also believe we ought to do these things, so it will not do to say that using 'ought' statements is more likely to prevent these things from occurring than dispensing with them.

Look at it this way. We happen to believe in democracy, freedom, we are opposed to totalitarianism, etc. It does not matter here whether we say we ought to believe in or want democracy. How do we go about attaining this end? If we continue to use the 'ought' language we will continue to be stuck with finding the right 'ought' statements to begin with, or the 'is-ought' barrier. Remember, the totalitarians will also be using the 'ought' language for their own ends. In the case of finding the right 'ought' statements to begin with, the totalitarians will proclaim their self-evident truths just as we will. In the case of the is-ought barrier, we will be as unable to break through as they will.

Now suppose 'ought' statements are dispensed with, then what? We will no longer have to worry about and spend time finding the right 'ought' statements to begin with or bridging the gap between what 'is' and what 'ought' to be. We will be able to concentrate on finding 'is' and 'is supportable' statements, finding out why people want to persecute and enslave others, discovering the economic, social, political, psychological, etc., reasons for the existence of democracy, totalitarianism, etc.

We will be able to find out ways of promoting the one and preventing the other. Isn't this the sort of thing Dewey had in mind in reiterating the need for scientific method in ethics, in the social sciences?

Hold on. Saying we will be able to do these things, promote democracy, etc., does not mean we will *do* these things or even want to do them. And it does not mean that the totalitarians will not be able to or not actually try to promote totalitarianism. Also, all this talk about obtaining more knowledge, etc., and using it to promote democracy and prevent totalitarianism, how do we know that people will do this sort of thing or even desire to do this?

Oh well. Of course there is no guarantee they will do this, any more than there is that a world of 'ought' believers will. But without 'ought' statements or the gap between 'is' and 'ought' statements to bridge and the hindering results therefrom, the only thing they will have left to fall back on will be the search for 'is supportable' statements, the acquisition of more knowledge, and so on. People will not spend their time telling each other they ought to support or destroy democracy, they ought to fight or adopt totalitarianism, etc. They will not spend their time giving 'is' reasons why they 'ought' or 'ought not' to do such and such, and finding themselves unable to show how from the 'is' reasons they offer it follows that they 'ought' or 'ought not' to do such and such.

Yes, but what is wrong with doing both? Why can't we continue using 'ought' statements, as well as 'is' statements, thereby getting the benefit of both, just as we have been doing all along?

But the whole point has been to consider not merely whether we can do just as well without 'ought' statements, but whether we can do even better without the long history of trying to break through the insufferable 'is-ought' barrier. The point is that if we think we have to rely on 'ought' statements, if we find it impossible to get from an 'is' to an 'ought' then we will have the kind of situation we do in fact have in the present impasse in ethics and morality. It is not a question of getting the benefit of both but rather getting the benefit of one without the hindrance of the other.

Well, this whole thing seems very odd, does it not? I mean, this attempt to show that we ought to do away with 'ought' statements because of the is-ought barrier, and trying to show this by using 'is' statements.

Not at all, there is no need to think we are trying to show that we 'ought' to do away with ought statements. Rather we are merely wondering about what would happen if we dispensed with 'ought' statements as compared to what we can expect if we do not.

But there seems to be another paradox here. After all, have not we presupposed all along that we ought to believe 'is-supportable' statements only? And we cannot say that it is self-evident that we ought to do this, or that we have 'is' reasons for doing this, can we?

True, but this is the same thing, for we have been merely considering what is likely to happen if we rely on 'is-supportable' statements only, as compared to what we can expect if we do not.

VIII Zimmerman's 'is-is': A schizophrenic monism

Kenneth Hanly

In a recent paper[1] Mr Zimmerman proposes that we can do without 'ought' statements. He maintains that if we do so, we will no longer need to worry about the is-ought barrier. There will be no need to wonder how we can infer what we ought to do or what ought to be from what is, since 'ought' will no longer appear in our language. Furthermore, we can get on with the important task of promotng democracy, and generally making the world a better place, instead of spending our time arguing over questions of theoretical ethics which need not concern us.

My main criticism of Zimmerman's position is that we do not really crash the is-ought barrier by removing 'ought' from our language. What happens is that our 'is' statements take on a dual personality: that is, they perform not only the old tasks which they did before the revolution, but also all the tasks that 'ought' used to do. And because they do this, all the difficulties concerning the is-ought barrier now appear as difficulties concerning how our two types of 'is' statements are to be connected. Let us look at one section where Zimmerman tries to eliminate 'ought', in order to see how having eliminated 'ought' his troubles are not really over.

Zimmerman thinks that it makes no difference if we say (*a*) that since an insane man could not help doing what he did this is a sufficient reason that we ought not to punish him, or (*b*) that since he could not help doing what he did, this is a sufficient reason for us not wanting to punish him, not wanting others to punish him, not punishing him, and trying to persuade others not to punish him.

It would seem at first sight that it does make a difference. We say that someone 'ought' not to do something when we think doing that thing would be violating some rule of behaviour. It is accepted as a rule in our society that one does not punish people when they could

[1] Paper VII.

not help doing what they did; and when we say that someone 'ought' not to punish an insane man because he could not have done other than he did, we are in effect showing that this rule would be violated if such an action were performed. We assume that the rule not to punish those who could not have done otherwise is accepted, and having shown that this case falls under that rule, we can infer that the act 'ought' not to be done.

It is true that since we accept the rule, we want, in some sense of 'want', not to punish a man who could not do otherwise than he did. But what if the insane man is very much disliked by us? What if he has done us great wrong? Would we still be able to say so easily that we want him not to be punished?

We would be inclined to say, I think, that we want him to be punished, although he ought not to be. How would Zimmerman's 'oughtless' language function here?

There are, it seems to me, many cases in which we do not want to do those things which our rules of behaviour enjoin us to do. We hold it as a rule that we spend our money wisely on what is most likely to benefit us; but we are attracted by what tickles our fancy, and find that we spend our money on things which are actually of little benefit to us. We could say that we want to spend our money on the latter, although we ought not to; but in Zimmerman's language this course is not open to us. We would have to say that we both want and do not want to spend our money on what is most likely to benefit us. This at least would get rid of 'ought', but only at the expense of a seeming contradiction.

Whenever we have a situation where we would often say, 'I want to do X, but I ought not to do X', Zimmerman would, I think, have to say, 'I want to do X, but I do not want to do X'. There is really nothing so very strange about statements like the latter, even though they may be offensive to those logicians who cannot see anything of the form 'P and not P', without immediately associating it with a contradiction. In ordinary language it does not always hold that if we want to do something then we cannot both want and not want to do that thing; and the same holds when we do not want to do something. But this 'oddness' of our own language erects again the barrier that Zimmerman just tore down.

If it is to serve as an acceptable reason for our not wanting an insane man to be punished that he could not have done otherwise than he did, then we must regard it as *right* under these circumstances not to punish. If we are speaking of wanting in a non-evaluative sense; that is, if we are simply saying that we have a

strong desire or inclination not to punish such a man, then it makes
no sense whatever to talk of reasons for wanting. If we try to justify
what we want, we are subsuming what we want under some value.
Otherwise, we can only look for causes of what we want. It does not
necessarily follow that since punishing an insane man leads to no
change in his behaviour that we do not want to punish him. This
only follows because we hold it as a rule not to punish anyone when
punishing him cannot possibly alter his behaviour. If we do not hold
such a rule then it would not follow that we would not want to
punish the man. Hence, we are unable to argue from what is to
what we want unless what is already has a value. You cannot show
someone that nothing is gained by punishing an insane man by
noting that the man's behaviour is not altered, if the person with
whom you are arguing is not interested in altering his behaviour. We
would have the same difficulty in trying to show someone that he
really does not want to punish an insane man as we had before in
showing that he really ought not.

What we have is a situation quite analogous to that which pre-
vailed before we removed 'ought'. We cannot infer simply from
descriptive statements what we want to do. What makes it look as if
we can, is that it is tacitly assumed that our 'descriptive' premises
are values rather than simply facts. For example, I might argue that
smoking results in poor health, therefore I do not want to smoke;
but this only follows if poor health has a negative value for me,
otherwise I cannot infer that I do not want to smoke. A second
reason why we might think such an inference valid is that 'want' is
often a purely descriptive word. But then the premise is only a
proposed causal explanation of why I do not want to smoke, *not* a
justification.

If you have already decided what you want and do not want –
and this corresponds to the old-fashioned what you ought to do and
ought not to do – then you can cheerfully turn to science to realise
your ideals. But this does not negate the fact that we cannot infer
what we want from what simply is. We must first give what is some
value, attribute to it some importance, before anything at all follows
concerning what we want to do. It is to this gulf that the is-ought
barrier calls attention. Zimmerman does not remove this barrier but
merely obscures it by using 'want', which looks like a purely descriptive or 'is' term, in an evaluative sense.

IX A note on the 'is-ought' barrier

M. Zimmerman

In an interesting criticism[1] of my paper,[2] Kenneth Hanly takes me to task for proposing to do away with 'ought' statements. He suggests that the difficulties associated with the is-ought barrier reappear in the use of 'is' statements.

He objects to my giving as a reason for not wanting to punish an insane man that he could not help doing what he did, on the grounds that there might be cases where we would want to punish him anyway. In such cases, he contends, retaining the use of 'ought' statements makes it possible to say that we ought not to punish him though we want to, whereas elimination of the 'ought' language rules this out.

But nothing is gained and something is lost in saying we ought not to punish him, since we are faced with the problem of 'showing' that we ought not to (this is the main theme of my paper). If our belief that we ought not to punish him is sufficient to prevent us from punishing him, even if we want to for whatever reasons (repulsion towards his horrible crime, etc.), then we will not punish him even if we eliminate 'ought' statements, and we will not be faced with the problem of justifying 'ought' statements. If it is insufficient to prevent us from punishing him, then retaining 'ought' statements will gain us nothing while confronting us with the burden of 'ought' statements all over again.

Hanly thinks that our justification for not wanting to punish an insane man is based on our accepting a rule of our society not to, and this is another way of saying we 'ought' not to. But we can just as well say that we want to act in accordance with the desires or approval of our society, without facing the barrier of the 'ought' language. If society does desire or approve of our not wanting to punish an insane man and we want to act in accordance with such desires or approval, then it does follow that we do not want to punish an insane man.

[1] Paper VIII.   [2] Paper VII.

PART THREE

Attempts to derive ought
from is

X The gap between 'is' and 'should'

Max Black

It has often been held that ethical statements cannot follow from premises consisting exclusively of statements of fact. Thus Karl Popper once said:

> Perhaps the simplest and most important point about ethics is purely logical. I mean the impossibility to derive [*sic*] nontauto-logical ethical rules – imperatives; principles of policy; aims; or however we may describe them – from statements of facts. Only if this fundamental logical position is realized can we begin to formulate the real problems of moral philosophy, and to appreciate their difficulty.[1]

Popper would presumably wish to make a similar claim about all non-factual statements: like many other philosophers, he believes that only statements of fact can follow from statements of fact. This is the contention that I wish to examine in what follows. I shall try to show that there is a good sense in which some statements about what should be done do follow from factual premises.

Contemporary writers, such as R. M. Hare [2] and P. H. Nowell-Smith,[3] who agree with Popper, usually quote a famous passage from Hume's *Treatise*.[4] Hume maintains that all the moralists he knows make an imperceptible transition from observations about human affairs or assertions about the existence of God, all expressed

---

[1] *Aristotelian Society Proceedings*, supp. vol. XXII (1948) p. 154.

[2] Hare says: 'Popper rightly refers to the rule as "perhaps the simplest and most important point about ethics" ' [*The Language of Morals* (Oxford, 1952 p. 31]. In Hare's treatment, the autonomy principle takes the special form that no imperative conclusions can be validly drawn from premises that do not contain at least one imperative (p. 28).

[3] Nowell-Smith says that an argument from factual premises to an ethical conclusion 'must be illegitimate reasoning, since the conclusion of an argument can contain nothing which is not in the premises, and there are no "oughts" in the premises' [*Ethics* (1954) p. 37].

[4] *A Treatise on Human Nature*, III. i. i.

with 'the usual copulations of propositions, *is* and is *not*', to normative conclusions 'connected with an *ought* or *ought not*'. He says that this transition is 'of the last consequence' and needs to be explained: 'it is necessary ... that a reason should be given for what seems altogether inconceivable, how this new relation can be a deduction from others, which are entirely different from it.'

As a tribute to the remarkable influence this passage has exerted, I propose to assign to the principle that only factual statements can follow from exclusively factual statements the title 'Hume's Guillotine'. 'By 'factual statements' here and throughout, I mean such as can be expressed by sentences whose copula is 'is' or 'is not' but cannot be expressed by sentences containing 'should', 'must', 'ought', and so forth.

It is not clear whether Hume is intending to offer an argument or is merely insinuating sceptical doubts.[5] Considered as argument, what he says is singularly unconvincing. He implies that it is fallacious reasoning to introduce into a conclusion 'some new relation or affirmation', expressed by 'ought' or 'ought not', that is 'entirely different' from the relations or affirmations occurring in the premises. The strength of his position depends upon the interpretation that is given to the expression 'entirely different'; 'ought' is different from 'is', of course, but if Hume thought this was sufficient to disqualify the 'ought'-conclusion, he himself was committing an error of reasoning. The sense of 'entirely different' that Hume needs is one in which *A* counts as entirely different from *B* when and only when a statement containing *A* cannot be logically derived from premises containing *A*, but not *B*. Now whether 'ought' is entirely different from 'is' in this sense is the very question at issue. Hume, if taken to be offering an argument, is assuming what needs to be established, namely, that an 'ought' can never be derived from an 'is'.

Why are modern readers predisposed to endorse Hume's Guillotine? One reason may be the widespread but mistaken view that no term may occur in the conclusion of a valid argument unless it occurs, or can be made to occur by suitable definitions, somewhere

[5] In Paper I, A. C. MacIntyre argues against the customary interpretation of Hume's remarks. He contends that Hume was only raising a *question* about the derivation of an 'ought' from an 'is', which is subsequently answered affirmatively in Hume's own ethical theory. I side with MacIntyre's critics in holding this reading to be unsound in spite of its ingenuity. See Papers II, III, IV, V; and M. J. Scott-Taggart in *Philosophical Review*, LXX (1961).

in the premises. If 'valid argument' meant the same as 'valid syllogism', the view would be correct – but it is easily shown not to be so in general. Consider, for instance, the following simple argument. A citizen is a person; therefore a married citizen is a married person. Here, the word 'married' occurs for the first time in the conclusion, yet the argument is valid as it stands, without benefit of suppressed premises. One obstacle to the recognition of this elementary point is an unfortunate but popular metaphor of the conclusion being 'contained' in the premises.[6] But there is no useful sense in which the conclusion of a valid argument can be said to be 'contained' in the premises; that is merely a misleading way of saying that the conclusion really does follow from the given premises, without the addition of supplementary assumptions.

It is in fact quite easy to show that some kinds of 'ought'-statements, *pace* Hume, really do follow from 'is'-premises. Consider, for instance, the following valid argument:

Vivisection causes gratuitous suffering to animals.
Nothing that causes gratuitous suffering ought to be done.
Therefore, vivisection ought not to be done.

From this argument, we can easily derive another valid argument proceeding from 'is' to 'ought':

Vivisection causes gratuitous suffering to animals.
Therefore, if nothing that causes gratuitous suffering ought to be done, vivisection ought not to be done.

And in general, 'If A then B' entails 'If B ought not to be done, A ought not to be done.'[7]

Although this example may serve to discredit the dogma that an 'ought' is never derivable from an 'is', I do not attach much importance to it and shall not rely upon it in my argument. For when 'If B ought not to be done, A ought not to be done' is entailed by 'If A then B', the former statement will serve no useful purpose in an ethical argument. Our only reason for asserting it will be our knowledge of the truth of the factual statement 'If A then B' from which we can derive any consequences that follow from the trivial ethical

[6] It is interesting to find G. E. Moore in his *Commonplace Book* (1962) taking 'p contains q' to mean that p is a conjunction having q as one of its conjuncts (p. 342). Upon this literal construction of the metaphor of 'containing', it is not surprising that Moore speedily concludes that p can entail q without containing it.

[7] For further examples of this sort, see A. N. Prior, 'The Autonomy of Ethics', *Australasian Journal of Philosophy*, vol. 38 (1960) pp. 199–206.

statement that it entails.[8] (Contrast a non-trivial ethical hypothetical such as 'If something ought to be done, one ought not to boast of having done it', whose truth is not guaranteed by a corresponding factual hypothetical.) I shall say nothing more about cases in which the 'ought'-conclusion is complex, because I want to discuss the more fundamental case in which the normative conclusion is free from sentential connectives.

A second reason that may predispose modern philosophers to accept Hume's Guillotine is the view, more popular in our own time than in his, that 'ought'-statements make no truth claims at all and are therefore disqualified to serve either as premises or as conclusions. I take it as certain, however, that we can reason, for example, from expressed to unstated orders, which I choose as undoubtedly having a primary function other than that of making a truth claim. From the orders 'Answer questions on every page' and 'Initial page on which questions are answered', I can infer the unstated order 'Initial every page.' The conjunction of the first two orders logically implies the third, in the sense that it would be impossible to obey the first two orders and not to behave *as if* one were obeying the third, unstated, order.[9] We can exhibit logical relations between orders – or, for that matter, between promises, resolutions, and so forth – which are the same as, or at least closely analogous to, the familiar relations of implication, equivalence, compatability, and the like, that are involved in all arguments.

With these preliminaries out of the way, we should now be able to take a fresh and unprejudiced look at Hume's Guillotine.

To those who claim the existence of an unbridgeable logical gap between 'ought' and 'is', I offer for consideration the following counter-example:

Fischer wants to mate Botwinnik.[10]
The one and only way to mate Botwinnik is for Fischer to move the Queen.
Therefore, Fischer should move the Queen.

[8] I owe this point to J. M. Shorter. See his article, 'Professor Prior on the Autonomy of Ethics'. *Australian Journal of Philosophy*, vol. 39 (1961) pp. 286–7.
[9] Of course, there is more to *obeying* an order than performing the action prescribed by it. Cf. the recent discussion, 'Imperative Inference' by B. A. O. Williams and P. T. Geach, *Analysis*, vol. 23 (supp., 1963) pp. 30–42.
[10] One might wish to qualify the premise to read 'Fischer wants to mate Botwinnik, *if that is possible*', but there is no point in the addition and the subsequent discussion is in any case unaffected.

I am assuming that these statements refer to some game in progress.

Here, it seems to me, both premises state matters of fact, while the conclusion is a non-factual 'should'-statement. (An 'ought'-statement might have been used instead, the differences between 'should' and 'ought' being immaterial here.)

I hope it will be agreed that the first premise, 'Fischer wants to mate Botwinnik', is factual. The relevant sense of 'want' is that of actively wanting, as it were – being in a state of already taking or being set to take the necessary steps to achieve the end in question – not a free-floating desire, wish, or aspiration.[11] Were Fischer himself to make the corresponding first-person utterance, 'I want to mate Botwinnik', he might perhaps be taken to be expressing only a resolution to achieve the end and so to be making no truth claim. But the third-person statement used as a premise in the example is a straightforward statement of fact about Fischer, supported by the usual sort of evidence about human behaviour.

Anybody wishing to deny that the example discredits Hume's Guillotine will probably contend that the correct conclusion is really factual. He might say that the proper conclusion should run 'Fischer's best move is the Queen move' or, perhaps, 'The one and only way in which Fischer can win is by moving the Queen', both of which statements are 'factual' in the broad sense in which that term is here being used. The objection might run that the conclusion of my counter-example really follows from the premises only if that conclusion is itself given a factual interpretation.

For example, Professor Von Wright, in his recent paper on 'Practical Inference',[12] argues in just this way. He considers the following 'practical' argument:

A wants to make the hut habitable.
Unless *A* heats the hut it will not become habitable.
Therefore, *A* must heat the hut.

He asks whether the argument is 'valid', even though *A* may be unaware of the practical necessity of the action to be performed. Von Wright replies:

The answer depends upon how we interpret the 'must'. If we understand the phrase '*A* must heat the hut' *to mean the same as*

[11] Cf. G. E. M. Anscombe: 'The wanting that interests us, however, is neither wishing nor hoping nor the feeling of desire, and cannot be said to exist in a man who does nothing towards getting what he wants' [*Intention* (Oxford 1957) p. 67].

[12] *Philosophical Review*, LXXII (1963) pp. 159–79.

'unless *A* heats the hut, he will fail to attain some end of his action' or to mean the same as 'there is something *A* wants but will not get, unless he heats the hut', then the answer is affirmative. (p. 164, italics added).

Thus Von Wright manages to certify his practical inference as valid only by interpreting its conclusion as factual. I agree that if we are asked what we mean by saying that so-and-so 'must' do such and such, or 'should' do such and such (the differences between the meanings of the two words being unimportant here) we should sometimes answer in the way that Von Wright has claimed. But I disagree with his implication, if it is intended, that in so doing we should be giving *the meaning* of our 'must'-statement.

If I say to someone, 'Do your best', he might ask me whether I meant 'Work as hard as you can, without worrying about success', and I might reasonably agree that I did mean that – but the alternative forms of words do not mean the same. To say what the speaker meant may be only to specify the implications of his utterance in a given context. Now, 'must', 'should', and similar words used with normative force in practical inferences are highly schematic and admit of various specifications in alternative contexts; but to admit this is not to concede that the 'must'-statements are synonymous with their appropriate specifications – nor is it to concede that the meaning of 'must' varies from context to context.

I wish to argue that the 'should'-conclusion of the counter-example is not intended to be merely another way of saying that the best move is such and such or that the only way the player can achieve his end is by making that move. My object is to stress the distinctively performative aspect of the utterance 'Fischer should move the Queen', while trying to show that the 'should'-statement, so understood, without reduction to its factual implications in context, still follows from the premises.

In saying that there is a performative aspect to saying 'Fischer should move the Queen', I mean that a speaker who uses this form of words counts as doing something more than, or something other than, saying something having truth value.[13] He is not just saying something that is true or false, but is doing, and counts as doing, something more than that. But what does such a speaker count as doing when he makes a 'should'-statement? An adequate account of the linguistic act in question, involving an examination of the

[13] I am drawing here on Austin's discussion of performatives. Cf. my paper in 'Austin on Performatives', *Philosophy*, xxxviii (1963) pp. 217–26.

various interrelated functions of 'should' (in the special kinds of contexts relevant here), would make for too lengthy a digression.

The beginnings of an answer might, however, be obtained by taking the second-person use, '*You* should do such and such', as primary, in the hope of explaining the first- and third-person uses in terms of their relations to that second-person use. It is plausible to hold that the prime function of the second-person formula is to urge the hearer to adopt a course of action selected by the speaker as preferable, optimal, or correct. That the implied valuation of the courses of action available to the hearer is subordinate to the urging function can be seen in the following way. The speaker's evaluation of a selected action as preferable or obligatory gives him a reason for urging his hearer to perform that action. Now, contrary to what is sometimes said, there seems to be no linguistic violation in urging a man to do something, even when the speaker has no reason with which to back the recommendation.[14] There is no linguistic or conceptual impropriety about saying 'I feel you should do *A*, though I can't give you any reason why you should.' It might be said that the use of the second-person 'should'-formula normally arouses a presumption that the speaker has reasons for saying what he does, but since the same might be said about any kind of statement whatever, this cannot be a distinctive peculiarity of the meaning or function of 'should'. A further presumption is that the speaker normally wants his hearer to do what he says that he should do, but this presumption, like the one concerning the existence of supporting reasons, can be defeated in special circumstances. If I have bet heavily on your losing the game of chess in which you are engaged, I shall not want you to win, but if you ask my advice and I see that you can win by moving the Queen, I am still required to say, 'You should move the Queen.'

Consider the following sequence of possible utterances:

'The one and only way in which you can mate is by moving the Queen.'
'Your best move is the Queen move.'
'You should move the Queen.'
'Move the Queen.'

[14] Thus Charles E. Caton says, ' "ought"-judgements are logically a kind of statement which must be supportable by reasons...if he [the speaker] cannot give reasons, he should hesitate to reiterate his assertion or should retract it' [*Philosophical Quarterly*, vol. 13 (1963) p. 150].

The first of these is a neutral, non-performative comment on the situation, while the last is a straightforward imperative – a forthright verbal push: the 'should'-utterance stands between these, as a sort of hybrid, implying an evaluation based upon matters of fact, but partaking also of the imperative force of the bare incitement to action. According to circumstances, the use of the 'should'-utterance would count as advising, inciting, admonishing, urging, suggesting, and so on. Although we have no single word to cover all such activities, I think we can see that there is something common to all of them: in default of a better word, I shall use 'advising', in an extended sense, to cover everything we do in telling another what he should do. I want to emphasise that 'should', in second-person uses, has the practical function of 'advising' (prodding, or whatever you may choose to call it), the same in all such uses. I shall not say anything here about the interestingly different third- and first-person uses of 'should'.

In order to render prominent the 'performative' aspect of the conclusion of my counter-example, I shall now switch to a second-person variant. Consider, therefore, any argument of the following form:

> You want to achieve *E*.
> Doing *M* is the one and only way to achieve *E*.
> Therefore, you should do *M*.

Here the conclusion is intended to express 'advice', and not to be merely another way of restating the factual conditions expressed by the premises. With this understanding, can we properly say that the conclusion follows by logical necessity from the premises?

It is often said that any argument of the above form is really an enthymeme with an unstated premise, possibly of the form:

> Everybody should do anything which is the one and only way to achieve anything that he wants to achieve.

Since this general premise is held to be 'normative' or 'practical', its addition is held to convert the original inference into a formally correct one still conforming to Hume's Guillotine. My answer is that the proposed additional premise must be held to be analytic, in the sense of being guaranteed correct by virtue of the meanings or functions of the terms it contains. If so, its presence is unnecessary, as in the parallel case of an argument from contingent premises to a contingent conclusion. (If such an argument is valid when an analytical premise is imported, it remains so when that premise is removed.) I need not insist upon this, however. For if somebody still wishes to insert the additional general premise, I would urge upon him that the very reasons making him reluctant to agree that non-factual conclusions might follow from exclusively factual premises ought to make him reject the idea of a necessarily true conditional having a factual antecedent but a non-factual consequent. Hume's Guillotine applies to such a conditional statement just as plausibly as it does to an argument. Indeed, by rendering the original argument formally valid, we are simply smuggling in the principle of inference as an extra premise and are leaving all the substantial questions of validity unsettled. (We may here recall similar moves in connection with questions about the validity of inductive inferences. Those who say that such inferences are enthymematic and insist upon adding a general premise merely shift the question of validity to that of the validity of the imported premise.)

Another misconception, traceable to Kant, consists in thinking of the conclusion of any 'practical' argument as 'hypothetical'. This may be intended to mean that the only correct conclusion from the given premises must have the conditional form '*If* you want to achieve E, you should do M.' But how can we stop there? Given, as we are, the premise that 'you' do want to achieve E, *modus ponens* requires us to go all the way to the 'categorical' conclusion 'You *should* do M.' Unless we did intend to 'go all the way', there would be no point in invoking the first premise; for the genuinely hypothetical or conditional statement 'If you want to achieve E, you should do M' follows from the second premise alone. (And of course such a conditional statement, made in ignorance of the other's actual end, has none, or almost none, of the 'prodding' force that I have ascribed to the categorical 'should'-statement.)

Equally untenable is the more drastic view that 'should', as used in the contexts here considered, has a variable condition as part of its meaning. On this view, 'You should do M' is elliptical and really means the same as 'If you want to achieve E, you should do M.' But then what does the 'should' in the expanded sentence mean? It would be absurd to repeat the manoeuvre by arguing that what is really meant is 'If you want to achieve E, you should, if you want to achieve E, do M.' For this way lies an infinite regress. On the other hand, there is no good reason to suppose that 'should' means two different things in 'You should do M' and 'You should do M, if you want to achieve E', respectively. A good reason against supposing this is that, were it true, arguments by *modus ponens* in which the categorical and the hypothetical statements occur together would have to count as invalid. If we want to use the traditional terminology, we must say that the conclusion of my counter-example is categorical: a man who, knowing his hearer's end, says 'You should do *M*' is advising him unconditionally, without qualifications or reservations. Those who resist this conclusion usually have in mind what might be called a 'terminating' or 'definitive' use of 'should', in which the speaker advises an action only after considering the case in the broadest possible perspective, including any moral considerations arising. But this kind of case is exceptional.

Those who insist on the so-called 'hypothetical' nature of the 'should'-conclusion have seen an important point, nevertheless. Consider the following case: *A*, playing chess with *B*, asks me for advice. I see that the one and only way to checkmate is to move the Queen and say 'You should move the Queen.' A bystander, *C*, however, who has overheard this, objects that *B* is in such precarious health that the shock of being suddenly mated by an inferior player might induce a stroke and kill him. *C*, therefore, says to *A*: 'You should not move the Queen – perhaps you ought to break off the game.' Is *C*'s advice or admonition in conflict with mine? If it is, I cannot properly argue that my advice follows from the two factual premises about *A*'s purpose and the necessary and sufficient condition for achieving it. For the addition of further premises – for example, about *B*'s state of health and the probable consequences to him of defeat – would produce a conclusion contrary to mine.

It seems to me that *C*'s comment involves a change of subject. When *A* asked me for advice, I rightly supposed he was consulting me as a chess player and answered accordingly. It would have been an objection to my remark to point out some other mating move, or to argue that the move I recommended would not have the desired effect. But to introduce moral considerations is to change the topic. *A* asks, 'What shall I do *in this game*?' but *C* replies, in effect, 'Don't play the game at all!' Of course, I am not suggesting that moral considerations are subordinate to those of chess strategy; nor am I implying that it was wrong for *C* to answer as he did because he was not asked for moral advice. It may be morally right to answer irrelevantly – as when asked for technical advice on firearms by a would-be murderer.

The truth behind the view that the conclusions of 'practical' arguments are hypothetical seems to be about as follows. The use of 'should' and its normative cognates in such contexts is specified in a certain way, usually made plain by the nature of the context. 'You should do *M*' has the force of 'You should do *M* – given that you are playing chess and that the question is about *that*.' One might say it is a presupposition that the advice, according to circumstances, is restricted to answering a question about game strategy, a legal question, a prudential one, and so on. (It is no doubt an important point about moral injunctions that they cannot be restricted or limited in a parallel fashion. It is normally absurd to say, 'It is your duty to do *M* – given . . .'. Given *what*? Nothing seems to fit except 'given that you are a moral agent' and even that imposes no restriction analogous to those I have mentioned.) Henry Sidgwick stated the point accurately when he said of Kant's so-called hypothetical imperatives that 'they are not *addressed* to anyone who has not accepted the end.'[15]

I turn now to my main question. Given that you want to achieve *E* and that doing *M* is the one and only way of achieving *E*, does it follow as a logical necessity that you should do *M*? It is obvious that the truth of the factual premises provides at least a good reason for saying 'You should do *M*.' Indeed, the truth of the premises constitutes a conclusive reason for saying, in the given context, 'You should do *M*.' Given that my interlocutor is playing chess and solicits advice about the game, the fact, if it is a fact, that he can mate the opponent only by moving the Queen provides me with a *conclusive* reason for urging him to do that rather than anything else. It would be absurd to say 'The one and only way you can mate the opponent is by moving your Queen – and that's why I say you should move the Queen!' If we heard someone say this, apparently in earnest, we should reasonably suppose him to have made a slip of the tongue, to be joking, transmitting a code message, making some esoteric allusion, or otherwise using his words in some unusual way. Were all other suppositions to fail, we might even conclude that he did not understand what he was saying. But no sense could be made of the supposition that he did understand what he said, spoke literally, and still meant what he seemed to be saying. The test I have been applying here parallels a test we might apply to an argument with factual premises and a factual conclusion. Given a simple argument patently invalid, say of the form '*P*, if *P* then *Q*, therefore not-*Q*', we could make no sense of the supposition that somebody might utter it, understand what he was saying, and mean what he seemed to be saying. If this test does not fully express what we mean by saying that the factual premises entail the factual conclusion, it at least constitutes a strong criterion of entailment.[16]

[15] *The Methods of Ethics*, 4th ed. (1890) p. 6 (italics added).
[16] R. M. Hare *defines* entailment as follows: 'A sentence *P* entails a sentence *Q* if and only if the fact that a person assents to *P* but dissents

There is one important difference between the case I have just cited and that of a practical inference from 'is' to 'should'. When a man thinks that P and also that if P then Q, it is logically impossible for him not to think also that Q: he may of course assert the premises explicitly without uttering the conclusion, but it is impossible that he should fail to think Q – say it 'in his heart' as it were. To assert the premise in question while showing signs of doubting or wondering about the conclusion would be an indication of stupidity, failure to understand, or some other cognitive deficiency. (This case needs to be distinguished from that previously discussed, in which the speaker seems to be asserting not-Q.) But a man might refuse to say 'You should do M', even though he had affirmed the factual premises whose truth constituted a conclusive reason for making the 'should'-statement: having conscientious scruples about giving advice in such cases, he might have trained himself so well to abstain from giving it that he did not even think 'You should do M' in his heart. We could not properly call such a man irrational or ignorant of the language. Because giving advice is performing a voluntary action, a man may in general abstain from the activity without incurring a charge of irrationality. Giving advice by means of 'should'-formulas is a linguistic practice just as much as the making of promises is; and just as a man may have reasons so good for making a certain promise that it would be irrational for him to give a contrary promise but might choose not to make a promise at all, so also in the case of 'advice'.

This important point of difference between the two cases may help to explain the common insistence that moral conclusions cannot follow from factual premises. Suppose for the sake of argument that a moral injunction of the form 'I ought to do such and such' might be related to non-moral premises in a manner analogous to the relation I have claimed to obtain between the conclusion and the premises of my counter-example: then a man accepting the non-moral premises would not, as a matter of logical necessity, have to accept the moral conclusion and so be required to think it. For he might in such cases refrain from drawing the moral implications from the facts: this would not be an indication of incapacity to reason or failure to understand the meaning of 'ought' but might be a sign of moral deficiency. (One can sometimes blamelessly abstain

---

from Q is a sufficient criterion for saying that he has misunderstood one or other of the sentences' (*Language of Morals*, p. 25). This is unsatisfactory, for fairly obvious reasons.

from non-moral practices, but nobody has the right in general to neglect relevant moral considerations.)

Too much must not be made of this admission. If a moral conclusion is ever related to non-moral premises in the fashion I have imagined, then, given that a moral conclusion is to be drawn, we have no choice as to which conclusion it shall be. Or, to return to my original example, given that the speaker is committed to offering some advice or other, the only advice that he can rationally offer is 'You should do *M*.' That is why, upon being asked to consider the complex conditional question 'Given that *A* wants to achieve *E* and that *M* is the one and only way for him to achieve that end, should he do *M*?' we feel the compulsion to answer 'Of course!' Courtesy, if nothing else, obliges us to consider the question raised and so to adopt the posture of a judge. It would have to be a very exceptional kind of person who could evade the question by saying 'I never pass judgement.'

For the reasons now before us, I am reluctant to say that the practical 'should'-conclusion is entailed by its factual premises: the important contrast with straightforward cases of entailment might indeed be marked by using some such label as '*latent* necessity' or '*virtual* necessity'. On my view, the practical conclusion is 'hypothetical' in quite another way from that in which Kant thought of the matter: between the factual premises and the practical conclusion there is a sort of gap, bridgeable only by an agent's willingness to engage in the relevant activity or practice. The truth of the premises restricts the performance, whether that of 'advising' or something else, to a single possibility, but there will be no performance at all unless the agent chooses to follow the path.

Given the truth of the factual premises concerning a man's end and the necessary and sufficient condition for attaining that end, and given that one is to make some second-person 'should'-statement, one must say 'You should do *M*' – and nothing else will do. What kind of a 'must' is this? It seems to mean here precisely what 'must' means when we say that anybody affirming the premises of a valid deductive argument must also affirm that argument's conclusion. Choice of the given 'should'-statement is enforced by the rules, understandings, or conventions governing the correct uses of 'should' and the other words occurring in the argument: nobody who understands the premises of the practical argument and knows the rules for the proper use of 'should' can honestly offer any other 'should'-conclusion. In this respect, the parallel with 'theoretical' arguments is strong. Accordingly, no special 'practical' logic is needed in such cases: the relevant principles are the familiar ones employed throughout deductive reasoning.

The general pattern for other cases of the relation between a practical or performative utterance and factual reasons for making that utterance may be explained as follows. In the case of some performatives, though not in all, some of the conventions governing the correct use of the performatives prescribe that if certain factual conditions obtain, only a determinate, specifiable performative of the type in question may properly be used.[17] If we form a practical argument, whose premises state the factual conditions in question while its conclusion expresses the relevant performative, we shall then have a case analogous to those I have been discussing. For instance, the following seems to me a 'strict' practical argument:

> Unless I do something about it, you will take action *A*.
> If you take action *A*, you will be killed.
> Therefore, I warn you not to take action *A*.

If I am to warn you at all – which is not necessary, except possibly on moral grounds – I must use the negative warning formula, on pain of misusing language. Indeed, the case is very close to the earlier ones discussed in this paper, since one way of giving the warning would be to say 'You should not do *A*.'

My conclusion, therefore, comes to this: some non-factual conclusions do follow and can be shown to follow from factual premises, even when proper allowance has been made for the 'performative' aspects of such conclusions.

Very little might be held to have been accomplished by making such trivial arguments as I have considered logically respectable. But once Hume's Guillotine has been discredited, we may hope to find more important arguments containing valid transitions from 'is' to 'should' or from 'is' to 'ought'. If I am not mistaken, the following argument from factual premises to a moral conclusion is valid:

[17] In terms of Austin's analysis of the 'infelicities' of performatives in his *How to Do Things with Words* (Oxford 1962) pp. 14–15, what I am calling 'factual conditions' fall under what he calls the 'circumstances ... [which] ... must be appropriate for the invocation of the particular procedure invoked' (p. 15). Austin would count the use of the wrong performative in the circumstances I envisage as a 'misinvocation' (p. 18) of the special sort that he calls a 'misapplication' (ibid.). It is an understatement to say, as Austin does, that the act is then 'disallowed' (ibid.). I am urging that logic requires the act to be rejected as improper.

Doing *A* will produce pain.

Apart from producing the pain resulting from *A*, doing *A* will have the same consequence that not doing *A* would have had.

Therefore, *A* ought not to be done.

In other words, if the consequences of doing some action differ from those of abstaining from that action only by producing avoidable pain, that action ought not to be done. If I am to be shown mistaken in this claim, somebody will have to demonstrate that a person ready to make a moral judgement and accepting the premises could decline to make the moral judgement expressed by the conclusion, without thereby convicting himself of failure to understand the terms used, or some other cognitive defect. A detailed demonstration is required – not an appeal to a dogma which ought by now to have been finally exploded.

XI The possibilities of moral advice

D. Z. Phillips

Professor Max Black tells us[1] that as a recognition of its remarkable philosophical influence, he proposes 'to assign to the principle that only factual statements can follow from exclusively factual statements the title "Hume's Guillotine"' (p. 100). He ends his paper by describing this principle as 'a dogma which ought by now to have been finally exploded' (p. 113). I assume that the 'by now' refers, not to the end of the article, but to the present state of contemporary moral philosophy, where the number of those prepared to assist in exploding the principle in question increases quarterly.

I want to consider the way in which Black thinks moral advice can be deduced from factual premises. Certainly, in some contexts, it seems that one can argue from 'is' to 'should'. For example, as Black argues, if I know that A wants to checkmate his opponent B in a game of chess, and I see that he can only do so by moving the Queen, if A then asks me for advice, it follows that I *should* say 'Move the Queen'. But is there a transition from the chess example to an example of *moral* advice? Professor Black asks us to consider the following case:

> A, playing chess with B, asks me for advice. I see that the one and only way to checkmate is to move the Queen and say 'You should move the Queen'. A bystander, C, however, who has overheard this, objects that B is in such precarious health that the shock of being suddenly mated by an inferior player might induce a stroke and kill him. C, therefore, says to A: 'You should not move the Queen – perhaps you ought to break off the game.' Is C's advice or admonition in conflict with mine? If it is, I cannot properly argue that my advice follows from the two factual premises about A's purpose and the necessary and sufficient condition for achieving it. For the addition of further premises – for example, about B's state of health and the probable consequences to him of defeat – would produce a conclusion contrary to mine. (p. 108)

[1] Paper X.

Black underestimates the significance of his own example. As a first reaction to it, he suggests that *C*'s comment involves a change of subject. The introduction of moral considerations takes one away from the question of what should be done *in this game*. I do not want to press the point here, but the distinction between games and morality is not as rigid as Black would make it. Consider, for example, the conflict between attitudes such as 'Win at all costs' and 'Observe the spirit of the game'. Black says that it is no doubt an important point that moral injunctions cannot be limited in the same way as advice on strategy during a game, but it is doubtful whether he has recognised the nature of the importance involved. Had he done so, he would not have tried to establish an analogy between advice in chess, granted the absence of so-called moral intrusions, and moral advice. In trying to do this he is guilty of serious confusions.

Black begins by stating that *within* a given context, such as a game, the way in which the question 'What should I do?' should be answered may be generally agreed upon. But given that you want to achieve *E* and that doing *M* is the one and only way of achieving *E*, does it follow as a logical necessity that you should do *M*? Black says that in the context of a game of chess, the facts already mentioned constitute a *conclusive* reason for doing *M*. We should not understand someone who, given the facts, advised 'You should not move the Queen'. The facts bind one to the *should*-conclusion as much as the facts bind one to a factual conclusion in an argument of the form '*P*, if *P* then *Q*, therefore *Q*'. If someone said 'Therefore not-*Q*' in this context, we should be at a loss to know what he was up to.

Black is prepared to admit that there are differences between the two pieces of advice. For example, in the latter, to think *P* is also to think *Q*. Failure to think *Q* entails failure to understand *P*. Yet, it is not so in the case of a moral *should*-conclusion. Giving moral advice, unlike thinking *Q* given *P*, is a voluntary activity. A man may train himself to abstain from giving moral advice, or he may refrain from drawing a moral conclusion from the facts because of moral deficiency. For these reasons, Black is reluctant to say that the *should*-conclusion is entailed by the factual premises. But once a man chooses to be involved in moral practices, the differences, for all practical purposes, are unimportant. Black says

> If a moral conclusion is ever related to non-moral premises in the fashion I have imagined, then, given that a moral conclusion is to be drawn, we have no choice as to which moral conclusion it shall be. (p. 111)

Clearly, the conclusion of this argument is false, and so is its
initial hypothesis. To see this one need only elaborate a little on the
situation in which advice is sought during a game of chess. As well
as knowing of B's precarious health, and the probable effect of sudden defeat by an inferior player on him, let us suppose that various
bystanders also know that B takes his chess very seriously indeed,
and that he would be terribly upset if he thought that he had been
'given' a game; indeed, upset enough to induce a stroke. They also
know, let us say, that B had been told by his doctor to give up playing chess because of the tension it caused in him, to which advice B
had replied, 'In that case I'll die with my boots on'. A not only asks
C, but all the bystanders, what he should do. They all know the
facts I have mentioned, plus the fact that the only way to checkmate is to move the Queen. What advice should the bystanders give?
Black tells us that 'The truth of the premises restricts the performance, whether that of "advising" or something else, to a single
possibility' (p. 111). Well, then, what is 'the single possibility' in the
situation I have outlined?

If we ask, 'What advice *could* the bystanders give which would
count as *moral* advice?' we can see that there are *many* possibilities.
Here are some which come readily to mind.

Bystander D argues: 'What is more important than a man's life?
After all, chess is only a game. I know that B has disregarded medi-
cal advice in order to play, but he is wrong in taking this attitude,
and so I feel I am doing the right thing in overruling it. After all,
he may never find out that he was given the game, whereas the
consequences of his sudden defeat are very real. You should not
move the Queen.'

Bystander E argues: 'How I admire B. He is one of the few who
have seen through the shallowness of this life-at-all-cost attitude.
What is life stripped of everything worthwhile? I do not share his
passion for chess, but I understand it. I too should prefer to die with
my boots on, rather than carry on in some kind of pretence. You
should move the Queen.'

Bystander F argues: 'I agree with B. I understand him perfectly.
We have played chess together for years. You should move the
Queen.'

Bystander G argues: 'I disagree strongly with B's attitude to his
health, but I also think that every man has a right to his moral
opinions. You should move the Queen.'

Bystander H argues: 'I do not propose to give positive advice. A
man's life may be at stake whatever you do. I am prepared to clarify

the issues involved as I see them, but you must draw your own moral conclusion.'

All these are *moral* reactions. Whether one agrees with them or not is another matter. Of course, the situation can be far more complicated; by the introduction of the fact that B has a family, for instance. But given that the situation is as I have described it, what is 'the single possibility' to which the facts bind me?

Black says

> Given the truth of the factual premises concerning a man's end and the necessary and sufficient condition for attaining that end, and given one is to make some second-person 'should'-statement, one must say 'You should do *M*' – and nothing else will do. What kind of a 'must' is this? It seems to mean here precisely what 'must' means when we say that anybody affirming the premises of a valid deductive argument must also affirm that argument's conclusion. Choice of the given 'should'-statement is enforced by the rules, understandings, or conventions governing the correct uses of 'should' and other words occurring in the argument: nobody who understands the premises of the practical argument and knows the rules for the proper use of 'should' can honestly offer any other 'should'-conclusion. In this respect, the parallel with 'theoretical' arguments is strong. Accordingly, no special 'practical' logic is needed in such cases: the relevant principles are the familiar ones employed throughout deductive reasoning. (pp. 111–112)

The confusions in the above argument are due in part to a mistaken view of 'facts'. True, *within* a given moral viewpoint, the facts will bind those who share it to similar moral conclusions. But, for them, the facts already have moral import. It is not a case of moral conclusions being deduced from non-evaluative factual premises. Black thinks that the facts bind one to moral advice which he regards as 'the single possibility' in the situation. But as I have tried to show in my five examples, the moral advice one thinks one ought to give will be determined by one's moral beliefs; it is such beliefs which give the facts their relevance and significance. There are no 'theoretical' rules for the 'proper' use of 'should' which make one piece of advice the only honest possibility. To talk of 'the proper use of "should"' is simply to beg the question: to equate one's own moral views with 'the single possibility'. In case my five examples of possible moral advice in the above situation are interpreted as a sign of theoretical disinterestedness, I had better put my cards on the table and say that at the moment I do not know what advice ought to be given in the situation I have described, or whether positive advice should be given at all.

Another curious feature of Black's argument is his stress on a man's end and the necessary and sufficient condition for attaining that end. He thinks these facts bind one to a specific moral conclusion. Clearly, this is not the case. Morality does not wait on these facts. On the contrary, people's aims and their methods of attaining them wait on morality. A bystander would indicate his lack of moral concern if he advised *A* as follows: '*B*'s health is irrelevant. You want to win this game; that's all that matters. You can only checkmate by moving the Queen, so move it.' Again, it may be true that someone wants to extend his business, and that the one and only way of doing so is by ruining his friend's business. But morality says 'Not that way.' On the other hand, where a person's aims and methods of attaining them are moral, it is always possible, as we have seen, for someone else to disagree and put forward other moral proposals. There are no 'single possibilities'.

Finally, a word about the challenge Professor Black puts to his readers at the end of his paper. He says that

> Once Hume's Guillotine has been discredited, we may hope to find more important arguments containing valid transitions from 'is' to 'should' or from 'is' to 'ought'. If I am not mistaken, the following argument from factual premises to a moral conclusion is valid:
> Doing *A* will produce pain.
> Apart from producing the pain resulting from *A*, doing *A* will have the same consequences that not doing *A* would have had.
> Therefore, *A* ought not to be done. (pp.112-13)

On one interpretation, the conclusion of this argument can be shown to be false. If by 'consequences' Professor Black means the kind of thing Mill had in mind, it is clear that many people have thought that they ought to do *A* on moral grounds despite the absence of such consequences. For example, a man may feel that he ought to die for a cause although the cause is lost. Again, a soldier may refuse to give details of plans to the enemy under torture, although he may know that they have already discovered them. Such actions can certainly be given a *moral* point, though in Mill's sense they would be pointless.

But Black may want to include in his 'consequences' the agent's regard for his moral convictions (as opposed to the success or failure which may attend standing by them), and his remorse at failing in the time of trial. The second premise of Black's argument could then be reworded as follows: 'Apart from producing the pain resulting from *A*, doing *A* will have the same point that not doing *A* would have had.' The challenge is then to show that pointless pain has a point. No wonder Professor Black feels confident about the argument! But confidence is bought at the price of triviality. Certainly, Hume's point is unaffected by the argument. Black tells us that pointless pain is bad, but this is to say nothing at all, since the whole moral issue concerns *what is to count* as pointless pain, and this is not something that the facts will tell us. There will be moral disagreement over what is and what is not to count as pointless. Is dying for a lost cause pointless? Black's second premise, once it is given a *positive* content, will be a premise which already has moral import; that is, it will say that such-and-such is pointless. Those who disagree about this pointlessness will not feel bound to the moral conclusion. There are no deductive moves to 'single possibilities' which will change this situation.

Morality is not a game, and philosophers are not people who have special insight into its 'rules'. I think Professor Black ought to take another look at Hume's Guillotine, for, unless I am mistaken, his arguments are on the block.

XII How to derive 'ought' from 'is'[1]

John R. Searle

I

It is often said that one cannot derive an 'ought' from an 'is'. This thesis, which comes from a famous passage in Hume's *Treatise*, while not as clear as it might be, is at least clear in broad outline: there is a class of statements of fact which is logically distinct from a class of statements of value. No set of statements of fact by themselves entails any statement of value. Put in more contemporary terminology, no set of *descriptive* statements can entail an *evaluative* statement without the addition of at least one evaluative premise. To believe otherwise is to commit what has been called the naturalistic fallacy.

I shall attempt to demonstrate a counter-example to this thesis.[2] It is not of course to be supposed that a single counter-example can refute a philosophical thesis, but in the present instance if we can present a plausible counter-example and can in addition give some account or explanation of how and why it is a counter-example, and if we can further offer a theory to back up our counter-example – a theory which will generate an indefinite number of counter-examples – we may at the very least cast considerable light on the original thesis; and possibly, if we can do all these things, we may even incline ourselves to the view that the scope of that thesis was more restricted than we had originally supposed. A counter-example must proceed by taking a statement or statements which any proponent of

---

[1] Earlier versions of this paper were read before the Stanford Philosophy Colloquium and the Pacific Division of the American Philosophical Association. I am indebted to many people for helpful comments and criticisms, especially Hans Herzberger, Arnold Kaufmann, Benson Mates, A. I. Melden, and Dagmar Searle.

[2] In its modern version. I shall not be concerned with Hume's treatment of the problem.

the thesis would grant were purely factual or 'descriptive' (they need not actually contain the word 'is') and show how they are logically related to a statement which a proponent of the thesis would regard as clearly 'evaluative'. (In the present instance it will contain an 'ought'.)[3]

Consider the following series of statements:

(1) Jones uttered the words 'I hereby promise to pay you, Smith, five dollars.'

(2) Jones promised to pay Smith five dollars.

(3) Jones placed himself under (undertook) an obligation to pay Smith five dollars.

(4) Jones is under an obligation to pay Smith five dollars.

(5) Jones ought to pay Smith five dollars.

I shall argue concerning this list that the relation between any statement and its successor, while not in every case one of 'entailment', is none the less not just a contingent relation; and the additional statements necessary to make the relationship one of entailment do not need to involve any evaluative statements, moral principles, or anything of the sort.

Let us begin. How is (1) related to (2)? In certain circumstances, uttering the words in quotation marks in (1) is the act of making a promise. And it is a part of or a consequence of the meaning of the words in (1) that in those circumstances uttering them is promising. 'I hereby promise' is a paradigm device in English for performing the act described in (2), promising.

Let us state this fact about English usage in the form of an extra premise:

(1a) Under certain conditions C anyone who utters the words (sentence) 'I hereby promise to pay you, Smith, five dollars' promises to pay Smith five dollars.

What sorts of things are involved under the rubric 'conditions C?' What is involved will be all those conditions, those states of affairs, which are necessary and sufficient conditions for the utterance of the words (sentence) to constitute the successful performance of the act of promising. The conditions will include such things as that the

---

[3] If this enterprise succeeds, we shall have bridged the gap between 'evaluative' and 'descriptive' and consequently have demonstrated a weakness in this very terminology. At present, however, my strategy is to play along with the terminology, pretending that the notions of evaluative and descriptive are fairly clear. At the end of the paper I shall state in what respects I think they embody a muddle.

speaker is in the presence of the hearer Smith, they are both conscious, both speakers of English, speaking seriously. The speaker knows what he is doing, is not under the influence of drugs, not hypnotised or acting in a play, not telling a joke or reporting an event, and so forth. This list will no doubt be somewhat indefinite because the boundaries of the concept of a promise, like the boundaries of most concepts in a natural language, are a bit loose.[4] But one thing is clear; however loose the boundaries may be, and however difficult it may be to decide marginal cases, the conditions under which a man who utters 'I hereby promise' can correctly be said to have made a promise are straightforwardly empirical conditions.

So let us add as an extra premise the empirical assumption that these conditions obtain.

(1b) Conditions *C* obtain.

From (1), (1a), and (1b) we derive (2). The argument is of the form: If *C* then (if *U* then *P*): *C* for conditions, *U* for utterance, *P* for promise. Adding the premises *U* and *C* to this hypothetical we derive (2). And as far as I can see, no moral premises are lurking in the logical woodpile. More needs to be said about the relation of (1) to (2), but I reserve that for later.

What is the relation between (2) and (3)? I take it that promising is, by definition, an act of placing oneself under an obligation. No analysis of the concept of promising will be complete which does not include the feature of the promiser placing himself under or undertaking or accepting or recognising an obligation to the promisee, to perform some future course of action, normally for the benefit of the promisee. One may be tempted to think that promising can be analysed in terms of creating expectations in one's hearers, or some such, but a little reflection will show that the crucial distinction between statements of intention on the one hand and promises on the other lies in the nature and degree of commitment or obligation undertaken in promising.

I am therefore inclined to say that (2) entails (3) straight off, but I can have no objection if anyone wishes to add – for the purpose of formal neatness – the tautological premise:

(2a) All promises are acts of placing oneself under (undertaking) an obligation to do the thing promised.

[4] In addition the concept of a promise is a member of a class of concepts which suffer from looseness of a peculiar kind, viz. defeasibility. Cf. H. L. A. Hart, 'The Ascription of Responsibility and Rights', *Logic and Language*, first series, ed. A. Flew (Oxford 1951).

How is (3) related to (4)? If one has placed oneself under an obligation, then, other things being equal, one is under an obligation. That I take it also is a tautology. Of course it is possible for all sorts of things to happen which will release one from obligations one has undertaken and hence the need for the *ceteris paribus* rider. To get an entailment between (3) and (4) we therefore need a qualifying statement to the effect that:

(3a) Other things are equal.

Formalists, as in the move from (2) to (3), may wish to add the tautological premise:

(3b) All those who place themselves under an obligation are, other things being equal, under an obligation.

The move from (3) to (4) is thus of the same form as the move from (1) to (2): If E then (if PUO then UO): E for other things are equal, PUO for place under obligation and UO for under obligation. Adding the two premises E and PUO we derive UO.

Is (3a), the *ceteris paribus* clause, a concealed evaluative premise? It certainly looks as if it might be, especially in the formulation I have given it, but I think we can show that, though questions about whether other things are equal frequently involve evaluative considerations, it is not logically necessary that they should in every case. I shall postpone discussion of this until after the next step.

What is the relation between (4) and (5)? Analogous to the tautology which explicates the relation of (3) and (4) there is here the tautology that, other things being equal, one ought to do what one is under an obligation to do. And here, just as in the previous case, we need some premise of the form:

(4a) Other things are equal.

We need the *ceteris paribus* clause to eliminate the possibility that something extraneous to the relation of 'obligation' to 'ought' might interfere.[5] Here, as in the previous two steps, we eliminate the appearance of enthymeme by pointing out that the apparently suppressed premise is tautological and hence, though formally neat, it

[5] The *ceteris paribus* clause in this step excludes somewhat different sorts of cases from those excluded in the previous step. In general we say, 'He undertook an obligation, but none the less he is not (now) under an obligation' when the obligation has been *removed*, e.g. if the promisee says, 'I release you from your obligation.' But we say, 'He is under an obligation, but none the less ought not to fulfil it' in cases where the obligation is *overridden* by some other consideration, e.g. a prior obligation.

is redundant. If, however, we wish to state it formally, this argument is of the same form as the move from (3) to (4): If E then (if UO then O); E for other things are equal, UO for under obligation, O for ought. Adding the premises E and UO we derive O.

Now a word about the phrase 'other things being equal' and how it functions in my attempted derivation. This topic and the closely related topic of defeasibility are extremely difficult and I shall not try to do more than justify my claim that the satisfaction of the condition does not necessarily involve anything evaluative. The force of the expression 'other things being equal' in the present instance is roughly this. Unless we have some reason (that is, unless we are actually prepared to give some reason) for supposing the obligation is void (step 4) or the agent ought not to keep the promise (step 5), then the obligation holds and he ought to keep the promise. It is not part of the force of the phrase 'other things being equal' that in order to satisfy it we need to establish a universal negative proposition to the effect that no reason could ever be given by anyone for supposing the agent is not under an obligation or ought not to keep the promise. That would be impossible and would render the phrase useless. It is sufficient to satisfy the condition that no reason to the contrary can in fact be given.

If a reason is given for supposing the obligation is void or that the promiser ought not to keep a promise, then characteristically a situation calling for an evaluation arises. Suppose, for example, we consider a promised act wrong, but we grant that the promiser did undertake an obligation. Ought he to keep the promise? There is no established procedure for objectively deciding such cases in advance, and an evaluation (if that is really the right word) is in order. But unless we have some reason to the contrary, the *ceteris paribus* condition is satisfied, no evaluation is necessary, and the question whether he ought to do it is settled by saying 'he promised'. It is always an open possibility that we may have to make an evaluation in order to derive 'he ought' from 'he promised', for we may have to evaluate a counter-argument. But an evaluation is not logically necessary in every case, for there may as a matter of fact be no counter-arguments. I am therefore inclined to think that there is nothing necessarily evaluative about the *ceteris paribus* condition, even though deciding whether it is satisfied will frequently involve evaluations.

But suppose I am wrong about this: would that salvage the belief in an unbridgeable logical gulf between 'is' and 'ought'? I think not, for we can always rewrite my steps (4) and (5) so that they include the *ceteris paribus* clause as part of the conclusion. Thus from our premises we would then have derived 'Other things being equal Jones ought to pay Smith five dollars', and that would still be sufficient to refute the tradition, for we would still have shown a relation of entailment between descriptive and evaluative statements. It was not the fact that extenuating circumstances can void obligations that drove philosophers to the naturalistic fallacy fallacy; it was rather a theory of language, as we shall see later on.

We have thus derived (in as strict a sense of 'derive' as natural languages will admit of) an 'ought' from an 'is'. And the extra premises which were needed to make the derivation work were in no cause moral or evaluative in nature. They consisted of empirical assumptions, tautologies, and descriptions of word usage. It must be pointed out also that the 'ought' is a 'categorical' not a 'hypothetical' ought. (5) does not say that Jones ought to pay up if he wants such and such. It says he ought to pay up, period. Note also that the steps of the derivation are carried on in the third person. We are not concluding 'I ought' from 'I said "I promise" ', but 'he ought' from 'he said "I promise" '.

The proof unfolds the connection between the utterance of certain words and the speech act of promising and then in turn unfolds promising into obligation and moves from obligation to 'ought'. The step from (1) to (2) is radically different from the others and requires special comment. In (1) we construe 'I hereby promise . . .' as an English phrase having a certain meaning. It is a consequence of that meaning that the utterance of that phrase under certain conditions is the act of promising. Thus by presenting the quoted expressions in (1) and by describing their use in (1a) we have as it were already invoked the institution of promisng. We might have started with an even more ground-floor premise than (1) by saying:

(1b) Jones uttered the phonetic sequence:/ai⁺hirbai⁺pramis⁺ təpei⁺yu⁺smiθ⁺faiv⁺dalərz/

We would then have needed extra empirical premises stating that this phonetic sequence was associated in certain ways with certain meaningful units relative to certain dialects.

The moves from (2) to (5) are relatively easy. We rely on definitional connections between 'promise', 'obligate', and 'ought', and the only problem which arises is that obligations can be overridden or removed in a variety of ways and we need to take account of that fact. We solve our difficulty by adding further premises to the effect that there are no contrary considerations, that other things are equal.

II

In this section I intend to discuss three possible objections to the
derivation.

First Objection

Since the first premise is descriptive and the conclusion evaluative, there must be a concealed evaluative premise in the description
of the conditions in (1b).

So far, this argument merely begs the question by assuming the
logical gulf between descriptive and evaluative which the derivation
is designed to challenge. To make the objection stick, the defender
of the distinction would have to show how exactly (1b) must contain
an evaluative premise and what sort of premise it might be. Uttering certain words in certain conditions just *is* promising and the
description of these conditions needs no evaluative element. The
essential thing is that in the transition from (1) to (2) we move from
the specification of a certain utterance of words to the specification
of a certain speech act. The move is achieved because the speech
act is a conventional act; and the utterance of the words, according
to the conventions, constitutes the performance of just that speech
act.

A variant of this first objection is to say: all you have shown is
that 'promise' is an evaluative, not a descriptive, concept. But this
objection again begs the question and in the end will prove disastrous to the original distinction between descriptive and evaluative. For that a man uttered certain words and that these words have
the meaning they do are surely objective facts. And if the statement
of these two objective facts plus a description of the conditions of the
utterance is sufficient to entail the statement (2) which the objector
alleges to be an evaluative statement (Jones promised to pay Smith
five dollars), then an evaluative conclusion is derived from descriptive premises without even going through steps (3), (4), and (5).

Second Objection

Ultimately the derivation rests on the principle that one ought to
keep one's promises and that is a moral principle, hence evaluative.

I don't know whether 'one ought to keep one's promises' is a 'moral' principle, but whether or not it is, it is also tautological; for it is nothing more than a derivation from the two tautologies:

> All promises are (create, are undertakings of, are acceptances of) obligations,
>
> and
>
> One ought to keep (fulfil) one's obligations.

What needs to be explained is why so many philosophers have failed to see the tautological character of this principle. Three things I think have concealed its character from them.

The first is a failure to distinguish external questions about the institution of promising from internal questions asked within the framework of the institution. The questions 'Why do we have such an institution as promising?' and 'Ought we to have such institutionalised forms of obligation as promising?' are external questions asked about and not within the institution of promising. And the question 'Ought one to keep one's promises?' can be confused with or can be taken as (and I think has often been taken as) an external question roughly expressible as 'Ought one to accept the institution of promising?' But taken literally, as an internal question, as a question about promises and not about the institution of promising, the question 'Ought one to keep one's promises?' is as empty as the question 'Are triangles three-sided?' To recognise something as a promise is to grant that, other things being equal, it ought to be kept.

A second fact which has clouded the issue is this. There are many situations, both real and imaginable, where one ought not to keep a promise, where the obligation to keep a promise is overridden by some further considerations, and it was for this reason that we needed those clumsy *ceteris paribus* clauses in our derivation. But the fact that obligations can be overridden does not show that there were no obligations in the first place. On the contrary. And these original obligations are all that is needed to make the proof work.

Yet a third factor is the following. Many philosophers still fail to realise the full force of saying that 'I hereby promise' is a performative expression. In uttering it one performs but does not describe the act of promising. Once promising is seen as a speech act of a kind different from describing, then it is easier to see that one of the features of the act is the undertaking of an obligation. But if one thinks the utterance of 'I promise' or 'I hereby promise' is a peculiar kind of description – for example, of one's mental state – then the relation between promising and obligation is going to seem very mysterious.

Third Objection

The derivation uses only a factual or inverted-commas sense of the evaluative terms employed. For example, an anthropologist observing the behaviour and attitudes of the Anglo-Saxons might well go through these derivations, but nothing evaluative would be included. Thus step (2) is equivalent to 'He did what they call promising' and step (5) to 'According to them he ought to pay Smith five dollars.' But since all of the steps (2) to (5) are in *oratio obliqua* and hence disguised statements of fact, the fact-value distinction remains unaffected.

This objection fails to damage the derivation, for what it says is only that the steps *can* be reconstrued as in *oratio obliqua*, that we can construe them as a series of external statements, that we can construct a parallel (or at any rate related) proof about reported speech. But what I am arguing is that, taken quite literally, without any *oratio obliqua* additions or interpretations, the derivation is valid. That one can construct a similar argument which would fail to refute the fact-value distinction does not show that this proof fails to refute it. Indeed it is irrelevant.

III

So far I have presented a counter-example to the thesis that one cannot derive an 'ought' from an 'is' and considered three possible objections to it. Even supposing what I have said so far is true, still one feels a certain uneasiness. One feels there must be some trick involved somewhere. We might state our uneasiness thus: How can my granting a mere fact about a man, such as the fact that he uttered certain words or that he made a promise, commit *me* to the view that *he* ought to do something? I now want briefly to discuss what broader philosophic significance my attempted derivation may have, in such a way as to give us the outlines of an answer to this question.

I shall begin by discussing the grounds for supposing that it cannot be answered at all.

The inclination to accept a rigid distinction between 'is' and 'ought', between descriptive and evaluative, rests on a certain picture of the way words relate to the world. It is a very attractive picture, so attractive (to me at least) that it is not entirely clear to what extent the mere presentation of counter-examples can challenge it. What is needed is an explanation of how and why this classical empiricist picture fails to deal with such counter-examples. Briefly, the picture is constructed something like this: first we present examples of so-called descriptive statements ('my car goes eighty miles an hour', 'Jones is six feet tall', 'Smith has brown hair'), and we contrast them with so-called evaluative statements ('my car is a good car', 'Jones ought to pay Smith five dollars', 'Smith is a nasty man'). Anyone can see that they are different. We articulate the difference by pointing out that for the descriptive statements the question of truth or falsity is objectively decidable, because to know the meaning of the descriptive expressions is to know under what objectively ascertainable conditions the statements which contain them are true or false. But in the case of evaluative statements the situation is quite different. To know the meaning of the evaluative expressions is not by itself sufficient for knowing under what conditions the statements containing them are true or false, because the meaning of the expressions is such that the statements are not capable of objective or factual truth or falsity at all. Any justification a speaker can give of one of his evaluative statements essentially involves some appeal to attitudes he holds, to criteria of assessment he has adopted, or to moral principles by which he has chosen to live and judge other people. Descriptive statements are thus objective, evaluative statements subjective, and the difference is a consequence of the different sorts of terms employed.

The underlying reason for these differences is that evaluative statements perform a completely different job from descriptive statements. Their job is not to describe any features of the world but to express the speaker's emotions, to express his attitudes, to praise or condemn, to laud or insult, to commend, to recommend, to advise, and so forth. Once we see the different jobs the two perform, we see that there must be a logical gulf between them. Evaluative statements must be different from descriptive statements in order to do their job, for if they were objective they could no longer function to evaluate. Put metaphysically, values cannot lie in the world, for if they did they would cease to be values and would just be another part of the world. Put in the formal mode, one cannot define an evaluative word in terms of descriptive words, for if one did, one would no longer be able to use the evaluative word to commend, but only to describe. Put yet another way, any effort to derive an 'ought' from an 'is' must be a waste of time, for all it could show even if it succeeded would be that the 'is' was not a real 'is' but only a disguised 'ought' or, alternatively, that the 'ought' was not a real 'ought' but only a disguised 'is'.

This summary of the traditional empirical view has been very brief, but I hope it conveys something of the power of this picture. In the hands of certain modern authors, especially Hare and Nowell-Smith, the picture attains considerable subtlety and sophistication.

What is wrong with this picture? No doubt many things are wrong with it. In the end I am going to say that one of the things wrong with it is that it fails to give us any coherent account of such notions as commitment, responsibility, and obligation.

In order to work towards this conclusion I can begin by saying that the picture fails to account for the *different types* of 'descriptive' statements. Its paradigms of descriptive statements are such utterances as 'my car goes eighty miles an hour', 'Jones is six feet tall', 'Smith has brown hair', and the like. But it is forced by its own rigidity to construe 'Jones got married', 'Smith made a promise', 'Jackson has five dollars', and 'Brown hit a home run' as descriptive statements as well. It is so forced, because whether or not someone got married, made a promise, has five dollars, or hit a home run is as much a matter of objective fact as whether he has red hair or brown eyes. Yet the former kind of statement (statements containing 'married', 'promise', and so forth) seem to be quite different from the simple empirical paradigms of descriptive statements. How are they different? Though both kinds of statements state matters of objective fact, the statements containing words such as 'married', 'promise', 'home run', and 'five dollars' state facts whose existence presupposes certain institutions: a man has five dollars, given the institution of money. Take away the institution and all he has is a rectangular bit of paper with green ink on it. A man hits a home run only given the institution of baseball; without the institution he only hits a sphere with a stick. Similarly, a man gets married or makes a promise only within the institutions of marriage and promising. Without them, all he does is utter words or make gestures. We might characterise such facts as institutional facts, and contrast them with non-institutional, or brute, facts: that a man has a bit of paper with green ink on it is a brute fact, that he has five dollars is an institutional fact.[6] The classical picture fails

[6] For a discussion of this distinction see G. E. M. Anscombe, 'On Brute Facts', *Analysis*, 18 (1958).

to account for the differences between statements of brute fact and statements of institutional fact.

The word 'institution' sounds artificial here, so let us ask: what sorts of institutions are these? In order to answer that question I need to distinguish between two different kinds of rules or conventions. Some rules regulate antecedently existing forms of behaviour. For example, the rules of polite table behaviour regulate eating, but eating exists independently of these rules. Some rules, on the other hand, do not merely regulate but create or define new forms of behaviour: the rules of chess, for example, do not merely regulate an antecedently existing activity called playing chess; they, as it were, create the possibility of or define that activity. The activity of playing chess is constituted by action in accordance with these rules. Chess has no existence apart from these rules. The distinction I am trying to make was foreshadowed by Kant's distinction between regulative and constitutive principles, so let us adopt his terminology and describe our distinction as a distinction between regulative and constitutive rules. Regulative rules regulate activities whose existence is independent of the rules; constitutive rules constitute (and also regulate) forms of activity whose existence is logically dependent on the rules.[7]

Now the institutions that I have been talking about are systems of constitutive rules. The institutions of marriage, money, and promising are like the institutions of baseball or chess in that they are systems of such constitutive rules or conventions. What I have called institutional facts are facts which presuppose such institutions.

Once we recognise the existence of and begin to grasp the nature of such institutional facts, it is but a short step to see that many forms of obligations, commitments, rights, and responsibilities are similarly institutionalised. It is often a matter of fact that one has certain obligations, commitments, rights, and responsibilities, but it is a matter of institutional, not brute, fact. It is one such institutionalised form of obligation, promising which I invoked above to derive an 'ought' from an 'is'. I started with a brute fact, that a man uttered certain words, and then invoked the institution in such a way as to generate institutional facts by which we arrived at the institutional fact that the man ought to pay another man five dollars. The whole proof rests on an appeal to the constitutive rule that to make a promise is to undertake an obligation.

[7] For a discussion of a related distinction see J. Rawls, 'Two Concepts of Rules', *Philosophical Review*, LXIV (1955).

We are now in a position to see how we can generate an indefinite number of such proofs. Consider the following vastly different example. We are in our half of the seventh inning and I have a big lead off second base. The pitcher whirls, fires to the shortstop covering, and I am tagged out a good ten feet down the line. The umpire shouts, 'Out!' I, however, being a positivist, hold my ground. The umpire tells me to return to the dugout. I point out to him that you can't derive an 'ought' from an 'is'. No set of descriptive statements describing matters of fact, I say, will entail any evaluative statements to the effect that I should or ought to leave the field. 'You just can't get orders or recommendations from facts alone.' What is needed is an evaluative major premise. I therefore return to and stay on second base (until I am carried off the field). I think everyone feels my claims here to be preposterous, and preposterous in the sense of logically absurd. Of course you can derive an 'ought' from an 'is', and though to actually set out the derivation in this case would be vastly more complicated than in the case of promising, it is in principle no different. By undertaking to play baseball I have committed myself to the observation of certain constitutive rules.

We are now also in a position to see that the tautology that one ought to keep one's promises is only one of a class of similar tautologies concerning institutionalised forms of obligation. For example, 'one ought not to steal' can be taken as saying that to recognise something as someone else's property necessarily involves recognising his right to dispose of it. This is a constitutive rule of the institution of private property.[8] 'One ought not to tell lies' can be taken as saying that to make an assertion necessarily involves undertaking an obligation to speak truthfully. Another constitutive rule. 'One ought to pay one's debts' can be construed as saying that to recog-

---

[8] Proudhon said: 'Property is theft.' If one tries to take this as an internal remark it makes no sense. It was intended as an external remark attacking and rejecting the institution of private property. It gets its air of paradox and its force by using terms which are internal to the institution in order to attack the institution.

Standing on the deck of some institutions one can tinker with constitutive rules and even throw some other institutions overboard. But could one throw all institutions overboard (in order perhaps to avoid ever having to derive an 'ought' from an 'is')? One could not and still engage in those forms of behaviour we consider characteristically human. Suppose Proudhon had added (and tried to live by): 'Truth is a lie, marriage is infidelity, language is uncommunicative, law is a crime', and so on with every possible institution.

nise something as a debt is necessarily to recognise an obligation to pay it. It is easy to see how all these principles will generate counter-examples to the thesis that you cannot derive an 'ought from an 'is'.

My tentative conclusions, then, are as follows:

1. The classical picture fails to account for institutional facts.
2. Institutional facts exist within systems of constitutive rules.
3. Some systems of constitutive rules involve obligations, commitments, and responsibilities.
4. Within those systems we can derive 'ought's' from 'is's' on the model of the first derivation.

With these conclusions we now return to the question with which I began this section: How can my stating a fact about a man, such as the fact that he made a promise, commit me to a view about what he ought to do? One can begin to answer this question by saying that for me to state such an institutional fact is already to invoke the constitutive rules of the institution. It is those rules that give the word 'promise' its meaning. But those rules are such that to commit myself to the view that Jones made a promise involves committing myself to what he ought to do (other things being equal).

If you like, then, we have shown that 'promise' is an evaluative word, but since it is also purely descriptive, we have really shown that the whole distinction needs to be re-examined. The alleged distinction between descriptive and evaluative statements is really a conflation of at least two distinctions. On the one hand there is a distinction between different kinds of speech acts, one family of speech acts including evaluations, another family including descriptions. This is a distinction between different kinds of illocutionary force.[9] On the other hand there is a distinction between utterances which involve claims objectively decidable as true or false and those which involve claims not objectively decidable, but which are 'matters of personal decision' or 'matters of opinion'. It has been assumed that the former distinction is (must be) a special case of the latter, that if something has the illocutionary force of an evaluation, it cannot be entailed by factual premises. Part of the point of my argument is to show that this contention is false, that factual premises can entail evaluative conclusions. If I am right, then the alleged distinction between descriptive and evaluative utterances is useful only as a distinction between two kinds of illocutionary force,

[9] See J. L. Austin, *How to Do Things with Words* (Cambridge, Mass. 1962) for an explanation of this notion.

describing and evaluating, and it is not even very useful there, since if we are to use these terms strictly, they are only two among hundreds of kinds of illocutionary force; and utterances of sentences of the form (5) – 'Jones ought to pay Smith five dollars' – would not characteristically fall in either class.

XIII On not deriving 'ought' from 'is'

Antony Flew

In *How to do Things with Words* (Oxford 1962) there is a promise which Austin, unfortunately, did not live to try to fulfil. In introducing his fivefold classification into verdictives, exercitives, commissives, behabitives, and expositives Austin suggests that this classification is 'quite enough to play Old Harry with two fetishes which I admit to an inclination to play Old Harry with, viz. (1) the true/false fetish (2) the value/fact fetish' (p. 150). Perhaps it is; but Austin made there no attempt to show why the possibility of making his fivefold classification must qualify or undermine the possibility of distinguishing issues of fact from issues of value, or the need sometimes to insist on the difference. Indeed from what he actually says it is not clear precisely what he wished to play Old Harry with; and hence even less clear how the exercise was to be performed.

The word nevertheless seems to have gone round that the idea that there is a radical difference between *ought* and *is* is old hat, something which though still perhaps cherished by out-group backwoodsmen has long since been seen through and discarded by all with-it mainstream philosophers. For instance, in a penetrating article on 'Do illocutionary forces exist?'[1] Mr L. Jonathan Cohen offers some provocative asides: 'the statement-evaluation dichotomy, whatever it may be, is as erroneous on my view as on Austin's'; and 'Indeed there is a case for saying that Austin's recommendation about the word "good" is itself a hangover from the fact-value dichotomy' (pp. 136 and 137). Cohen gives no hint as to where and how this dichotomy was so decisively liquidated. But a recent paper by Mr John R. Searle, on 'How to derive "ought" from "is"'[2] can perhaps be seen as an attempt to plug the gap. Searle's stated aim is to show that the Naturalistic Fallacy is not a fallacy, and he gives many signs of thinking of his aspirations in Austinian terms. My

[1] *Philosophical Quarterly*, 14 (1964).
[2] Paper XII.

object is to show that Searle is entirely unsuccessful, and to suggest
that anyone who hopes to succeed where he has failed will have to
find other and more powerful arguments.

2. The first point to remark about Searle's article is that he
chooses to start from his own characterisation of what the Naturalistic Fallacy is supposed to consist in; and that he neither quotes nor
gives precise references to any statements by the philosophers with
whom he wishes to disagree. His characterisation runs (p. 120):

> It is often said that one cannot derive an 'ought' from an 'is'.
> This thesis, which comes from a famous passage in Hume's
> *Treatise*, while not as clear as it might be, is at least clear in broad
> outline: there is a class of statements of fact which is logically dis-
> tinct from a class of statements of value. No set of statements of
> fact by themselves entails any statement of value. Put in more
> contemporary terminology, no set of *descriptive* statements can
> entail an *evaluative* statement without the addition of at least one
> evaluative premise. To believe otherwise is to commit the natural-
> istic fallacy. (Italics here and always as in original.)

Let us consider alongside this paragraph from Searle some sen-
tences written by a contemporary protagonist of the view which
Searle is supposed to be challenging. These quotations come from
K. R. Popper and – significantly – they come from *The Open
Society* (1945):

> The breakdown of magic tribalism is closely connected with the
> realization that taboos are different in various tribes, that they are
> imposed and enforced by man, and that they may be broken with-
> out unpleasant repercussions if one can only escape the sanctions
> imposed by one's fellow-men.... These experiences may lead to a
> conscious differentiation between the man-enforced normative
> laws or conventions, and the natural regularities which are be-
> yond his power.... In spite of the fact that this position was
> reached a long time ago by the Sophist Protagoras ... it is still so
> little understood that it seems necessary to explain it in some
> detail.... It is we who impose our standards upon nature, and
> who introduce in this way morals into the natural world, in spite
> of the fact that we are part of this world.... It is important for
> the understanding of this attitude to realize that decisions can
> never be derived from facts (or statements of facts), although they
> pertain to facts. The decision, for instance to oppose slavery does
> not depend upon the fact that all men are born free and equal,
> and no man is born in chains ... even if they were born in chains,
> many of us might demand the removal of these chains.... The
> making of a decision, the adoption of a standard, is a fact. But the
> norm which has been adopted, is not. That most people agree with
> the norm 'Thou shalt not steal' is a sociological fact. But the norm

'Thou shalt not steal' is not a fact; and it can never be inferred from sentences describing facts. . . . *It is impossible to derive a sentence stating a norm or a decision from a sentence stating a fact*; this is only another way of saying that it is impossible to derive norms or decisions from facts. (Vol. 1, pp. 50–3)

Popper's account, even in this abbreviated form, is of course much fuller than that given by Searle; and, partly for that reason, it says or suggests many things which are not comprised in Searle's short paragraph. It presents the idea of the Naturalistic Fallacy as involved in the clash of world-outlooks and personal commitments; and it is governed throughout by the notion that 'we are free to form our own moral opinions in a much stronger sense than we are free to form our own moral opinions as to what the facts are.[3] But the most relevant and important difference is that Popper at least suggests, what is true, that the fundamental discrimination in terms of which the Naturalistic Fallacy is being characterised is not, and does not have to be thought to be, a clearcut feature of all actual discourse. It is not something which you cannot fail to observe everywhere as already there and given, if once you have learnt what to look for. There is, rather, a differentiation which has to be made and insisted upon; and the distinction is one the development of which may go against the grain of set habits and powerful inclinations. Our situation in this case is not at all like that represented in the second chapter of the book of *Genesis*, where God presents to Adam the beasts of the field and the fowl of the air, leaving it to him merely to supply names for each natural kind.

Searle's account of the opposing position seems to suggest, what his later criticism appears to be assuming, that its misguided spokesmen must be committed to the notion: that an *is/ought* dichotomy is something which the alert natural historian of utterances could not fail to notice, as somehow already given; and that no utterances can either combine, or be ambiguous as between, these two sorts of claim. Yet when we turn to Popper, and allow him to speak for himself, we find in his account nothing at all to suggest any commitment to the erroneous ideas: that all the utterances which are

[3] R. M. Hare, *Freedom and Reason* (Oxford 1963) p. 2. The same author's *The Language of Morals* (Oxford 1952) is another excellent source for the sophisticated and flexible handling of the idea of the Naturalistic Fallacy; and Hare is, of course, perfectly well aware that the same terms and expressions may combine both descriptive and normative meanings – and hence that normative standards are incapsulated in certain uses of such terms. See, for instance, especially *LM* pp. 119–21 and pp. 145–50 and *FR* pp. 188ff. and pp. 25ff. Cf. Hare, Paper XIV.

actually made must already be clearly and unambiguously either statements of fact or expressions of value; or that every actual utterance is either purely a statement of fact or purely normative. What Popper emphasises is, rather, the epoch-marking importance of the development of this sort of distinction, the great need to insist upon it, and the difficulty of appreciating fully what it does and what it does not imply.

It is perhaps possible that Searle here, like so many others else-where, has been misled by Hume's irony; notwithstanding that Searle himself disclaims concern 'with Hume's treatment of the problem'. For Hume does indeed write as if he was quite modestly claiming only to have noticed, and to have become seized of the vast importance of, a distinction which, however unwittingly, every-one was always and systematically making already:[4]

> I cannot forbear adding to these reasonings an observation, which may, perhaps, be found of some importance. In every system of morality, which I have hitherto met with, I have always remarked, that the author proceeds for some time in the ordinary way of reasoning, and establishes the being of a God, or makes observations concerning human affairs; when of a sudden I am surprised to find, that instead of the usual copulations of propositions *is*, and *is not*, I meet with no proposition that is not connected with an *ought*, or an *ought not*.

3. After this somewhat protracted introduction, designed to refresh memories about what is and is not involved in the position which Searle is supposed to be attacking, we can now at last turn to his arguments. He works with the example of promising: 'The proof unfolds the connection between the utterance of certain words and the speech act of promising and then in turn unfolds promising into obligation and moves from obligation to "ought" ' (p. 125). The idea is to start with a purely descriptive premise such as 'Jones uttered the words "I hereby promise to pay you, Smith, five dollars" ', or that Jones uttered the corresponding phonetic sequence, and to proceed by a series of deductive moves to the purely normative conclusion 'Jones ought to pay Smith five dollars'. Considerable elaboration is necessary, and is provided, in the attempt to deal with the compli-cations arising: because the utterance of such words or sounds will not always rate as a making of the promise; and because the prima facie obligation to keep a promise can be nullified or overridden.

[4] D. Hume, *Treatise*, III. i. 1. For discussion of the issues of Humean interpretation see Papers I, II, III, IV, V, VI.

It will, in the light of what has been said in section 2, be sufficiently obvious what sort of moves the critic must make if he hopes to drive a wedge into such a proposed proof. He has to distinguish normative and descriptive elements in the meaning of words like *promise*; and to insist that, however willing we may be to accept the package deal in this particular uncontentious case of promising, it is nevertheless still not possible to deduce the normative from the descriptive part of the combination. The best place to insert the wedge in Searle's argument seems to be where he maintains: 'one thing is clear; however loose the boundaries may be, and however difficult it may be to decide marginal cases, the conditions under which a man who utters "I hereby promise" can correctly be said to have made a promise are straightforwardly empirical conditions' (p. 122). The weakness becomes glaring if we summon for comparison some obnoxious contentions of the same form. Terms such as *nigger* or *Jewboy*, *apostate* or *infidel*, *colonialist* or *kulak* no doubt carry, at least when employed in certain circles, both normative and descriptive meanings; and, presumably, the descriptive element of that meaning can correctly be said to apply whenever the appropriate 'straightforwardly empirical conditions' are satisfied. But in these parallel cases most of us, I imagine, would be careful to use one of the several linguistic devices for indicating that we do not commit ourselves to the norms involved, or that we positively repudiate them. Thus, to revert to Searle's example, one could, without any logical impropriety, say of the man who had in suitable circumstances uttered the words 'I hereby promise . . .' that he had done what is called (by those who accept the social institution of promising) promising. The oddity of this non-committal piece of pure description would lie simply in the perversity of suggesting a policy of non-involvement in an institution which is surely essential to any tolerable human social life.

4. It remains to ask either why these moves do not impinge on Searle as considerable objections or how he thinks to dispose of them. We have already in section 2 offered suggestions bearing on these questions. But more light is to be found by considering in the second part of his article his discussion of 'three possible objections to the derivation'.

(a) The first of these objections consists in simply asserting that 'Since the first premise is descriptive and the conclusion evaluative, there must be a concealed evaluative premise in the description of the conditions . . .' (p. 126). To which Searle replies that as it stands this objection just begs the question: it requires to be supplemented with some account of the precise location and nature of the concealed evaluative premise. So far, so unexceptionable. The crunch comes when he continues: 'Uttering certain words in certain conditions just *is* promising and the description of these conditions needs no evaluative element' (p. 126). For, as we have been urging in section 3, the normative element enters: not with the neutral description of the conditions in which those who accept the social institution of promise-making and promise-keeping would say that someone had made what they call a promise; but at the moment when, by using the word *promise* without reservation, we commit ourselves to that institution.

(b) The second objection considered runs: 'Ultimately the derivation rests on the principle that one ought to keep one's promises and that is a moral principle, hence evaluative.' To this Searle responds that, whether or not this is a moral principle, 'it is also tautological'. He then proceeds to offer three suggestions to explain 'why so many philosophers have failed to see the tautological character of this principle' (pp. 126–7). This is, perhaps, to go rather too fast. For the sentence 'One ought to keep one's promises' is not in itself and unequivocally either tautological or not. It could without too much strain be given either tautological or substantial or even equivocal employments. If the user is prepared to accept that the absence of obligation is a sufficient reason for withdrawing the word *promise*, then the employment is clearly tautological. But if he is to be taken to be referring to certain specific descriptive conditions, and maintaining that, granted those, certain specific things ought to be done, then, surely, the employment is substantial. And if he is insisting that, granted these specific descriptive conditions, then necessarily those things ought to be done; then he would seem to be equivocating between a substantial and a tautological employment.

The first of Searle's suggestions is that some of his opponents have failed 'to distinguish external questions about the institution of promising from internal questions asked within the framework of the institution' (p. 127). No doubt some have: though it would be slightly surprising and wholly deplorable to find that many philosophers in an Humean tradition had neglected a distinction of a kind for which one of the classical sources is to be found in the third appendix of the second *Inquiry*. Even so this particular charge rings very badly in the present context. For, as we were urging in section 3, the weakness of Searle's attempted derivation lies precisely in the refusal to allow that the acceptance of a social institution must come between any statement of the purely descriptive conditions for saying that a promise was made, and the drawing of the normative conclusion that something ought to be done.

A more subtle version of the same fault can be seen in Searle's reply to a variant of his first proposed objection, which would protest: 'all you have shown is that "promise" is an evaluative, not a descriptive, concept.' This variant, he claims, 'in the end will prove disastrous to the original distinction between descriptive and evaluative. For that a man uttered certain words and that these words have the meaning that they do are surely objective facts. And if the statement of these two objective facts plus a description of the conditions of the utterance is sufficient to entail the statement... which the objector alleges to be an evaluative statement... then an evaluative conclusion is derived from descriptive premises...' (p. 126). But here again it is both necessary and decisive to insist on distinguishing: between a detached report on the meanings which some social group gives to certain value words; and the unreserved employment of those words by an engaged participant. For it is between the former and the latter that there comes exactly that commitment to the incapsulated values which alone warrants us to draw the normative conclusions.

Searle's other two suggestions both refer to peculiarities which make his chosen example especially tricky to handle: the second notices the difficulties which arise because the prima facie obligation to keep a promise made may sometimes properly be overridden by other claims: and the third takes cognisance of the fact that the first person present tense 'I promise' is performative. It is not perhaps altogether clear why failure to take the measure of this insight – for which again a classical source can be found in Hume[5] – is supposed to encourage the idea that 'One ought to keep one's promises' is not tautological. What Searle says is: 'If one thinks the utterance of "I promise" or "I hereby promise" is a peculiar kind of description ... then the relation between promising and obligation is going to seem very mysterious' (p. 127). Certainly if one thinks that, then there will be a mystery as to why the utterance of these words is construed, by anyone who accepts the institution of promising, as involving the incurring of an obligation. But this is no reason at all for saying that the same misguided person must also by the same token find something mysterious about the notion that, supposing that someone has promised, it follows necessarily that he is obliged.

This is a good occasion to say that where we have spoken of a descriptive element in the meaning of *promise*, we were, of course,

[5] *Treatise*, III. ii. 5, 'Of the obligation of promises'.

intending to include only uses other than the first person present performative. Fortunately the complications connected with that use can for present purposes be largely ignored. For in Searle's candidate proof 'I promise' is mentioned, not used; and so our criticism insists that the normative premise is to be found at the point where the performance is characterised, unreservedly, as a promise.

(c) The third objection considered is that: 'The derivation uses only a factual or inverted-commas sense of the evaluative terms employed.' This discussion is the most interesting for us. It is here that Searle comes nearest to recognising, and to trying to deal with, the rather obvious sort of criticism which we have been deploying. In formulating this objection Searle recognises the distinction: between the employment of a term like *promise* in a detached anthropological description of a social practice; and the use of the same term, without reservation, by a committed participant. His reply is: 'This objection fails to damage the derivation, for what it says is only that the steps *can* be reconstrued as in *oratio obliqua*. . . . That one can construct a similar argument which would fail to refute the fact-value distinction does not show that this proof fails to refute it. Indeed it is irrelevant' (p. 128).

This, of course, is true. And if all spokesmen for the opposition were such men of straw it would be a very easy matter to consign them to the garbage dump. What is so extraordinary is that, having apparently allowed the crucial distinction, Searle fails to notice the decisive objection: that his step from 1, 'Jones uttered the words "I hereby promise to pay you, Smith, five dollars"' to 2, 'Jones promised to pay Smith five dollars' is fallacious; unless, that is, we are supposed, as we are not, to construe 2 as being purely descriptive, as being, as it were, in *oratio obliqua*.

To explain Searle's oversight the only philosophically relevant suggestions we can offer are those indicated in section 2. Yet it really is extremely hard to believe that he is attributing to his opponents the assumptions: that all our discourse is already divided into elements which are either purely normative or exclusively descriptive; and that no legitimate expression could combine in its meaning both normative and descriptive components. For, though such misconceptions could conceivably be derived from a wooden and unsophisticated reading of some of those sentences in the *Treatise*, such a construction must at once make a mystery of any claim that attention to this distinction 'would subvert all the vulgar systems of morality'. This sort of thing could scarcely even be thought – as quite clearly it has been thought by many of the most distinguished protagonists of the idea of the Naturalistic Fallacy – if what was at stake really was just a matter of noticing a division already clearly and universally obtaining; rather than, as of course it is, a matter of insisting on making discriminations where often there is every sort of combination and confusion.

5. In the issue of the *Philosophical Review* immediately following that which contains Searle's paper, Professor Max Black published one of his own taking a very similar line and ending with a strong challenge to protagonists of the opposite view to, so to speak, show up or shut up. I shall not try here to deal with his article too. One thing at a time. But at least I have taken the first available opportunity to show up!

XIV The promising game
R. M. Hare

One of the most fundamental questions about moral judgements is whether they, and other value-judgements, can be logically derived from statements of empirical fact. Like most important philosophical questions, this one has reached the stage at which its discussion is bound to proceed piecemeal, in terms of particular examples, arguments and counter-arguments. This article is intended as a contribution to one such controversy. In a recent article, 'How to derive "ought" from "is"',[1] Professor J. R. Searle attempts a feat which many before him have thought to perform. His argument, though it seems to me unsound, is set out with such clarity and elegance as amply to repay examination.

He asks us to consider the following series of statements:

(1) Jones uttered the words 'I hereby promise to pay you, Smith, five dollars'.
(2) Jones promised to pay Smith five dollars.
(3) Jones placed himself under (undertook) an obligation to pay Smith five dollars.
(4) Jones is under an obligation to pay Smith five dollars.
(5) Jones ought to pay Smith five dollars.

He then argues concerning this list that 'the relation between any statement and its successor, while not in every case one of "entailment", is nonetheless not just a contingent relation; and the additional statements necessary to make the relationship one of entail-

[1] Paper XII. I must acknowledge the help I have received from an unpublished paper which Professor A. G. N. Flew kindly lent me, as well as from several enjoyable arguments with Professor Searle himself. Searle's argument, though I cannot accept it, is both more plausible, and sets a higher moral tone, than that recently supplied by Mr MacIntyre and repeated in an unimportantly different form by Professor Black (Papers I and X). While Searle seeks to demonstrate logically that we ought to keep our promises, Black and MacIntyre seek to demonstrate that we ought to do whatever is the one and only means to achieving *anything* that we happen to want, or avoiding *anything* that we want to avoid. I have discussed Black's arguments in a paper 'Wanting, some Pitfalls' contributed to the proceedings of the 1968 Colloquium of the University of Western Ontario (ed. R. Binkley, forthcoming).

ment do not need to involve any evaluative statements, moral principles, or anything of the sort' (p. 121).

Though there may be other steps in the argument that are open to question, I shall concentrate on those from (1) to (2) and from (2) to (3). One of the 'additional statements' which Searle supplies between (1) and (2) is

> (1a) Under certain conditions C anyone who utters the words (sentence) 'I hereby promise to pay you, Smith, five dollars' promises to pay Smith five dollars.

This, he says, in conjunction with the further premiss,

> (1b) Conditions C obtain,

turns the step from (1) to (2) into an entailment (pp. 121ff.). Next, he similarly inserts between (2) and (3), in order to show that that step is an entailment, what he calls the 'tautological'[2] premiss,

> (2a) All promises are acts of placing oneself under (undertaking) an obligation to do the thing promised.

This premiss is 'tautological' because 'No analysis of the concept of promising will be complete which does not include the feature of the promiser placing himself under an obligation' (p. 122).

Later, Searle puts what appears to be the same point in terms of what he calls 'constitutive rules'. There are some institutions which are not merely regulated but constituted by the rules governing them. Thus 'the rules of chess, for example, do not merely regulate an antecedently existing activity called playing chess; they, as it were, create the possibility of or define that activity' (p. 131). The rules of chess and baseball are examples of constitutive rules, and so is 'the constitutive rule that to make a promise is to undertake an obligation' (p. 131).

I wish to consider the relations between (1a) and (2a). In order to clarify them, I shall appeal to the 'baseball' analogy with which Searle has helpfully provided us (p. 131). He describes a set of empirical conditions such that, if they obtain, a baseball-player is out, and is obliged to leave the field. I will call these conditions 'E', in order to conceal my ignorance of the rules of baseball in which they are specified. What correspond, in the 'promising' case, to conditions E in the baseball case, are conditions C *together with* the condition that the person in question should have uttered the words 'I promise, etc.'. Let us number the propositions in the 'baseball' case to correspond with Searle's numbering in the 'promising' case, distinguish-

---

[2] 'Analytic' seems to me preferable; but I will use Searle's term.

ing them by the addition of a 'prime'. There will then be a constitutive rule of baseball to the effect that

(1a′) Whenever a player satisfies conditions E, he is out.

And, since no analysis of the concept *out* will be complete which does not include the feature of the player who is out being obliged to leave the field, we can add the 'tautological' premiss,

(2a′) All players who are out are obliged to leave the field.

We can simplify the argument by combining (1a′) and (2a′) into the single constitutive rule,

(1a′*) Whenever a player satisfies conditions E, he is obliged to leave the field.

For, if the definition in virtue of which (2a′) is a tautology is applied direct to (1a′), it turns into (1a′*). And similarly in the 'promising' case, the argument will be simplified if we combine (1a) and (2a) into the single constitutive rule,

(1a*) Under certain conditions C anyone who utters the words (sentence) 'I hereby promise to pay you, Smith, five dollars' places himself under (undertakes) an obligation to pay Smith five dollars.

The rule could be put in a general form, leaving out the reference to Smith; but we need not trouble with this.

What then is the status of (1a*)? Five answers seem plausible enough to merit discussion:

(a) It is a tautology;
(b) It is a synthetic empirical statement about English word-usage;
(c) It is a synthetic prescription about word-usage in English;
(d) It is a synthetic empirical statement about something other than word-usage;
(e) It is, or implicitly contains, a synthetic evaluation or prescription, not merely about word-usage.

Searle would appear to maintain (b). I shall argue for (e). Since the arguments which I shall use against (a), (b) and (c) are all the same, I shall not need to detail them separately for the three answers; (d) will require to be rebutted independently, but this will not take long.

Let us start by discussing the status of the analogous statement (1a′*). Is it a tautology? There certainly is a tautology with which it can be easily confused, namely

(1a′*+) *In (i.e. according to the rules of) baseball*, whenever a player satisfies conditions E, he is obliged to leave the field.

This is a tautology because a definition of 'baseball' would have to run 'a game with the following rules, viz. . . .' followed by a list of rules, including (1a′*) or its equivalent. But this does not make (1a′*) itself, in which the italicised part is omitted, into a tautology. (1a′*) is a summary of part of the rules of baseball; and, although it may be that some of the rules of a game are tautologies, it is impossible that they should all be. For if they were, what we should have would be, not the rules for playing a game, but rules (or, more strictly, exemplifications of rules) for speaking correctly about the game. To conform to the rules of a game it is necessary to act, not merely speak, in certain ways. Therefore the rules are not tautologies.

For the same reasons, as we shall see, the rules of baseball [and in particular (1a′) and (1a′*)] cannot be treated as synthetic statements, or even as synthetic prescriptions, about word-usage. They are about how a game is, or is to be, played.

Let us now apply all this to the 'promising' case. By parity of reasoning it is clear that (1a*) is not a tautology, although it is easy to confuse it with another proposition (1a*⁺), which *is* a tautology. (1a*⁺) will consist of (1a*), preceded by the words 'In the institution of promising' – we might say, if it were not liable to misinterpretation, 'In the promising game'. This is a tautology, because it is expansible into 'According to the rules of an institution whose rules say "Under conditions *C* anyone who utters the words . . . [etc., as in (1a*)]", under conditions *C* anyone who utters the words . . . [etc., as in (1a*)]'. But (1a*) itself is not a tautology. As before, the constitutive rules of an institution may contain some tautologies, but they cannot all be tautologies, if they are going to prescribe that people *act* in certain ways and not in others. And, as before, we must not be misled into thinking that, because it is a tautology that promising is an institution of which (1a*) is a constitutive rule, (1a*) itself is a tautology.

As before, and for analogous reasons, (1a*) is neither a synthetic statement nor a synthetic prescription about how English is, or is or ought to be, spoken. Just because it has the consequences which Searle claims for it, it is more than this.

There is one apparent disparity between the 'promising' and 'baseball' cases which might be a source of confusion. In the 'baseball' case the word 'baseball' does not occur in (1a′*); and therefore, though (1a′*) is in a sense definitive of 'baseball', it is not thereby made tautologous. But in the 'promising' case, (1a*) does contain the word 'promise'; and this makes it much more plausible to suggest that (1a*), since it is in a sense explicative of the notion of promising, is a tautology. This plausibility is even stronger in the case of (1a). The answer to this objection may help to clarify the whole procedure of introducing a word like 'promise' into the language. The word is introduced by means of such a proposition as (1a*). But we must not be misled into thinking that this makes (1a*) a tautology, or a mere statement about word-usage. For, as we shall see, it is a characteristic of words like 'promise', which have meaning only within institutions, that they can be introduced into language only when certain synthetic propositions about how we should *act* are assented to. (1a*) is such a proposition. The word 'promise' depends for its meaning upon the proposition, but the proposition is not true solely in virtue of the meaning of 'promise'. Similarly, a word like 'out' is dependent for its meaning upon the rules of base-ball or cricket; but those rules are not tautologies in virtue of the meaning of 'out' and other such words.

However, this may not seem to go to the root of the objection. For Searle's argument could be stated without mentioning the word 'promise' at all. He could simply, in (1a), substitute the words 'place upon himself an obligation' for the word 'promise' throughout. The proposition then becomes:

> Under certain conditions C anyone who utters the words (sentence) 'I hereby place upon myself an obligation to pay you, Smith, five dollars' places upon himself an obligation to pay Smith five dollars.

Surely, it might be said, I cannot deny that *this* is a tautology, or, alternatively, a statement about word-usage. But this is just what I do wish to deny. For, to begin with, if the mere repetition of the words 'place ... an obligation' in the proposition made it into a tautology, it is hard to see what the words 'Under certain conditions C' are doing; one might think that under any conditions whatever a person who says 'I hereby place upon myself an obligation, etc.' must necessarily have thereby placed upon himself an obligation, etc. But once we have seen that this is not so (for example, the man might be under duress or mad), we see that the appearance of tautology is deceptive. It is not in general true (let alone tautologous) that the man who says 'p' makes it the case that p. Something like this does happen in the case of what used to be called performative verbs; it happens in our present case with the verb 'promise'. The man who says 'I promise', promises (under certain conditions). But it is not a tautology that he does so, nor is it a tautology that the man who says 'I hereby place myself under an obligation' places himself under an obligation, even under certain (empirical) conditions. Nor are either of these merely remarks about word-usage. For it is a necessary condition for the adoption of these performative expressions that certain synthetic constitutive (and not merely linguistic) rules be also adopted, thus creating the institution within which the expressions have meaning.

To make this clearer, let us suppose that we have already in our language the word 'obligation' (and kindred words like 'ought'), but that none of our obligations has been, as Searle puts it, 'institutionalised' (p. 132). That is to say, we can speak of our having obligations (e.g. to feed our children) and even of our placing upon ourselves obligations (e.g. by having children we place upon ourselves the obligation to feed them); but we cannot yet speak of placing upon ourselves an obligation just by saying, merely, 'I place upon myself the obligation, etc.'. Then suppose that some inventive person suggests the adoption of this useful expression (or rather its conversion to this new use). The other members of society may well stare at him and say 'But we don't see how you can place upon yourself an obligation just by saying these words'. What he will then have to say, in order to sell this device to them, and therewith the institution of which it is a part, is something like this: 'You have to adopt the constitutive rule or moral principle that one has an obligation to do those things of which one has said "I (hereby) place upon myself an obligation to do them".' When they have adopted this principle, or in adopting it, they can introduce the new use for the expression. And the principle is a synthetic one. It is a new synthetic moral principle, and not merely a new way of speaking, that is being introduced; this shows up in the fact that, if they adopt the principle, they will have acquired obligations to do things that they have not done before, not merely to speak in ways that they have not spoken before.

There may be, indeed, an interpretation on which (1a), (1a*) and their analogues could be said to be statements 'about' the English language. They could be treated as statements which say, or imply, that the English have in their language the performative expression 'I promise', or the performative expression 'I place myself under an obligation', whose use is tied to the institution of promising (or undertaking obligations); and which therefore imply also that the English (or sufficient of them) subscribe to the rules of this institution. The latter half of this would be an anthropological statement about the English. But it is obvious that such a statement cannot generate the entailments which Searle requires. For the conclusions which will then follow will be, at most, of the type: 'The English subscribe to the view that Jones is under an obligation'; 'The English subscribe to the view that Jones ought', etc. For the required non-anthropological, moral (or at least prescriptive) conclusions to follow, (1a) must, interpreted in the light of (2a), be taken as expressing the speakers' own subscription to the rules of the institution of promising, i.e. to moral principles. I do not wish to argue which is the most natural way to take these statements; all I need to say is that *unless* they are taken in this way, the derivation will not work.

It is often the case that performative expressions cannot be introduced without the adoption of synthetic constitutive rules. Thus it would be impossible to introduce the expression 'I stake a claim to this land' unless there were adopted, at the same time, a principle that by saying this, under the appropriate conditions, if the claimant has not been forestalled by somebody else, he acquires at least some claim to the land. In pioneering days in America one could do this; but try doing it in modern Siberia, where they do not have that principle.

Another way of showing that (1a*) is not a tautology, and is not made so by the fact that it is used for introducing the word 'promise' into the language, is the following. If (1a*) were true in virtue of the meaning of the word 'promise', and therefore tautologous, then both (1a) and (2a) would have to be tautologous. For (1a*) was arrived at by applying to (1a) the definition which made (2a) tautologous; and it is impossible to get a tautology out of a synthetic proposition by definitional substitution. But (1a) and (2a) cannot both be made tautologous without an equivocation on the word 'promise'. For (2a) is tautologous, if it is, in virtue of *one* definition of 'promise', and (1a) is tautologous, if it is, in virtue of *another* definition of 'promise' (or, on the alternative suggestion that (1a) is a statement about language, it can be so only in virtue of *another* definition of 'promise'). If we take (1a) as tautologous, or as a usage-statement, it will have to be in virtue of some such definition as the following:

(D1) Promising is saying, under certain conditions *C*, 'I hereby promise, etc.'

But (2a), if it is tautologous, is so in virtue of a *different* definition, namely

Promising is placing oneself under an obligation....

How the definition is completed does not matter; it has at any rate to start like this. To make (1a*) tautologous, or a usage-statement, we have to take 'promise' simultaneously in these two different senses. And the trouble cannot be escaped by completing the last definition thus:

> (D2) Promising is placing oneself under an obligation by saying, under certain conditions *C*, 'I hereby promise, etc.'.

This definition sounds attractive, and may be more or less correct; but it does not make (1a) a tautology, and would make it into more than a statement about word-usage. According to (D2), a man who says 'I hereby promise, etc.' has satisfied only one of the conditions of promising, but may not have satisfied the other; he may have said the words, but may not have thereby placed upon himself any obligation. We can only say that he has succeeded in doing this if we assent to the *synthetic* principle (1a*). The necessity of assenting to this synthetic principle before the trick works may be concealed by taking (D2), not as a verbal definition of the modern type, but as that old device of synthetic-a-priorists, an 'essential' or 'real' definition of promising. But then it will be synthetic.

I conclude, for these reasons, that (1a*) cannot be tautologous or a statement about word-usage, but must be a synthetic constitutive rule of the institution of promising. If the constitutive rules of the institution of promising are moral principles, as I think they are, then (1a*) is a synthetic moral principle. It follows that, if Searle sticks to it that (2a) is tautologous, he must allow that (1a) either is or implicitly contains a synthetic moral principle. But this would destroy his argument; and indeed he says that it is not; for, after introducing it, he says 'As far as I can see, no moral premises are lurking in the logical woodpile' (p. 122). He says this, in spite of the fact that he is going on immediately to make (1a) by definition equivalent to (1a*), which we have seen to be a synthetic moral principle.

It might be suggested that (1a) is an empirical statement of some non-linguistic sort. I am assured by Searle that he does not think this; but the suggestion is worth examining. If it were true, it might save his argument, which is, essentially, that no moral or other non-empirical, non-tautological, premises have to be included. He spends some effort in showing that conditions *C*, to which (1a) alludes, are empirical conditions – and this may be granted for the sake of argument. But, although this would make the proposition (1b), 'Conditions *C* obtain', into an empirical statement, it by no means makes (1a) into one. For however empirical these conditions *C* may be, it is possible to construct non-empirical propositions, and even imperatives, of the form 'Under conditions C, p' – e.g. 'Under conditions C, switch off (*or* you ought to switch off) the motor'. Nevertheless, it is easy to be misled into thinking that, if the conditions under which a man who utters 'I hereby promise' can correctly be said to have made a promise are empirical conditions, this proves that (1a) is not a moral statement.

I said that I would concentrate my attack on steps (1) to (3) of Searle's argument. But I may mention here that an analogous attack could be made against steps (3) to (5). These too depend on a non-tautologous rule of the institution of promising, or in general of (performatively) placing oneself under obligations. This non-tautological rule is as follows:

> (3a) If anybody has placed himself under an obligation (in the past) he is (still) under an obligation, unless he has done already what he was obliged to do.

To find out whether this is a tautology, we should have, as before, to rewrite it with the aid of the definition or tautology which is required to make the step from (4) to (5) into an entailment, viz. the definition

> (D3) For one to be under an obligation to do a thing is for it to be the case that one ought to do that thing

(I shall not enquire whether this definition is a sufficient one; it is probably not); or the tautology

> (4a) All people who are under obligations to do things ought to do them.

(3a) then turns into

> (3a*) If anybody has placed himself under an obligation (in the past), it is (still) the case that he ought to do the thing that he placed himself under an obligation to do, unless he has already done it.

That this is not a tautology (or for that matter a statement about word-usage) could be shown, if it is not plain already, by an argument analogous to the preceding.

I will conclude with some general remarks about the nature of the mistake that Searle seems to me to have made in this paper. There are many words which could not have a use unless certain propositions were assented to by the users or a sufficient number of them.

The possibility of using a word can depend on assent to synthetic propositions. This will apply especially to many words whose use is dependent upon the existence of institutions, though not only to them.[3] Unless there were laws of property, we could not speak of 'mine' and 'thine'; yet the laws of property are not tautologies. Unless there were a readiness to accept currency in exchange for goods, words like 'dollar' and 'pound' would pass out of use; yet to be ready to accept currency in exchange for goods is not to assent to a tautology or to a statement about language. In a community which did not play, or accept the rules of, baseball, the word 'out', as it is used by umpires, would lack a use (though not as used by anthropologists, if they were discussing the ways of a community which did have the game); but this does not make the rules of baseball into tautologies or statements about word-usage.

In the case of promising we have a similar phenomenon. Unless a sufficient number of people were prepared to assent to the moral principles which are the constitutive rules of the institution of promising, the word 'promise' could not have a use. To take the extreme case: suppose that nobody thought that one ought to keep promises. It would then be impossible to make a promise; the word 'promise' would become a mere noise (except, as before, in the mouths of anthropologists), unless it acquired some new use. But it does not follow from this that the moral principles, assent to which by a sufficient number of people is a condition for the remaining in use of the word 'promise', are themselves analytic.

It is necessary, moreover, only that a sufficiently large number of people should assent to the constitutive rule. If they do so, and if the word in question comes into use, it is possible for people who do not assent to the rules to use the word comprehensibly. Thus an anarchist can use the word 'property'; a man who for reasons of his own has no confidence in paper money, and is therefore not prepared to exchange goods for it, can still use the word 'pound'; and a Macchiavellian politician who recognises no duty to keep promises can still use the word 'promise'. He can even use it to make promises, always provided that his moral opinions are not too well known.

Such people are, admittedly, parasites; but not all parasites are

[3] What Kant was driving at, without the synthetic-a-priorism, might possibly be hinted at by pointing out that many words that we use in physics and in everyday life, such as 'table', and in general 'material object', would lack a use unless we made certain assumptions about the regularity of the universe.

reprehensible. Let us suppose that somebody is opposed to fox-hunting. This does not stop him engaging in fox-hunting, in the sense of going to meets, following hounds, etc., and using all the terminology of the chase. He may think it his duty, whenever he can get away with it, to help the fox to escape (that may be why he goes fox-hunting); but this does not involve him in any self-contradiction. It may be that to try to help foxes escape is contrary to the constitutive rules for fox-hunting;[4] for unless there were among these rules one which said that the object of the game was to kill the fox, it would not be fox-*hunting*. But this does not stop our opponent of blood sports masquerading as a person who accepts this rule; nor does it mean that, by so masquerading, he lays upon himself any obligation to abide by it. And in just the same way the Macchiavellian politician can, without self-contradiction, think it his duty to break some of the promises he makes (and think this even while he is making them). He could not have made them unless the word 'promise' were in use; and it could not be in use unless a sufficient number of people assented to the moral principles governing promising; but this does not mean that a person who, while making promises, dissents, silently, from the principles contradicts himself. In using the word 'promise' indeed, he is masquerading as one who thinks that one ought to keep promises, just as one who lies is masquerading as one who thinks that p, when he does not. But neither the liar nor the man who makes lying promises is contradicting himself. And when the lying promiser comes to break his promise, he is still not contradicting himself, he can say 'I pretended to think, when I made the promise, that one ought to keep promises; but I don't really think this and never have'.

Talking about 'institutional facts', though it can be illuminating, can also be a peculiarly insidious way of committing the 'naturalistic fallacy'. I do not think that Searle actually falls into this particular trap; but others perhaps have. There are moral and other principles, accepted by most of us, such that, if they were not generally accepted, certain institutions like property and promising could not exist. And if the institutions do exist, we are in a position to affirm certain 'institutional facts' (for example, that a certain piece of land is my property), on the ground that certain 'brute facts' are the

---

[4] It might be objected that the rules of fox-hunting are not constitutive but regulative. This would depend on establishing some relevant difference between the chasing of foxes and the chasing of cricket balls – a question into which I shall not go, but whose investigation might cast doubt on this distinction.

case (for example, that my ancestors have occupied it from time immemorial). But from the 'institutional facts' certain obviously prescriptive conclusions can be drawn (for example, that nobody ought to deprive me of the land). Thus it looks as if there could be a straight deduction, in two steps, from brute facts to prescriptive conclusions via institutional facts. But the deduction is a fraud. For the brute fact is a ground for the prescriptive conclusion only if the prescriptive principle which is the constitutive rule of the institution be accepted; and this prescriptive principle is not a tautology. For someone (a communist for example) who does not accept this non-tautologous prescriptive principle, the deduction collapses like a house of cards – though this does not prevent him from continuing to use the word 'property' (with his tongue in his cheek).

Similarly with promising. It may seem as if the 'brute fact' that a person has uttered a certain phonetic sequence entails the 'institutional fact' that he has promised, and that this in turn entails that he ought to do a certain thing. But this conclusion can be drawn only by one who accepts, in addition, the non-tautologous principle that one ought to keep one's promises. For unless one accepts this principle, one is not a subscribing member of the institution which it constitutes, and therefore cannot be compelled logically to accept the institutional facts which it generates in such a sense that they entail the conclusion, though of course one must admit their truth, regarded purely as pieces of anthropology.

If I do not agree with Searle's reasons for maintaining that we ought to keep our promises, what are my own reasons? They are of a fundamentally different character, although they take in parts of Searle's argument in passing. To break a promise is, normally, a particularly gross form of deception. It is grosser than the failure to fulfil a declaration of intention, just because (if you wish) our society has, *pari passu* with the introduction of the word 'promise', adopted the moral principle that one ought to keep promises, thus constituting the institution called 'promising'. My reason for thinking that I ought not to take parasitic advantage of this institution, but ought to obey its rules, is the following. If I ask myself whether I am willing that I myself should be deceived in this way, I answer unhesitatingly that I am not. I therefore cannot subscribe to any moral principle which permits people to deceive other people in this way (any general principle which says 'It is all right to break promises'). There may be more specific principles which I could accept, of the form 'It is all right to break promises in situations of type *S*'. Most people accept some specific principles of this form. What anybody can here substitute for '*S*' he will determine, if he follows my sort of reasoning, by asking himself, for any proposed value of '*S*', whether he can subscribe to the principle when applied to all cases, including cases in which he is the person to whom the promise is made. Thus the morality of promise-keeping is a fairly standard application of what I have called elsewhere[5] the 'golden-rule' type of moral argument; it needs no 'is'-'ought' derivations to support it – derivations whose validity will be believed in only by those who have ruled out a priori any questioning of the existing institutions on whose rules they are based.

[5] *Freedom and Reason* (Oxford 1963), esp. pp. 86–125.

XV On deriving 'ought' from 'is'

J. E. McClellan and B. P. Komisar

A new hand turns to an old task when John R. Searle joins those others who purport to offer transport from 'is' to 'ought' without using such vehicles as 'evaluative statements, moral principles, or anything of the sort.'[1] Mr Searle's demonstration has two steps. The first presents and defends an instance of an evaluation derived exclusively from descriptive premises. The second step sketches a theory of language capable of generating an indefinite number of cases of the sort given in step one.

The project is unsuccessful at both ends. Concerning step one we will show that either the derivation is invalid or else that it requires the use of an obviously evaluative premise. Concerning step two we will suggest that all attempts to find a faultless instance would be equally futile.

I

The derivation of 'ought' from 'is' is achieved through a series of premises as follows:

(1) Jones uttered the words 'I hereby promise to pay you, Smith, five dollars'.
(2) Jones promised to pay Smith five dollars.
(3) Jones placed himself under (undertook) an obligation to pay Smith five dollars.
(4) Jones is under an obligation to pay Smith five dollars.
(5) Jones ought to pay Smith five dollars. (p. 121)

[1] Paper XII. Numbers within parentheses, following quotations, refer to pages above.

Searle provides the necessary additional sub-premises, consisting in
... empirical assumptions, tautologies, and descriptions of word
usage. (p. 125)

The inferences from steps (3) to (4) and (4) to (5) invoke a *ceteris
paribus* clause and a presumably descriptive statement that, indeed,
things are equal.[2] According to Searle:

> The force of the expression 'other things being equal' in the
> present instance is roughly this. Unless we have some reason (that
> is, unless we are actually prepared to give some reason) for sup-
> posing the obligation is void (step 4) or the agent ought not to
> keep the promise (step 5), then the obligation holds and he ought
> to keep the promise. ... It is sufficient to satisfy the condition that
> no reason to the contrary can in fact be given. (p. 124)

Searle seems to take this factual interpretation of the *ceteris
paribus* clause in order to avoid the uncomfortable alternative that
the force of the clause depends on establishing a 'universal negative
proposition to the effect that no reason could ever be given by anyone for supposing the agent is not under an obligation or ought not
to keep the promise' (p. 124). *That* could be satisfied only if (in the
present case) (5) were logically necessary (or true independently of
all contingent premises such as (1) – (4)), which it is not.

But between saying that (5) is logically necessary and saying, in a
particular case, that we are prepared to give reasons for denying that
things are equal, many options obtain. The use of the weasel-words
'prepared' and 'in fact' conceals the distinction between (a) there
being some person or persons in a given situation, such as that por-
trayed in (1) to (5), who *does* state and defend a rejection of the
clause, and (b) there existing a reason, relevant to that situation, for
rejecting the clause.

Does Searle's argument require the denial of (b), a stronger claim,
in order to validate the assertion of (5) given (1) to (4), or is the
denial of (a), a weaker claim, sufficient for his logical move? Let us
assume here that he *must* deny (b); later we will demonstrate that
otherwise his case is absurd.

Searle distinguishes the positive case (asserting *ceteris paribus*,
thus validating the move from (4) to (5)) from the negative case
(denying *ceteris paribus*, thus voiding the final 'ought'). The negative case he readily acknowledges to be 'a situation calling for an

---

[2] We ignore Searle's *ceteris paribus* clause in the transition from (3) to
(4) and also the unacknowledged presence of that clause in the transit from
(2) to (3). Our concern is exclusively with the movement from (4) to
(5), though our argument would apply at several points.

evaluation ...' (p. 124). But the positive case is different, for 'unless we have some reason to the contrary, the *ceteris paribus* condition is satisfied, no evaluation is necessary ...' (p. 124). On our present assumption that 'we have some reason' means the same as 'there is some reason', it is clear that the form of the statement, i.e. whether it contains or does not contain a negative operator, is irrelevant to the matter of its being evaluative. Consider:

(A) There is reason to deny *ceteris paribus*.
(B) It is not the case that there is reason to deny *ceteris paribus*.

If (A) is evaluative, then (B) must be also. And Searle's own positive case, viz., 'the *ceteris paribus* condition is satisfied', *implies* (B). ('Unless X, Y' is equivalent to 'Y $\supset$ $\smallsmile$ X'.) Therefore the very use of the *ceteris paribus* condition invokes the evaluation, whether *ceteris paribus* is asserted or denied.

Although the argument above holds whatever analysis is made of 'being a reason to deny that the promise ought to be kept', still the force of the argument may be seen better if a rudimentary analysis is given. May we not say that an obligation-voiding reason factors into these two claims?

(i) The possible voiding condition is properly relevant (or being considered in a properly relevant aspect). That is, to say that C is a condition which *could* void a promise is an evaluative statement.

(ii) The possible voiding condition has been given its proper, i.e. rightful, voiding force. That is, in accepting that C voids a promise, we are evaluating it as good enough to do so.

Now surely to say that the situation contains *no* condition C properly relevant to an *ought*-judgement, or to say that there is such a C but that it *lacks* sufficient force to avoid this particular obligation, would appear to be evaluative in precisely the same way that the contradictories of these claims are evaluative. We would suggest that on any analysis Searle's argument is not only logically false but counter-intuitive as well.

Turn now to the other alternative, that Searle means such expressions as 'unless we are actually prepared to give some reason' and 'no reason to the contrary can in fact be given' in a direct, literal sense. Then, of course, there is a difference between the positive and the negative case.

Positive case: 'We' (whoever it is Searle has in mind) go through steps (1) – (4) and then simply assert 'Other things are equal and Jones ought to pay Smith five dollars.'

Negative case: We go through the argument, we then survey the situation, discover some potentially obligation-voiding condition C, we evaluate its force and judge it sufficient to void the claim that Jones ought to pay Smith five dollars.

The negative case is or requires an evaluation in a way that the positive case does not. But the conclusion reached in the positive case could never be taken seriously as a moral judgement. We are at dinner. Miller goes through steps (1) – (5) and lays the moral claim on Jones. We know very well that poor Jones ought to renege on this promise and spend the money on medicine for his son who will otherwise die a painful death. Jones, Smith, and Miller all happen to be either ignorant of the facts or unaware that such facts may well void the obligation to keep some promises. But we are not actually prepared to give this reason at the moment, for our mouths are stuffed with very hot mashed potatoes. Later, after we have drunk many glasses of wine, we forget the sad state of Jones's pocket-book and his son's health, and we shout with the rest 'Jones ought to pay Smith five dollars.' Still later we recall the actual circumstances and then deny that other things are equal and for that reason deny that Jones ought to pay Smith.

Now either Jones ought to pay Smith or he ought not, but it is absurd to hold that the truth of the matter depends on what we happen to be eating, the condition of our memory, or anything else affecting what reasons '*we are actually prepared to give*'. To hold a literal interpretation of Searle's position would require him both to affirm and to deny that Jones ought to pay. Hence he cannot be taken to mean both that (5) is a moral claim about Jones, the agent, *and* that 'giving reasons' be taken in a literal, descriptive sense.

At any point, Searle seems to recognise that his 'proof' is shaky. But he claims that being wrong on the point we have attacked will not void his argument, for, he says, 'we can always rewrite my steps (4) and (5) so that they include the *ceteris paribus* clause as part of the conclusion. Thus from our premises we would have derived "Other things being equal Jones ought to pay Smith..."' and, just below, 'the "ought" is a "categorical" not a "hypothetical" ought. (5) does not say that Jones ought to pay up if he wants such and such. It says he ought to pay up, period' (pp. 124–5).

Here, of course, Searle confuses the distinction between hypothetical and categorical judgements with the distinction between prudential and moral judgements. With the *ceteris paribus* attached, (5) is hypothetical, but is still a moral, not prudential judgement. With the rider, (5) does not say Jones ought to pay-up-period, but

that *if* other things are equal he ought to pay. But Searle's confusion is enlightening on one count: it explains why strict gram-
marians reject the ablative absolute construction in English prose.

Summary: Searle's presumed derivation is either fallacious, or
ceteris paribus is or implies an evaluation. It is only fair to add that
Searle was attacking the necessity for the *general* premise that one
ought to keep promises as part of the proof of (5). We believe he is
right in that thesis, but he has not shown it to be true. A fuller
analysis of what is logically required when 'obligations can be overridden or removed...' (p. 125) might *re*-introduce *some* general
moral premise in the argument.

II

Searle has been refuted when we display the evaluative premise(s)
in his example. It is left to him to substitute a faultless instance. But
we would like to point out a feature of his theory of language which
makes his success quite unlikely.

Searle's case rests on the presumed similarity among such 'institutions' as chess, baseball, promising, geometry, and others for which
rules are constitutive, not merely regulative. Table manners, on the
other hand, are among those sets of rules applying to behaviour
which exists independently of the rules regulating it. This distinction
may or may not be tenable in general, but it surely conceals what it
is that makes moral judgements philosophically interesting. Searle
says that 'the question "Ought one to keep one's promises?" is as
empty as the question "Are triangles three-sided?"' (p. 127). He says
that 'the tautology that one ought to keep one's promises is only one
of a class of similar tautologies...' (p. 132). From this we presume
that the questions are empty because in each case, given the constitutive rules for geometry and promising, the answer is a tautology.
But it is not so. Given the constitutive rules of geometry *and nothing
else*, the question 'Are triangles three-sided?' can be answered univocally. One may insult the question as much as he likes, but the
answer is still and simply yes. But given the rules constituting the
institution of promising *and nothing else*, the question 'Ought one to
keep one's promises?' cannot be answered univocally. One may say
either 'Yes, unless...' or 'No, if...' or 'As a general rule, but...'
where 'general rule' means one that does not necessarily apply to
every instance. It is that feature which makes it philosophically

puzzling just what kind of rules these are, as different from the rules of geometry or chess.[3]

We suspect that Searle was not altogether convinced by his own argument. In his supposed 'proof' of (5) he did not hesitate to use many tautologies (pp. 122–3). If he had regarded 'One ought to keep one's promise' as a tautology, he would have employed it *simpliciter* and thus made his derivation as neat as pie. Instead, he qualified it with *ceteris paribus*, and unsuccessfully concealed a whole raft of evaluative judgements. These particular evaluations are not of the sort Searle was seeking to avoid. But this difference is not pertinent to the nature of moral argument. What is pertinent is that they are there.

[3] Cf. David Shwayder: 'Moral Rules and Moral Maxims', *Ethics*, LXVII (1957), 269–85. Searle's illustrative reference to baseball as suggestive of another case of logical manoeuvre from 'is' ('He was off base.' 'He was tagged.' 'Umpire declared him out.' etc.) to 'ought' ('He ought to leave the field') exemplifies beautifully the necessity for Shwayder's distinction between rules and maxims. No such statement as 'He ought to leave the field (because tagged out)' could count as moral. But moral claims can be made within baseball, e.g. 'you ought to take your glove off the field, lest someone trip on it and be hurt'. These claims, however, are not derived from the rules constitutive of baseball, but employ the 'rules' (Shwayder's 'maxims') which undergird baseball, as well as other activities. These substratum 'rules' require, at the very least, *ceteris paribus* clauses in their FORMULATION, AND IF CONSTITUTIVE AT ALL (of any activity in any clear sense) are constitutive of social life itself.

XVI How not to derive 'ought' from 'is'

James and Judith Thomson

Two of the steps in Mr Searle's derivation[1] are from:

> (3) Jones placed himself under (undertook) an obligation to pay Smith five dollars,

to:

> (4) Jones is under an obligation to pay Smith five dollars,

and from that to:

> (5) Jones ought to pay Smith five dollars.

Since Searle says that the two steps are to be understood in the same way, we shall discuss only the latter.

Searle is aware that even if someone is under an obligation to do something, there may yet be overriding reasons why he ought not or need not do it; that is, reasons sufficient to make it false to say that he ought to do it; so that (4) does not by itself entail (5). But he says that (5) does follow from (4) and another premise (4a) – 'Other things are equal' – and he argues that this extra premise 'need not involve anything evaluative.' His line of argument seems to be this. Suppose that Jones is quite definitely under the obligation, and that the question arises for us whether he ought to pay. There may be reason to think that he need not or ought not, but equally there may not; no such reason may be apparent. And unless we are 'actually prepared to give some reason' why Jones ought not or need not keep his promise, then 'the obligation holds and he ought to keep the promise.' So here is one way in which, given (4), the truth of (4a), and thereby of (5), may get settled: the question is settled because no reason against (5) is apparent. But if the truth of (4a) gets settled in this way, then we shall not have had to evaluate any reasons against (5); so (4a) is 'not necessarily evaluative.'

This argument is put forward as an explanation of the 'force' of the phrase 'other things are equal'. The explanation seems to us

[1] Paper XII.

incoherent. Searle is vacillating between two interpretations of (4a). The weak interpretation is that other things are equal if we, who are considering Jones's case, see no reason or know of no reason why he ought not or need not pay. But if this is what (4a) comes to, then (4) and (4a) surely do not *entail* (5). That none of us sees or knows of a reason just does not entail that there is none.[2]

Searle has said, however, that the reason (4) does not by itself entail (5) is that, given (4), there may all the same be some over-riding reason why Jones ought not or need not pay. So one would expect him to say that, given (4), what we require for (5) is that this should not be the case. This suggests another, rather different, inter-pretation for (4a): that other things are equal only if there is nothing sufficient to make it false that Jones ought to pay. We could call this the strong interpretation of (4a). It seems to us that (4a) must say or by itself entail at least this much if it is, together with (4), to entail (5).

Now although Searle certainly seems to offer the weak interpreta-tion of (4a) – that is, seems to say that the truth of (4a) is settled if no one is actually prepared to offer counter-arguments to (5), and thus is settled without the evaluation of any counter-arguments – he also says that (4a) is settled when as a matter of fact there *are* no counter-arguments. That is not the same thing. He says that to establish (4a) we need not establish a universal negative proposition 'to the effect that no reason could ever be given by anyone'; it is sufficient, to establish it, that 'no reason to the contrary can in fact be given.' But what does this latter mean? It might mean that no one who is considering Jones's case is in fact in a position to give a reason; this would be the weak interpretation again. But it might mean that there just is no such reason to be given. Now plainly it would be an over-strong interpretation of (4a) to say that it is true only if there is no reason at all to think that (5) is false; all you would require is that there be no *conclusive* reason to think (5) false. Therefore we are inclined to think that Searle is not offering this over-strong interpretation. Nevertheless, it could be left open that he is, or that he is here offering only the strong interpretation and just pointing to what is a sufficient, but not necessary, condition of its truth – for if there is no reason at all to think (5) false, then there certainly is no conclusive reason to think (5) false. It does not matter at which of these two interpretations he is hinting here. Either would

[2] Still less is it enough that none of us is 'actually prepared to give' a reason. Mrs Jones may have a reason, and a good one, but may not be, for all kinds of reasons, prepared to give it (in public, out loud).

indeed help his case: it is plausible to say that (5) is entailed by (4) together with 'There is no conclusive reason to think it false to say that Jones ought to pay' (or 'There is no reason at all to think it false to say that Jones ought to pay'). But in establishing either of these extra premises, we should surely be establishing a universal negative proposition. And are they not evaluative? Are they not anyway as evaluative as (5)?[3]

In short, Searle's reason for saying that (4a) need not be evaluative is that it is true if no one offers any counter-arguments; thus we may settle its truth without having to evaluate any counter-arguments. But in so far as this fixes the meaning of (4a), it and (4) do not entail (5). Conversely, if (4a) is given a meaning such that it and (4) do entail (5), it is evaluative.

We suppose it obvious that nothing is gained for Searle's position by his device of rewriting (5) as 'Other things being equal, Jones ought . . .'. Let us call this (5'). One of two possibilities now applies. Either (a) (5') is a conditional with the old (4a) as antecedent; but then under the weak interpretation of its antecedent, (5') is not entailed by (4), and under the strong interpretation of its antecedent, (5') is analytic – if the Law of Excluded Middle is – and therefore not evaluative. Or (*b*) the *ceteris paribus* clause is meant, not as antecedent of a conditional, but as an adverbial clause.[4] But then its

[3] One of Searle's aims is to show that the terms 'evaluative' and 'descriptive' 'embody a muddle', and that 'the whole distinction needs to be re-examined.' But (one of?) the means by which he will do this is this: he will 'play along with the terminology', and show that there are counter-examples to the thesis that no set of purely descriptive premises can by itself entail an evaluative conclusion. (One might question this strategy, but we shall not stop to do so.) At all events, in this part of his paper, Searle is taking the notion 'evaluative' seriously – seriously enough to have been drawn to the weaker interpretation of (4a).

[4] It is of course an interesting question just what is the force or meaning of a *ceteris paribus* clause. Perhaps one should begin by distinguishing the cases in which it is prefixed to a general observation ('Other things being equal, a queen is worth more in the end game than two rooks') from cases in which it is prefixed to a particular statement (Searle's 'Other things being equal, Jones ought to pay Smith five dollars'). One might comment on the former remark by saying that other things seldom are equal, meaning that the remark is not a very helpful one, but one could not ask, 'But *are* other things equal?' One can ask this only with a particular case (application) in mind. It may be that there is the same difficulty about the inference 'Other things being equal, an S is a P; x is an S; so, other things being equal, x is a P' as there is about 'The probability of an S being a P is N; x is an S; so the probability that x is a P is N.'

sense, and its role in (5′), want some spelling out; since Searle offers nothing in this direction at all, we are inclined to think it is (a) rather than (b) which he has in mind.

The interest in this confusion lies in its diagnosis: we think that Searle has tried to adapt to his own purposes an observation that may well be true, but will not serve them.

We have a ring which looks like gold, weighs what a gold ring of that size would weigh, is hall-marked, was bought from a well-known jeweller. Moreover, there is no reason that we know of to think it is not gold. Then we are (in some sense) *entitled* to take it to be gold, to expose it for sale as such. We are entitled, being aware of these things, to say 'I know it is gold.' If someone says 'But for all you've said it still may not be gold', we shall want to ask him whether he has any positive ground for suspicion; and if he can only reply that the fact that these things are so does not entail that it is gold, his doubt can be ignored. We are entitled to go on doing and saying what we do unless and until the doubter is actually prepared to give a reason for thinking the ring is not gold.

Again, if Smith has an abscessed tooth, and is complaining bitterly, and if moreover there is no reason we know of to think he is not in pain, we are (in that same sense) entitled to take him to be in pain. If someone says 'But perhaps he isn't really, for these things don't entail pain', that doubt too can be ignored.

It seems to us that it must be this observation – which is more or less familiar, and has been so perhaps since the appearance of Austin's paper on 'Other Minds' – which Searle has in mind when he offers the weak interpretation of (4a), 'other things are equal.' But the observation does not support the point he wishes to make. For the admitted facts about the ring (about Smith – even where these include that we know of no reason to think the ring is not gold (Smith is not in pain) – do not after all entail that the ring is gold (Smith is in pain). Given that p we may be (in that sense) entitled to take it that (even give others our word that) q – but this will not make it be true to say that p entails q. Indeed, it was the whole point of this observation that in order to be (in this sense) entitled to take it that q we do *not* need to have grounds that entail q.

Searle's confusion, then, arises from his having conflated a question of entailment with a question of entitlement.

As we noted in footnote 3, Searle's aim is not merely to show that 'ought' can be derived from 'is', but thereby to cast doubt on the is-ought distinction. In part III of his paper, he says this distinction arose out of a certain theory of language, a theory which (he thinks) allows no place for statements of what he calls 'institutional fact'. Thus, for example, 'He promised' states an institutional fact, and it is a 'constitutive rule' of the institution of promising that 'to make a promise is to undertake an obligation.' And Searle thinks that when we see and properly understand that there are such statements, we shall no longer be puzzled by the question 'How can my stating a fact about a man, such as that he made a promise, commit me to a view about what he ought to do?' But in this part of his paper Searle seems quite to have forgotten how he claimed to derive 'ought' from 'is': for as he had granted, to say

(1) Jones uttered the words 'I hereby promise to pay you, Smith, five dollars.'

or even to say

(2) Jones promised to pay Smith five dollars.

is *not* to be logically committed to the view that Jones ought to pay Smith five dollars. So Searle's explanation of why moralists thought that you could not deduce an 'ought from an 'is' does not work. It would explain at most a reluctance to pass from (1) or (2) to

(3) Jones placed himself under (undertook) an obligation to pay Smith five dollars.

But many anti-naturalists would be relatively uninterested in the difference of status between (1) and (3), and most anti-naturalists would be completely unperturbed by the relations between them to which Searle points – that is, by the fact that, in certain circumstances, to say certain words is to commit oneself to do this or that. What does interest them is the difference of status between (1) and (5).

Or we could put it this way. Searle has, if you like, brought out that there is not so sharp a distinction in kind between (1) and (3) as might have been thought. But to show a continuity between (1) and (3) is not thereby to have shown a continuity between (1) and (5). There seems to us to be no reason at all for thinking that it was because they thought there was a sharp distinction in kind between (1) and (3) that the anti-naturalists supposed there to be a sharp distinction in kind between (1) and (5), and therefore that 'ought' is not derivable from 'is'.

XVII The 'is-ought' controversy

W. D. Hudson

Mr J. R. Searle recently (Paper XII) attempted to derive 'ought' from 'is'. Criticism of his attempt has revolved round two main objections: (i) that he is not clear on the difference between reporting the use of a word such as 'promise' and actually using it, (ii) that the premise 'Other things are equal', which he introduces at two stages of his derivation, either is evaluative, which he says it is not, or fails to secure the entailment which it is introduced to secure. [On (i) see Paper XIII; on (ii) see Papers XV and XVI.] What I wish to argue is that neither of these objections gets rid of Searle's main point. This is that a counter-example can be demonstrated to the thesis ' "Ought" cannot be derived from "is" ', *as this thesis has been understood* by those who have claimed to expose the 'naturalistic fallacy' (op. cit., p. 120).

The five principal steps in Searle's derivation are:

(1) Jones uttered the words 'I hereby promise to pay you, Smith, five dollars'.
(2) Jones promised to pay Smith five dollars.
(3) Jones placed himself under (undertook) an obligation to pay Smith five dollars.
(4) Jones is under an obligation to pay Smith five dollars.
(5) Jones ought to pay Smith five dollars.

He introduces some extra premises. Between (1) and (2) he has: '(1a) Under certain conditions C anyone who utters the words (sentence) "I hereby promise to pay you, Smith, five dollars" promises to pay Smith five dollars' and '(1b) Conditions C obtain.' Between (2) and (3) comes the tautological premise '(2a) All promises are acts of placing oneself under (undertaking) an obligation to do the thing promised.' Between (3) and (4), and between (4) and (5), there is a *ceteris paribus* clause and a tautological premise: '(3a) Other things are equal', '(3b) All those who place themselves under an obligation are, other things being equal, under an obligation'; '(4a) Other things are equal', (*sc.* 4b) 'Other things being equal, one ought to do what one is under an obligation to do.' These extra premises, Searle emphasises, are 'in no case moral or evaluative in nature'; they are simply 'empirical assumptions, tautologies, and decriptions of word usage' (p. 125).

I

Now to the criticisms. Professor Flew points out that Searle's move from (1) to (2) is fallacious, unless we take (2) as, in effect, *oratio obliqua* (above, p. 142). This is so, according to Flew, because of the 'necessary and decisive' distinction between 'a detached report on the meanings which some social group gives to certain value words' and 'the unreserved employment of these words by an engaged participant.' Between the former and the latter 'there comes exactly that commitment to the incapsulated values which alone warrants us to draw the normative conclusions' (p. 141). Flew, then, does not disagree with Searle's remark that 'to commit myself to the view that Jones made a promise involves committing myself to what he ought to do' (p. 133), provided only that I am using 'promise' as an engaged participant at the time.

Flew's distinction is, of course, a real one. A reporter could say '*A* said "I promise to do *X*" and in *A*'s society (or mine, or some other) the meaning of "promise" is such that, certain conditions being fulfilled (cf. Searle's (1a) and (1b)) *A*'s statement entails "I ought to do *X*"'; and yet this reporter could refuse to commit himself to the view that *A* made a promise. To report that he did what is called promising is not to say that he promised. If it has been said that *A* promised to do *X*, then the question 'Ought *A* to do *X*?' is self-answering. But if it has merely been reported that *A* did what is called promising to do *X*, this question is not self-answering.

The crux of the matter now is: Does the wedge which Flew drives in come at the point where exposers of the 'naturalistic fallacy' drove in, or sought to drive in, their wedge between 'is' and 'ought'? Flew seems to think that it does. While he allows that there may be descriptions which, in ordinary use, entail evaluations, he affirms that 'the fundamental discrimination in terms of which the Naturalistic Fallacy is being characterised . . . has to be made and insisted upon' (p. 137) and we are clearly intended to take it that this is what he is doing. I think it is not and offer two comments. (i) It is not in dispute, as Flew points out following Popper, that we can decide what norms to adopt as we cannot decide what the facts are. But, if this distinction is crucial in the 'is-ought' controversy, it should be noted that the two sorts of factual statement which Flew differentiates – that of the reporter and that of the engaged participant – both come on the same side of it. If whether 'Jones uttered the words "I promise to pay you, Smith, five dollars"' is true or false does not depend on a decision of mine or anyone else's, then neither does whether 'Jones promised to pay Smith five dollars' is true or false (and this if we take the latter as *oratio obliqua* and if we do not). What factual statements entail, or do not entail, is beside the present point. What distinguishes them, as factual, from evaluative statements so distinguishes them all. Is Flew saying that 'Jones promised to pay Smith five dollars' is not a factual statement?

(ii) If it is not in our power to decide whether 'Jones promised to pay Smith five dollars' is true or false, what can we decide here? Certainly not that 'promise' shall not entail what it does entail: claiming the right to do that is claiming a licence to talk nonsense. What we can do, if we do not like what a word entails, is to stop using it. This raises the interesting question whether there are some descriptive words which we can (logically or empirically) stop using and others which we cannot. But I leave that. All I want to bring out is that exposers of the 'naturalistic fallacy' were not concerned to show what Flew has shown, that where descriptions entail evaluations we can decide whether or not to use them as 'engaged participants'. Their point was that there is no description such that it validly entails an evaluation. In their several ways (cf. G. E. Moore, *Principia Ethica*, ch. i. or R. M. Hare, *The Language of Morals*, ch. v) they said that, whatever naturalistic definition (ND) is given to words like 'good' and 'ought', the questions 'Is ND good?' or 'Ought ND to be done?' are not self-answering.

II

Searle introduces the *ceteris paribus* clause to secure the entailment of (4) by (3) and of (5) by (4). He says that other things are equal when 'no reason ... can in fact be given' for supposing that the obligation [step (4)] is void, or the agent ought not to keep the promise [step (5)]. Where such is the case, he contends, no evaluation is necessarily involved. But, if, on the other hand, reason can in fact be given, then, he concedes, a situation calling for evaluation characteristically arises (p. 124). It has been pointed out that, if we take 'no reason ... can in fact be given' to mean simply that those concerned are unable to give a reason, this may be because of something as trivial as having their mouths stuffed with food at the time, and it is absurd to suggest that this makes actions obligatory which otherwise would not be. But if we take the clause to register a judgement, is not this necessarily evaluative? Searle argues that, even if his claim that the *ceteris paribus* is not necessarily evaluative is rejected, he can still rewrite his derivation in such a way that this clause is included in step (5) and so get 'ought' from 'is' (pp. 124–5). But could he do that without rendering (5) hypothetical (If other things are equal, then Jones ought to pay Smith five dollars) thus contradicting his insistence that it is categorical (ibid.)? I think that Searle's account of his *ceteris paribus* clause is vulnerable to these criticisms (McClellan and Komisar, above, p. 160 and J. and J. Thomson, above, pp. 164–6).

However, what I want to claim is that Searle could have got along very well without the *ceteris paribus*, both in deriving (4) from (3) and (5) from (4). Consider the cases which he introduces it to exclude (p. 123n.) (i) It is necessary between (3) and (4), he says, to exclude, for instance, a promisee's releasing the promiser from the obligation which he has undertaken. But cannot such cases be excluded perfectly well by Searle's (1a) and (1b) (see above) at an earlier stage? Searle's account of conditions *C*, referred to in those extra premises, runs as follows: '... such things as that the speaker is in the presence of the hearer Smith, they are both conscious, both speakers of English, speaking seriously. The speaker knows what he is doing, is not under the influence of drugs, not hypnotised or acting in a play, not telling a joke or reporting an event, and so forth) (pp. 121–2). All empirical assumptions, remember! Well, why not another empirical assumption: that the promisee has not released the promiser?

(ii) Between (4) and (5), Searle maintains, 'we need the *ceteris paribus* clause to eliminate the possibility that something extraneous to the relation of "obligation" to "ought" might interfere' (p. 123). Take this case. I promise *A* that I will tell *B* a lie. But I, as a moral being, am under an obligation to tell him the truth. I decide to tell him the truth. Obligation (b), to tell the truth, has here overridden obligation (a), to keep promises. But does this mean that obligation (b) now, in some way, blocks the entailment of 'I ought to keep my promise to *A*' by obligation (a)? Two lines of argument may suggest themselves in support of an affirmative answer, but I do not think that either will do. (1) It may be said that, once obligation (b) has overridden obligation (a), 'I ought to keep my promise to *A*' no longer makes sense. But why not? 'Overridden' *could* plausibly be

so defined that, if obligation (b) is said to have overridden obligation (a), it no longer makes sense to say that there is an obligation
(a). But this does not seem to be what Searle, or anyone else, is
saying. The overriding is not taken to eliminate obligations at
step (4), only to 'interfere' with 'the relation of "obligation" to
"ought"' (Searle, p. 123). But if it makes good sense to say that I am
under obligation (a) *and* obligation (b), I cannot see why it should
not make sense to say that I ought to keep my promise to *A and* tell
the truth to *B*. That seems to be just as legitimate an account of my
moral dilemma as that I am in a conflict of obligations. (2) It may
be pointed out that 'ought' implies 'can', and I cannot both keep
my promise to *A* and tell *B* the truth by one and the same action.
But if this fact does not eliminate either obligation (a) or obligation
(b), no more does it eliminate either of their consequent 'oughts'. I
can keep my promise to *A*. I can tell *B* the truth. It makes sense to
say that I ought to do both, so long as the phrase 'by one and the
same action' is not added. In such a situation I may have to decide
what to do. And I may ask 'What ought I to do?', the tacit presupposition of the question being that there is one action which is
what I ought to do. But notice how difficult it is to get an answer
which is reasoned, or can be discussed, to such a question in such
a situation. Sir David Ross said that we know the answer by an
altogether mysterious intuition. Sartre told his pupil, in effect, to
stop looking for an answer and act. The presupposition that, in a
conflict of obligations, there is one thing, and one only, which is
what we ought to do is false. Suppose I choose to tell *B* the truth.
Does that cancel my obligation to keep my promise to *A* or its
'ought'? If it did, then once I have decided to tell *B* the truth, it
would be nonsensical to blame me for having made the promise to
A. But that is not nonsensical. I cannot evade responsibility for
having promised to tell a lie by saying 'Ah but I ought no longer to
keep that promise because the "ought" has been overridden.' I am
still blameworthy because the fact that I ought to keep my promise
to *A*, having made it, is an element in my moral situation. So I
conclude that there is no call for a means, such as Searle's *ceteris
paribus* purports to be, for differentiating cases where (4) entails (5)
from cases where it does not.

I have not shown that Searle's derivation is valid. All I have tried
to show is that criticisms so far made of it fall wide of his main point.

_____

For Searle's reply to some of his critics see the Appendix, pp. 259ff.

PART FOUR

Description and Evaluation

XVIII Modern moral philosophy[1]

G. E. M. Anscombe

I will begin by stating three theses which I present in this paper. The first is that it is not profitable for us at present to do moral philosophy; that it should be laid aside at any rate until we have an adequate philosophy of psychology, in which we are conspicuously lacking. The second is that the concepts of obligation, and duty – *moral* obligation and *moral* duty, that is to say – and of what is *morally* right and wrong, and of the *moral* sense of 'ought', ought to be jettisoned if this is psychologically possible; because they are survivals, or derivatives from survivals, from an earlier conception of ethics which no longer generally survives, and are only harmful without it. My third thesis is that the differences between the well-known English writers on moral philosophy from Sidgwick to the present day are of little importance.

Anyone who has read Aristotle's *Ethics* and has also read modern moral philosophy must have been struck by the great contrasts between them. The concepts which are prominent among the moderns seem to be lacking, or at any rate buried or far in the background, in Aristotle. Most noticeably, the term 'moral' itself, which we have by direct inheritance from Aristotle, just doesn't seem to fit, in its modern sense, into an account of Aristotelian ethics. Aristotle distinguishes virtues as moral and intellectual. Have some of what he calls 'intellectual' virtues what *we* should call a 'moral' aspect? It would seem so; the criterion is presumably that a failure in an 'intellectual' virtue – like that of having good judgement in calculating how to bring about something useful, say in municipal government – may be *blameworthy*. But – it may reasonably be asked – cannot *any* failure be made a matter of blame or reproach? Any derogatory criticism, say of the workmanship of a product or the design of a machine, can be called blame or reproach. So we want to put in the word 'morally' again: sometimes such a failure may be

[1] This paper was originally read to the Voltaire Society in Oxford.

morally blameworthy, sometimes not. Now has Aristotle got this idea of *moral* blame, as opposed to any other? If he has, why isn't it more central? There are some mistakes, he says, which are causes, not of involuntariness in actions, but of scoundrelism, and for which a man is blamed. Does this mean that there is a *moral* obligation not to make certain intellectual mistakes? Why doesn't he discuss obligation in general, and this obligation in particular? If someone professes to be expounding Aristotle and talks in a modern fashion about 'moral' such-and-such, he must be very imperceptive if he does not constantly feel like someone whose jaws have somehow got out of alignment: the teeth don't come together in a proper bite.

We cannot, then, look to Aristotle for any elucidation of the modern way of talking about 'moral' goodness, obligation, etc. And all the best-known writers on ethics in modern times, from Butler to Mill, appear to me to have faults as thinkers on the subject which make it impossible to hope for any direct light on it from them. I will state these objections with the brevity which their character makes possible.

Butler exalts conscience, but appears ignorant that a man's conscience may tell him to do the vilest things.

Hume defines 'truth' in such a way as to exclude ethical judgements from it, and professes that he has proved that they are so excluded. He also implicitly defines 'passion' in such a way that aiming at anything is having a passion. His objection to passing from 'is' to 'ought' would apply equally to passing from 'is' to 'owes' or from 'is' to 'needs'. (However, because of the historical situation, he has a point here, which I shall return to.)

Kant introduces the idea of 'legislating for oneself', which is as absurd as if in these days, when majority votes command great respect, one were to call each reflective decision a man made a *vote* resulting in a majority, which as a matter of proportion is overwhelming, for it is always 1–0. The concept of legislation requires superior power in the legislator. His own rigoristic convictions on the subject of lying were so intense that it never occurred to him that a lie could be relevantly described as anything but just a lie (e.g. as 'a lie in such-and-such circumstances'). His rule about universalisable maxims is useless without stipulations as to what shall count as a relevant description of an action with a view to constructing a maxim about it.

Bentham and Mill do not notice the difficulty of the concept 'pleasure'. They are often said to have gone wrong through committing the 'naturalistic fallacy'; but this charge does not impress me, because I do not find accounts of it coherent. But the other point – about pleasure – seems to me a fatal objection from the very outset. The ancients found this concept pretty baffling. It reduced Aristotle to sheer babble about 'the bloom on the cheek of youth' because, for good reasons, he wanted to make it out both identical with and different from the pleasurable activity. Generations of modern philosophers found this concept quite unperplexing, and it reappeared in the literature as a problematic one only a year or two ago when Ryle wrote about it. The reason is simple: since Locke, pleasure was taken to be some sort of internal impression. But it was superficial, if that was the right account of it, to make it the point of actions. One might adapt something Wittgenstein said about 'meaning' and say 'Pleasure cannot be an internal impression, for no internal impression could have the consequences of pleasure.'

Mill also, like Kant, fails to realise the necessity for stipulation as to relevant descriptions, if his theory is to have content. It did not occur to him that acts of murder and theft could be otherwise described. He holds that where a proposed action is of such a kind as to fall under some one principle established on grounds of utility, one must go by that; where it falls under none or several, the several suggesting contrary views of the action, the thing to do is to calculate particular consequences. But pretty well any action can be so described as to make it fall under a variety of principles of utility (as I shall say for short) if it falls under any.

I will now return to Hume. The features of Hume's philosophy which I have mentioned, like many other features of it, would incline me to think that Hume was a mere – brilliant – sophist; and his procedures are certainly sophistical. But I am forced, not to reverse, but to add to, this judgement by a peculiarity of Hume's philosophising: namely that although he reaches his conclusions – with which he is in love – by sophistical methods, his considerations constantly open up very deep and important problems. It is often the case that in the act of exhibiting the sophistry one finds oneself noticing matters which deserve a lot of exploring: the obvious stands in need of investigation as a result of the points that Hume pretends to have made. In this, he is unlike, say, Butler. It was already well known that conscience could dictate vile actions; for Butler to have written disregarding this does not open up any new topics for us. But with Hume it is otherwise: hence he is a very profound and great philosopher, in spite of his sophistry. For example:

Suppose that I say to my grocer 'Truth consists in *either* relations of ideas, as that 20*s.* = £1, *or* matters of fact, as that I ordered potatoes, you supplied them, and you sent me a bill. So it doesn't apply to such a proposition as that I *owe* you such-and-such-a sum.'

Now if one makes this comparison, it comes to light that the relation of the facts mentioned to the description 'X owes Y so much money' is an interesting one, which I will call that of being 'brute relative to' that description. Further, the 'brute' facts mentioned here themselves have descriptions relative to which *other* facts are 'brute' – as, e.g. *he had potatoes carted to my house* and *they were left there* are brute facts relative to 'he supplied me with potatoes'. And the fact *X owes Y money* is in turn 'brute' relative to other descriptions – e.g. 'X is solvent.' Now the relation of 'relative bruteness' is a complicated one. To mention a few points: if xyz is a set of facts brute relative to a description A, then xyz is a set out of a range some set among which holds if A holds; but the holding of some set among these does not necessarily entail A, because exceptional circumstances can always make a difference; and what are exceptional circumstances relatively to A can generally only be explained by giving a few diverse examples, and *no* theoretically adequate provision can be made for exceptional circumstances, since a further special context can theoretically always be imagined that would reinterpret any special context. Further, though in normal circumstances, xyz would be a justification for A, that is not to say that A just comes to the same as 'xyz'; and also there is apt to be an institutional context which gives its point to the description A, of which institution A is of course not itself a description. (E.g. the statement that I give someone a shilling is not a description of the institution of money or of the currency of this country.) Thus, though it would be ludicrous to pretend that there can be no such thing as a transition from, e.g. 'is' to 'owes', the character of the transition is in fact rather interesting and comes to light as a result of reflecting on Hume's arguments.[2]

That I owe the grocer such-and-such a sum would be one of a set of facts which would be 'brute' in relation to the description 'I am a bilker'. 'Bilking' is of course a species of 'dishonesty' or 'injustice'. (Naturally the consideration will not have any effect on my actions unless I want to commit or avoid acts of injustice.)

So far, in spite of their strong associations, I conceive 'bilking', 'injustice' and 'dishonesty' in a merely 'factual' way. That I can do this for 'bilking' is obvious enough; 'justice' I have no idea how to define, except that its sphere is that of actions which relate to some-

[2] The above two paragraphs are an abstract of a paper 'On Brute Facts', in *Analysis* (1958).

one else, but 'injustice', its defect, can for the moment be offered as a generic name covering various species. E.g.: 'bilking', 'theft' (which is relative to whatever property institutions exist), 'slander', 'adultery' 'punishment of the innocent'.

In present-day philosophy an explanation is required how an unjust man is a bad man, or an unjust action a bad one; to give such an explanation belongs to ethics; but it cannot even be begun until we are equppped with a sound philosophy of psychology. For the proof that an unjust man is a bad man would require a positive account of justice as a 'virtue'. This part of the subject-matter of ethics is, however, completely closed to us until we have an account of what *type of characteristic* a virtue is – a problem, not of ethics, but of conceptual analysis – and how it relates to the actions in which it is instanced: a matter which I think Aristotle did not succeed in really making clear. For this we certainly need an account at least of what a human action is at all, and how its description as 'doing such-and-such' is affected by its motive and by the intention or intentions in it; and for this an account of such concepts is required.

The terms 'should' or 'ought' or 'needs' relate to good and bad: e.g. machinery needs oil, or should or ought to be oiled, in that running without oil is bad for it, or it runs badly without oil. According to this conception, of course, 'should' and 'ought' are not used in a special 'moral' sense when one says that a man should not bilk. [In Aristotle's sense of the term 'moral' (ἠθικός), they are being used in connection with a *moral* subject-matter: namely that of human passions and (non-technical) actions.] But they have now acquired a special so-called 'moral' sense – i.e. a sense in which they imply some absolute verdict (like one of guilty/not guilty on a man) on what is described in the 'ought' sentences used in certain types of context: not merely the contexts that *Aristotle* would call 'moral' – passions and actions – but also some of the contexts that he would call 'intellectual'.

The ordinary (and quite indispensable) terms 'should', 'needs', 'ought', 'must' – acquired this special sense by being equated in the relevant contexts with 'is obliged, or 'is bound', or 'is required to', in the sense in which one can be obliged or bound by law, or something can be required by law.

How did this come about? The answer is in history: between Aristotle and us came Christianity, with its *law* conception of ethics. For Christianity derived its ethical notions from the Torah. (One might be inclined to think that a law conception of ethics could arise only among people who accepted an allegedly divine positive law; that this is not so is shown by the example of the Stoics, who also thought that whatever was involved in conformity to human virtues was required by divine law.)

In consequence of the dominance of Christianity for many centuries, the concepts of being bound, permitted, or excused became deeply embedded in our language and thought. The Greek word ἁμαρτάνειν, the aptest to be turned to that use, acquired the sense 'sin', from having meant 'mistake', 'missing the mark', 'going wrong'. The Latin *peccatum* which roughly corresponds to ἁμάρτημα was even apter for the sense 'sin', because it was already associated with 'culpa' – 'guilt' – a juridical notion. The blanket term 'illicit', 'unlawful', meaning much the same as our blanket term 'wrong', explains itself. It is interesting that Aristotle did not have such a blanket term. He has blanket terms for wickedness – 'villain', 'scoundrel'; but of course a man is not a villain or a scoundrel by the performance of one bad action, or a few bad actions. And he has terms like 'disgraceful', 'impious'; and specific terms signifying defect of the relevant virtue, like 'unjust'; but no term corresponding to 'illicit'. The extension of this term (i.e. the range of its application) could be indicated in his terminology only by a quite lengthy sentence: that is 'illicit' which, whether it is a thought or a consented-to passion or an action or an omission in thought or action, is something contrary to one of the virtues the lack of which shows a man to be bad *qua* man. That formulation would yield a concept co-extensive with the concept 'illicit'.

To have a *law* conception of ethics is to hold that what is needed for conformity with the virtues failure in which is the mark of being bad *qua* man (and not merely, say, *qua* craftsman or logician) – that what is needed for *this*, is required by divine law. Naturally it is not possible to have such a conception unless you believe in God as a law-giver; like Jews, Stoics, and Christians. But if such a conception is dominant for many centuries, and then is given up, it is a natural result that the concepts of 'obligation', of being bound or required as by a law, should remain though they had lost their root; and if the word 'ought' has become invested in certain contexts with the sense of 'obligation' it too will remain to be spoken with a special emphasis and a special feeling in these contexts.

It is as if the notion 'criminal' were to remain when criminal law and criminal courts had been abolished and forgotten. A Hume discovering this situation might conclude that there was a special sentiment, expressed by 'criminal', which alone gave the word its sense. So Hume discovered the situation in which the notion 'obligation' survived, and the notion 'ought' was invested with that peculiar force having which it is said to be used in a 'moral' sense, but in which the belief in divine law had long since been abandoned: for it was substantially given up among Protestants at the time of the Reformation.[3] The situation, if I am right, was the interesting one of the survival of a concept outside the framework of thought that made it a really intelligible one.

When Hume produced his famous remarks about the transition from 'is' to 'ought', he was, then, bringing together several quite different points. One I have tried to bring out by my remarks on the transition from 'is' to 'owes' and on the relative 'bruteness' of facts. It would be possible to bring out a different point by enquiring about the transition from 'is' to 'needs'; from the characteristics of an organism to the environment that it needs, for example. To say that it needs that environment is not to say, e.g. that you want it to have that environment, but that it won't flourish unless it has it. Certainly, it all depends whether you *want* it to flourish! as Hume would say. But what 'all depends' on whether you want it to flourish is whether the fact that it needs that environment, or won't flourish without it, has the slightest influence on your actions, Now *that* such-and-such 'ought' to be or 'is needed' is supposed to have an influence on your actions: from which it seemed natural to infer that to judge that it 'ought to be' was in fact to grant what you judged 'ought to be' influence on your actions. And no amount of truth as to what *is* the case could possibly have a logical claim to have influence on your actions. (It is not judgement as such that sets us in motion; but our judgement on how to get or do something we *want*.) Hence it *must* be impossible to infer 'needs' or 'ought to be' from 'is'. But in the case of a plant, let us say, the inference from 'is' to 'needs' is certainly not in the least dubious. It is interesting and worth examining; but not at all fishy. Its interest is similar to the interest of the relation between brute and less brute facts: these relations have been very little considered. And while you can contrast 'what it needs' with 'what it's got' – like contrasting *de facto* and *de jure* – that does not make its needing this environment less of a 'truth'.

Certainly in the case of what the plant needs, the thought of a

---

[3] They did not deny the existence of divine law; but their most characteristic doctrine was that it was given, not to be obeyed, but to show man's incapacity to obey it, even by grace; and this applied not merely to the ramified prescriptions of the Torah, but to the requirements of 'natural divine law'. Cf. in this connection the decree of Trent against the teaching that Christ was only to be trusted in as mediator, not obeyed as legislator.

need will only affect action if you want the plant to flourish. Here, then, there is no necessary connection between what you can judge the plant 'needs' and what you want. But there is some sort of necessary connection between what you think *you* need, and what you want. The connection is a complicated one; it is possible *not* to want something that you judge you need. But, e.g. it is not possible never to want *anything* that you judge you need. This, however, is not a fact about the meaning of the word 'to need', but about the phenomenon of *wanting*. Hume's reasoning, we might say, in effect, leads one to think it must be about the word 'to need', or 'to be good for'.

Thus we find two problems already wrapped up in the remark about a transition from 'is' to 'ought'; now supposing that we had clarified the 'relative bruteness' of facts on the one hand, and the notions involved in 'needing', and 'flourishing' on the other – there would *still* remain a third point. For, following Hume, someone might say: Perhaps you have made out your point about a transition from 'is' to 'owes' and from 'is' to 'needs': but only at the cost of showing 'owes' and 'needs' sentences to express a *kind* of truths, a *kind* of facts. And it remains impossible to infer *'morally ought'* from 'is' sentences.

This comment, it seems to me, would be correct. This word 'ought', having become a word of mere mesmeric force, could not, in the character of having that force, be inferred from anything whatever. It may be objected that it could be inferred from other 'morally ought' sentences: but that cannot be true. The appearance that this is so is produced by the fact that we say 'All men are ϕ' and 'Socrates is a man' implies 'Socrates is ϕ.' But here 'ϕ' is a dummy predicate. We mean that if you substitute a real predicate for 'ϕ' the implication is valid. A real predicate is required; not just a word containing no intelligible thought: a word retaining the suggestion of force, and apt to have a strong psychological effect, but which no longer signifies a real concept at all.

For its suggestion is one of a *verdict* on my action, according as it agrees or disagrees with the description in the 'ought' sentence. And where one does not think there is a judge or a law, the notion of a verdict may retain its psychological effect, but not its meaning. Now imagine that just this word 'verdict' *were* so used – with a characteristically solemn emphasis – as to retain its atmosphere but not its meaning, and someone were to say: 'For a *verdict*, after all, you need a law and a judge.' The reply might be made: 'Not at all, for if there were a law and a judge who gave a verdict, the question for us would be whether accepting that verdict is something that there is a *Verdict* on.' This is an analogue of an argument which is so frequently referred to as decisive: If someone does have a divine law conception of ethics, all the same, he has to agree that he has to have a judgement that he *ought* (morally ought) to obey the divine law; so his ethic is in exactly the same position as any other: he merely has a 'practical major premise':[4] 'Divine law ought to be obeyed' where someone else has, e.g. 'The greatest happiness principle ought to be employed in all decisions.'

I should judge that Hume and our present-day ethicists had done a considerable service by showing that no content could be found in the notion 'morally ought'; if it were not that the latter philosophers try to find an alternative (very fishy) content and to retain the psychological force of the term. It would be most reasonable to drop it. It has no reasonable sense outside a law conception of ethics; they are not going to maintain such a conception; and you can do ethics without it, as is shown by the example of Aristotle. It would be a great improvement if, instead of 'morally wrong', one always named a genus such as 'untruthful', 'unchaste', unjust'. We should no longer ask whether doing something was 'wrong', passing directly from some description of an action to this notion; we should ask whether, e.g. it was unjust; and the answer would sometimes be clear at once.

I now come to the epoch in modern English moral philosophy marked by Sidgwick. There is a startling change that seems to have taken place between Mill and Moore. Mill assumes, as we saw, that there is no question of calculating the particular consequences of an action such as murder or theft; and we saw too that his position was stupid, because it is not at all clear how an action *can* fall under just one principle of utility. In Moore and in subsequent academic moralists of England we find it taken to be pretty obvious that 'the right action' is the action which produces the best possible consequences (reckoning among consequences the intrinsic values ascribed to certain kinds of act by some 'Objectivists').[5] Now it follows from

[4] As it is absurdly called. Since major premise = premise containing the term which is predicate in the conclusion, it is a solecism to speak of it in connection with practical reasoning.

[5] Oxford Objectivists of course distinguish between 'consequences' and 'intrinsic values' and so produce a misleading appearance of not being 'consequentialists'. But they do not hold – and Ross explicitly denies – that the gravity of, e.g. procuring the condemnation of the innocent is such that it cannot be outweighed by, e.g. national interest. Hence their distinction is of no importance.

this that a man does well, subjectively speaking, if he acts for the best in the particular circumstances according to his judgement of the total consequences of this particular action. I say that this follows, not that any philosopher has said precisely that. For discussion of these questions can of course get extremely complicated: e.g. it can be doubted whether 'such-and-such is the right action' is a satisfactory formulation, on the grounds that things have to exist to have predicates – so perhaps the best formulation is 'I am obliged'; or again, a philosopher may deny that 'right' is a 'descriptive' term, and then take a roundabout route through linguistic analysis to reach a view which comes to the same thing as 'the right action is the one productive of the best consequences' (e.g. the view that you frame your 'principles' to effect the end you choose to pursue, the connection between 'choice' and 'best' being supposedly such that choosing reflectively means that you choose how to act so as to produce the best consequences); further, the roles of what are called 'moral principles' and of the 'motive of duty' have to be described; the differences between 'good' and 'morally good' and 'right' need to be explored, the special characteristics of 'ought' sentences investigated. Such discussions generate an appearance of significant diversity of views where what is really significant is an over-all similarity. The over-all similarity is made clear if you consider that every one of the best-known English academic moral philosophers has put out a philosophy according to which, e.g. it is not possible to hold that it cannot be right to kill the innocent as a means to any end whatsoever and that someone who thinks otherwise is in error. (I have to mention both points; because Mr Hare, for example, while teaching a philosophy which would encourage a person to judge that killing the innocent would be what he 'ought' to choose for overriding purposes, would also teach, I think, that if a man chooses to make avoiding killing the innocent for any purpose his 'supreme practical principle', he cannot be impugned for error: that just is his 'principle'. But with that qualification, I think it can be seen that the point I have mentioned holds good of every single English academic moral philosopher since Sidgwick.) Now this is a significant thing: for it means that all these philosophies are quite incompatible with the Hebrew-Christian ethic. For it has been characteristic of that ethic to teach that there are certain things forbidden whatever *consequences* threaten, such as: choosing to kill the innocent for any purpose, however good; vicarious punishment; treachery (by which I mean obtaining a man's confidence in a grave matter by promises of trustworthy friendship and then betraying him to his enemies);

idolatry; sodomy; adultery; making a false profession of faith. The prohibition of certain things simply in virtue of their description as such-and-such identifiable kinds of action, regardless of any further consequences, is certainly not the whole of the Hebrew-Christian ethic; but it is a noteworthy feature of it; and if every academic philosopher since Sidgwick has written in such a way as to exclude this ethic, it would argue a certain provinciality of mind not to see this incompatability as the most important fact about these philosophers, and the differences between them as somewhat trifling by comparison.

It is noticeable that none of these philosophers displays any consciousness that there is such an ethic, which he is contradicting: it is pretty well taken for obvious among them all that a prohibition such as that on murder does not operate in face of some consequences. But of course the strictness of the prohibition has as its point *that you are not to be tempted by fear or hope of consequences.*

If you notice the transition from Mill to Moore, you will suspect that it was made somewhere by someone; Sidgwick will come to mind as a likely name; and you will in fact find it going on, almost casually, in him. He is rather a dull author; and the important things in him occur in asides and footnotes and small bits of argument which are not concerned with his grand classification of the 'methods of ethics'. A divine law theory of ethics is reduced to an insignificant variety by a footnote telling us that 'the best theologians' (God knows whom he meant) tell us that God is to be obeyed in his capacity of a *moral* being. ἢ φορτικός ὁ ἔπαινος; one seems to hear Aristotle saying: 'Isn't the praise vulgar?'[6] – But Sidgwick *is* vulgar in that kind of way: he thinks, for example, that humility consists in underestimating your own merits – i.e. in a species of untruthfulness; and that the ground for having laws against blasphemy was that it was offensive to believers; and that to go accurately into the virtue of purity is to offend against its canons, a thing he reproves 'medieval theologians' for not realising.

From the point of view of the present enquiry, the most important thing about Sidgwick was his definition of intention. He defines intention in such a way that one must be said to intend any foreseen consequences of one's voluntary action. This definition is obviously incorrect, and I dare say that no philosopher would defend it now. He uses it to put forward an ethical thesis which would now be accepted by many people: the thesis that it does not make any difference to a man's responsibility for something that he foresaw,

[6] *Nicomachean Ethics*, 1 178b16.

that he felt no desire for it, either as an end or as a means to an end. Using the language of intention more correctly, and avoiding Sidgwick's faulty conception, we may state the thesis thus: it does not make any difference to a man's responsibility for an effect of his action which he can foresee, that he does not intend it. Now this sounds rather edifying; it is I think quite characteristic of very bad degenerations of thought on such questions that they sound edifying. We can see what it amounts to by considering an example. Let us suppose that a man has a responsibility for the maintenance of some child. Therefore deliberately to withdraw support from it is a bad sort of thing for him to do. It would be bad for him to withdraw its maintenance because he didn't want to maintain it any longer; *and* also bad for him to withdraw it because by doing so he would, let us say, compel someone else to do something. (We may suppose for the sake of argument that compelling that person to do that thing is in itself quite admirable.) But now he has to choose between doing something disgraceful and going to prison; if he goes to prison, it will follow that he withdraws support from the child. By Sidgwick's doctrine, there is no difference in his responsibility for ceasing to maintain the child, between the case where he does it for its own sake or as a means to some other purpose, and when it happens as a foreseen and unavoidable consequence of his going to prison rather than do something disgraceful. It follows that he must weigh up the relative badness of withdrawing support from the child and of doing the disgraceful thing; and it may easily be that the disgraceful thing is in fact a less vicious action than intentionally withdrawing support from the child would be; if then the fact that withdrawing support from the child is a side effect of his going to prison does not make any difference to his responsibility, this consideration will incline him to do the disgraceful thing; which can still be pretty bad. And of course, once he has started to look at the matter in this light, the only reasonable thing for him to consider will be the consequences and not the intrinsic badness of this or that action. So that, given that he judges reasonably that no *great* harm will come of it, he can do a much more disgraceful thing than deliberately withdrawing support from the child. And if his calculations turn out in fact wrong, it will appear that he was not responsible for the consequences, because he did not foresee them. For in fact Sidgwick's thesis leads to its being quite impossible to estimate the badness of an action except in the light of *expected* consequences. But if so, then *you* must estimate the badness in the light of the consequences *you* expect; and so it will follow that you can exculpate yourself

from the *actual* consequences of the most disgraceful actions, so long
as you can make out a case for not having foreseen them. Whereas
I should contend that a man is responsible for the bad consequences
of his bad actions, but gets no credit for the good ones; and con-
trariwise is not responsible for the bad consequences of good actions.

The denial of *any* distinction between foreseen and intended consequences, as far as responsibility is concerned, was not made by
Sidgwick in developing any one 'method of ethics'; he made this
important move on behalf of everybody and just on its own account;
and I think it plausible to suggest that *this* move on the part of
Sidgwick explains the difference between old-fashioned Utilitarianism and that *consequentialism*, as I name it, which marks him and
every English academic moral philosopher since him. By it, the kind
of consideration which would formerly have been regarded as a
temptation, the kind of consideration urged upon men by wives and
flattering friends, was given a status by moral philosophers in their
theories.

It is a necessary feature of consequentialism that it is a shallow
philosophy. For there are always borderline cases in ethics. Now if
you are either an Aristotelian, or a believer in divine law, you will
deal with a borderline case by considering whether doing such-and-
such in such-and-such circumstances is, say, murder, or is an act of
injustice; and according as you decide it is or it isn't, you judge it to
be a thing to do or not. This would be the method of casuistry; and
while it may lead you to stretch a point on the circumference, it will
not permit you to destroy the centre. But if you are a consequentialist, the question 'What is it right to do in such-and-such circumstances?' is a stupid one to raise. The casuist raises such a question
only to ask 'Would it be *permissible* to do so-and-so?' or 'Would it
be permissible *not* to do so-and-so?' Only if it would *not* be permissible *not* to do so-and-so could he say '*This* would be *the* thing to
do.'[7] Otherwise, though he may speak *against* some action, he cannot prescribe any – for in an *actual* case, the circumstances (beyond
the ones imagined) might suggest all sorts of possibilities, and you
can't know in advance what the possibilities are going to be. Now the
consequentialist has no footing on which to say 'This would be permissible, this not'; because by his own hypothesis, it is the consequences that are to decide, and he has no business to pretend that
he can lay it down what possible twists a man could give doing this

---

[7] Necessarily a rare case: for the positive precepts, e.g. 'Honour your
parents', hardly ever prescribe, and seldom even necessitate, any particular
action.

or that; the most he can say is: a man must not *bring about* this or that; he has no right to say he will, in an actual case, bring about such-and-such unless he does so-and-so. Further, the consequentialist, in order to be imagining borderline cases at all, has of course to assume some sort of law or standard according to which this is a borderline case. Where then does he get the standard from? In practice the answer invariably is: from the standards current in his society or his circle. And it has in fact been the mark of all these philosophers that they have been extremely conventional; they have nothing in them by which to revolt against the conventional standards of their sort of people; it is impossible that they should be profound. But the chance that a whole range of conventional standards will be decent is small. – Finally, the point of considering hypothetical situations, perhaps very improbable ones, *seems* to be to elicit from yourself or someone else a hypothetical decision to do something of a bad kind. I don't doubt this has the effect of predisposing people – who will never get into the situations for which they have made hypothetical choices – to consent to similar bad actions, or to praise and flatter those who do them, so long as their crowd does so too, when the desperate circumstances imagined don't hold at all.

Those who recognise the origins of the notions of 'obligation' and of the emphatic, 'moral', *ought*, in the divine law conception of ethics, but who reject the notion of a divine legislator, sometimes look about for the possibility of retaining a law conception without a divine legislator. This search, I think, has some interest in it. Perhaps the first thing that suggests itself is the 'norms' of a society. But just as one cannot be impressed by Butler when one reflects what conscience can tell people to do, so, I think, one cannot be impressed by this idea if one reflects what the 'norms' of a society can be like. That legislation can be 'for oneself' I reject as absurd; whatever you do 'for yourself' may be admirable, but is not legislating. Once one sees this, one may say: I have to frame my own rules, and these are the best I can frame, and I shall go by them until I know something better: as a man might say 'I shall go by the customs of my ancestors.' Whether this leads to good or evil will depend on the *content* of the rules or of the customs of one's ancestors. If one is lucky it will lead to good. Such an attitude would be hopeful in this at any rate: it seems to have in it some Socratic doubt where, from having to fall back on such expedients, it should be clear that Socratic doubt is good; in fact rather generally it must be good for anyone to think 'Perhaps in some way I can't see, I may be on a bad path, perhaps

I am hopelessly wrong in some essential way'. – The search for 'norms' might lead someone to look for laws of nature, as if the universe were a legislator; but in the present day this is not likely to lead to good results: it might lead one to eat the weaker according to the laws of nature, but would hardly lead anyone nowadays to notions of justice; the pre-Socratic feeling about justice as comparable to the balance or harmony which kept things going is very remote to us.

There is another possibility here: 'obligation' may be contractual. Just as we look at the law to find out what a man subject to it is required by it to do, so we look at a contract to find out what the man who has made it is required by it to do. Thinkers, admittedly remote from us, might have the idea of a *foedus rerum*, of the universe not as a legislator but as the embodiment of a contract. Then if you could find out what the contract was, you would learn your obligations under it. Now, you cannot be under a law unless it has been promulgated to you; and the thinkers who believed in 'natural divine law' held that it was promulgated to every grown man in his knowledge of good and evil. Similarly you cannot be in a contract without having contracted, i.e. given signs of entering upon the contract. Just possibly, it might be argued that the use of language which one makes in the ordinary conduct of life amounts in some sense to giving the signs of entering into various contracts. If anyone had this theory, we should want to see it worked out. I suspect that it would be largely formal; it might be possible to construct a system embodying the law (whose status might be compared to that of 'laws' of logic): 'what's sauce for the goose is sauce for the gander', but hardly one descending to such particularities as the prohibition on murder or sodomy. Also, while it is clear that you can be subject to a law that you do not acknowledge and have not thought of as law, it does not seem reasonable to say that you can enter upon a contract without knowing that you are doing so; such ignorance is usually held to be destructive of the nature of a contract.

It might remain to look for 'norms' in human virtues: just as *man* has so many teeth, which is certainly not the average number of teeth men have, but is the number of teeth for the species, so perhaps the species *man*, regarded not just biologically, but from the point of view of the activity of thought and choice in regard to the various departments of life – powers and faculties and use of things needed – 'has' such-and-such virtues; and this 'man' with the complete set of virtues is the 'norm', as 'man' with, e.g. a complete set of teeth is a norm. But in *this* sense 'norm' has ceased to be roughly equivalent to 'law'. In *this* sense the notion of a 'norm' brings us nearer to an Aristotelian than a law conception of ethics. There is, I think, no harm in that; but if someone looked in this direction to give 'norm' a sense, then he ought to recognise what has happened to the notion 'norm', which he wanted to mean 'law' – without bringing God in' – it has ceased to mean 'law' at all; and *so* the notions of 'moral obligation', 'the moral ought', and 'duty' are best put on the Index, if he can manage it.

But meanwhile – is it not clear that there are several concepts that need investigating simply as part of the philosophy of psychology and – as I should recommend – *banishing ethics totally* from our minds? Namely – to begin with: 'action', 'intention', 'pleasure', 'wanting'. More will probably turn up if we start with these. Eventually it might be possible to advance to considering the concept 'virtue'; with which, I suppose, we should be beginning some sort of a study of ethics.

I will end by describing the advantages of using the word 'ought' in a non-emphatic fashion, and not in a special 'moral' sense; of discarding the term 'wrong' in a 'moral' sense, and using such notions as 'unjust'.

It is possible, if one is allowed to proceed just by giving examples, to distinguish between the intrinsically unjust, and what is unjust given the circumstances. To arrange to get a man judicially punished for something which it can be clearly seen he has not done is intrinsically unjust. This might be done, of course, and often has been done, in all sorts of ways; by suborning false witnesses, by a rule of law by which something is 'deemed' to be the case which is admittedly not the case as a matter of fact, and by open insolence on the part of the judges and powerful people when they more or less openly say: 'A fig for the fact that you did not do it; we mean to sentence you for it all the same.' What is unjust given, e.g. normal circumstances is to deprive people of their ostensible property without legal procedure, not to pay debts, not to keep contracts, and a host of other things of the kind. Now, the circumstances can clearly make a great deal of difference in estimating the justice or injustice of these particular cases, and these circumstances may *sometimes* include expected consequences; for example, a man's claim to a bit of property can become a nullity when its seizure and use can avert some obvious disaster: as, e.g. if you could use a machine of his to produce an explosion in which it would be destroyed, but by means of which you could divert a flood or make a gap which a fire could not jump. Now this certainly does not mean that what would ordinarily be an act of injustice, but is not intrinsically unjust, can always be rendered just by a reasonable calculation of better consequences; far from it; but the problems that would be raised in an attempt to draw a boundary line (or boundary area) here are obviously complicated. And while there are certainly some general remarks which ought to be made here, and some boundaries that can be drawn, the decision on particular cases would for the most part be determined κατὰ τὸν ὀρθὸν λόγον 'according to what's reasonable.' – E.g. that *such-and-such* a delay of payment of a *such-and-such* debt to a person *so* circumstanced, on the part of a person *so* circumstanced, would or would not be unjust, is really only to be decided 'according to what's reasonable'; and for this there can *in principle* be no canon other than giving a few examples. That is to say, while it is because of a big gap in philosophy that we can give no general account of the concept of virtue and of the concept of justice, but have to proceed, using the concepts, only by giving examples; still there is an area where it is not because of any gap, but is in principle the case, that there is no account except by way of examples: and that is where the canon is 'what's reasonable': which of course is *not* a canon.

That is all I wish to say about what is just in some circumstances, unjust in others; and about the way in which expected consequences can play a part in determining what is just. Returning to my example of the intrinsically unjust: if a procedure *is* one of judicially executing a man for what he is clearly understood not to have done, there can be absolutely no argument about the description of this as unjust. No circumstances, and no expected consequences, which do *not* modify the description of the procedure as one of judicially executing a man for what he is known not to have done can modify the description of it as unjust. Someone who attempted to dispute this would only be pretending not to know what 'unjust' means: for this is a pardigm case of injustice.

And here we see the superiority of the term 'unjust' over the terms 'morally right' and 'morally wrong'. For in the context of English moral philosophy since Sidgwick it appears legitimate to discuss whether it *might* be 'morally right' in some circumstances to adopt that procedure; but it cannot be argued that the procedure would in any circumstances be just.

Now I am not able to do the philosophy involved – and I think that no one in the present situation of English philosophy *can* do the philosophy involved – but it is clear that a good man is a just man; and a just man is a man who habitually refuses to commit or partici-

pate in any unjust actions for fear of any consequences, or to obtain
any advantage, for himself or anyone else. Perhaps no one will disagree. But, it will be said, what *is* unjust is sometimes determined by
expected consequences; and certainly that is true. But there are
cases where it is not: now if someone says, 'I agree, but all this wants
a lot of explaining', then he is right, and, what is more, the situation
at present is that we can't do the explaining; we lack the philosophic
equipment. But if someone really thinks, *in advance*,[8] that it is open
to question whether such an action as procuring the judicial execution of the innocent should be quite excluded from consideration – I
do not want to argue with him; he shows a corrupt mind.

In such cases our moral philosophers seek to impose a dilemma
upon us. 'If we have a case where the term "unjust" applies purely
in virtue of a factual description, can't one raise the question
whether one sometimes conceivably ought to do injustice? If "what
is unjust" is determined by consideration of whether it is *right* to do
so-and-so in such-and-such circumstances, then the question whether
it is "right" to commit injustice can't arise, just because "wrong"
has been built into the definition of injustice. But if we have a case
where the description "unjust" applies purely in virtue of the facts,
without bringing "wrong" in, then the question can arise whether
one "ought" perhaps to commit an injustice, whether it might not
be "right" to? And of course "ought" and "right" are being used in
their *moral* senses here. Now either you must decide what is "morally
right" in the light of certain *other* "principles", or you make a
"principle" about *this* and decide that an injustice is never "right";
but even if you do the latter you are going beyond the facts; you are
making a decision that you will not, or that it is wrong to, commit
injustice. But in either case, *if* the term "unjust" is determined
simply by the facts, it is not the term "unjust" that determines that
the term "wrong" applies, but a decision that injustice is *wrong*,

---

[8] If he thinks it in the concrete situation, he is perhaps merely a normally tempted human being. In discussion when this paper was read, as
was perhaps to be expected, this case was produced: a government is required to have an innocent man tried, sentenced and executed under
threat of a 'hydrogen bomb war'. It would seem strange to me to have
much hope of so averting a war threatened by such men as made this
demand. But the most important thing about the way in which cases like
this are invented in discussions, is the assumption that only two courses are
open: here, compliance and open defiance. No one can say in advance of
such a situation what the possibilities are going to be – e.g. that there is
none of stalling by a feigned willingness to comply, accompanied by a
skilfully arranged 'escape' of the victim.

together with the diagnosis of the "factual" description as entailing injustice. But the man who makes an absolute decision that injustice is "wrong" has no footing on which to criticise someone who does *not* make that decision as judging falsely.'

In this argument 'wrong' of course is explained as meaning 'morally wrong', and all the atmosphere of the term is retained while its substance is guaranteed quite null. Now let us remember that 'morally wrong' is the term which is the heir of the notion 'illicit', or 'what there is an obligation *not* to do'; which belongs in a divine law theory or ethics. Here it really does add something to the description 'unjust' to say there is an obligation not to do it; for what obliges is the divine law – as rules oblige in a game. So if the divine law obliges not to commit injustice by forbidding injustice, it really does add something to the description 'unjust' to say there is an obligation not to do it. And it is because 'morally wrong' is the heir of this concept, but an heir that is cut off from the family of concepts from which it sprang, that 'morally wrong' *both* goes beyond the mere factual description 'unjust' *and* seems to have no discernible content except a certain compelling force, which I should call purely psychological. And such is the force of the term that philosophers actually suppose that the divine law notion can be dismissed as making no essential difference even if it is held – *because* they think that a 'practical principle' running 'I *ought* (i.e. am morally obliged) to obey divine laws' is required for the man who believes in divine laws. But actually this notion of obligation is a notion which only operates in the context of law. And I should be inclined to congratulate the present-day moral philosophers on depriving 'morally ought' of its now delusive appearance of content, if only they did not manifest a detestable desire to retain the atmosphere of the term.

It may be possible, if we are resolute, to discard the notion 'morally ought', and simply return to the ordinary 'ought', which, we ought to notice, is such an extremely frequent term of human language that it is difficult to imagine getting on without it. Now if we do return to it, can't it reasonably be asked whether one might ever need to commit injustice, or whether it won't be the best thing to do? Of course it can. And the answers will be various. One man – a philosopher – may say that since justice is a virtue, and injustice a vice, and virtues and vices are built up by the performances of the action in which they are instanced, an act of injustice will tend to make a man bad; and essentially the flourishing of a man *qua* man consists in his being good (e.g. in virtues); but for any X to which such terms apply, X needs what makes it flourish, so a man needs, or ought to perform, only virtuous actions; and even if, as it must be admitted may happen, he flourishes less, or not at all, in inessentials, by avoiding injustice, his life is spoiled in essentials by not avoiding injustice – so he still needs to perform only just actions. That is roughly how Plato and Aristotle talk; but it can be seen that philosophically there is a huge gap, at present unfillable as far as we are concerned, which needs to be filled by an account of human nature, human action, the type of characteristic a virtue is, and above all of human 'flourishing'. And it is the last concept that appears the most doubtful. For it is a bit much to swallow that a man in pain and hunger and poor and friendless is 'flourishing', as Aristotle himself admitted. Further, someone might say that one at least needed to stay alive to 'flourish'. Another man, unimpressed by all that, will say in a hard case: 'What we need is such-and-such, which we won't get without doing this (which is unjust) – so this is what we ought to do.' Another man, who does not follow the rather elaborate reasoning of the philosophers, simply says 'I know it is in any case a disgraceful thing to say that one had better commit this unjust action.' The man who believes in divine laws will say perhaps 'It is forbidden, and however it looks, it cannot be to anyone's profit to commit injustice'; he like the Greek philosophers can think in terms of 'flourishing'. If he is a Stoic, he is apt to have a decidedly strained notion of what 'flourishing' consists in; if he is a Jew or a Christian, he need not have any very distinct notion; the way it will profit him to abstain from injustice is something that he leaves to God to determine, himself only saying 'It can't do me any good to go against his law.' (But he also hopes for a great reward in a new life later on, e.g. at the coming of Messiah; in this, however, he is relying on special promises.)

It is left to modern moral philosophy – the moral philosophy of all the well-known English ethicists since Sidgwick – to construct systems according to which the man who says 'We need such-and-such, and will only get it this way' *may* be a virtuous character: that is to say, it is left open to debate whether such a procedure as the judicial execution of the innocent may not in some circumstances be the 'right' one to adopt; and though the present Oxford moral philosophers would accord a man *permission* to 'make it his principle' not to do such a thing, they teach a philosophy according to which the particular consequences of such an action *could* 'morally' be taken into account by a man who was debating what to do; and if they were such as to be needed for his 'ends', it might be a step in his moral education to frame a moral principle under which he 'managed' (to use Mr Nowell-Smith's phrase[9]) to bring the action; or it might be a new 'decision of principle', making which was an advance in the formation of his moral thinking (to adopt Mr Hare's conception), to decide: in such-and-such circumstances one ought to procure the judicial execution of the innocent. And that is my complaint.

[9] *Ethics*, p. 308.

XIX Moral beliefs

Philippa Foot

To many people it seems that the most notable advance in moral philosophy during the past fifty years or so has been the refutation of naturalism; and they are a little shocked that at this late date such an issue should be reopened. It is easy to understand their attitude: given certain apparently unquestionable assumptions, it would be about as sensible to try to reintroduce naturalism as to try to square the circle. Those who see it like this have satisfied themselves that they know in advance that any naturalistic theory must have a catch in it somewhere, and are put out at having to waste more time exposing an old fallacy. This paper is an attempt to persuade them to look critically at the premises on which their arguments are based.

It would not be an exaggeration to say that the whole of moral philosophy, as it is now widely taught, rests on a contrast between statements of fact and evaluations, which runs something like this: 'The truth or falsity of statements of fact is shown by means of evidence; and what counts as evidence is laid down in the meaning of the expressions occurring in the statement of fact. (For instance, the meaning of "round" and "flat" made Magellan's voyages evidence for the roundness rather than the flatness of the Earth; someone who went on questioning whether the evidence was evidence could eventually be shown to have made some linguistic mistake.) It follows that no two people can make the same statement and count completely different things as evidence; in the end one at least of them could be convicted of linguistic ignorance. It also follows that if a man is given good evidence for a factual conclusion he cannot just refuse to accept the conclusion on the ground that in his scheme of things this evidence is not evidence at all. With evaluations, however, it is different. An evaluation is not connected logically with the factual statements on which it is based. One man may say that a thing is good because of some fact about it, and another may refuse to take that fact as any evidence at all, for nothing is laid down in the meaning of "good" which connects it with one piece of "evidence" rather than another. It follows that a moral eccentric could argue to moral conclusions from quite idiosyncratic premises; he could say, for instance, that a man was a good man because he clasped and unclasped his hands, and never turned NNE after turning SSW. He could also reject someone else's evaluation simply by denying that his evidence was evidence at all.

'The fact about "good" which allows the eccentric still to use this term without falling into a morass of meaninglessness, is its "action-guiding" or "practical" function. This it retains; for like everyone else he considers himself bound to choose the things he calls "good" rather than those he calls "bad". Like the rest of the world he uses "good" in connection only with a "pro-attitude"; it is only that he has pro-attitudes to quite different things, and therefore calls them good.'

There are here two assumptions about 'evaluations', which I will call assumption (1) and assumption (2).

Assumption (1) is that some individual may, without logical error, base his beliefs about matters of value entirely on premises which no one else would recognise as giving any evidence at all. Assumption (2) is that, given the kind of statement which other people regard as evidence for an evaluative conclusion, he may refuse to draw the conclusion because *this* does not count as evidence for *him*.

Let us consider assumption (1). We might say that this depends on the possibility of keeping the meaning of 'good' steady through all changes in the facts about anything which are to count in favour of its goodness. (I do not mean, of course, that a man can make changes as fast as he chooses; only that, whatever he has chosen, it will not be possible to rule him out of order.) But there is a better formulation, which cuts out trivial disputes about the meaning which 'good' happens to have in some section of the community. Let us say that the assumption is that the evaluative function of 'good' can remain constant through changes in the evaluative principle; on this ground it could be said that even if no one can call a man *good* because he clasps and unclasps his hands, he can commend him or express his *pro-attitude* towards him, and if necessary can invent a new moral vocabulary to express his unusual moral code.

Those who hold such a theory will naturally add several qualifications. In the first place, most people now agree with Hare, against Stevenson, that such words as 'good' only apply to individual cases through the application of general principles, so that even the extreme moral eccentric must accept principles of commendation. In the second place 'commending', 'having a pro-attitude', and so on, are supposed to be connected with doing and choosing, so that it would be impossible to say, e.g. that a man was a good man only if he lived for a thousand years. The range of evaluation is supposed to be restricted to the range of possible action and choice. I am not here concerned to question these supposed restrictions on the use of evaluative terms, but only to argue that they are not enough.

The crucial question is this. Is it possible to extract from the meaning of words such as 'good' some element called 'evaluative meaning' which we can think of as externally related to its objects? Such an element would be represented, for instance, in the rule that when any action was 'commended' the speaker must hold himself bound to accept an imperative 'let me do these things'. This is externally related to its object because, within the limitation which we noticed earlier, to possible actions, it would make sense to think of anything as the subject of such 'commendation'. On this hypothesis a moral eccentric could be described as commending the clasping of hands as the action of a good man, and we should not have to look for some background to give the supposition sense. That is to say, on this hypothesis the clasping of hands could be commended without any explanation; it could be what those who hold such theories call 'an ultimate moral principle'.

I wish to say that this hypothesis is untenable, and that there is no describing the evaluative meaning of 'good', evaluation, commending, or anything of the sort, without fixing the object to which they are supposed to be attached. Without first laying hands on the proper object of such things as evaluation, we shall catch in our net either something quite different, such as accepting an order or making a resolution, or else nothing at all.

Before I consider this question, I shall first discuss some other mental attitudes and beliefs which have this internal relation to their object. By this I hope to clarify the concept of internal relation to an object, and incidentally, if my examples arouse resistance, but are eventually accepted, to show how easy it is to overlook an internal relation where it exists.

Consider, for instance, pride.

People are often surprised at the suggestion that there are limits to the things a man can be proud of, about which indeed he can feel pride. I do not know quite what account they want to give of pride; perhaps something to do with smiling and walking with a jaunty air, and holding an object up where other people can see it; or perhaps they think that pride is a kind of internal sensation, so that one might naturally beat one's breast and say 'pride is something I feel *here*'. The difficulties of the second view are well known;

the logically private object cannot be what a name in the public language is the name of.[1] The first view is the more plausible, and it may see reasonable to say that given certain behaviour a man can be described as showing that he is proud of something, whatever that something may be. In one sense this is true, and in another sense not. Given any description of an object, action, personal characteristic, etc., it is not possible to rule it out as an object of pride. Before we can do so we need to know what would be said about it by the man who is to be proud of it, or feels proud of it; but if he does not hold the right beliefs about it then whatever his attitude is it is not pride. Consider, for instance, the suggestion that someone might be proud of the sky or the sea: he looks at them and what he feels is *pride*, or he puffs out his chest and gestures with *pride* in their direction. This makes sense only if a special assumption is made about his beliefs, for instance, that he is under some crazy delusion and believes that he has saved the sky from falling, or the sea from drying up. The characteristic object of pride is something seen (*a*) as in some way a man's own, and (*b*) as some sort of achievement or advantage; without this object pride cannot be described. To see that the second condition is necessary, one should try supposing that a man happens to feel proud because he has laid one of his hands on the other, three times in an hour. Here again the supposition that it is pride that he feels will make perfectly good sense if a special background is filled in. Perhaps he is ill, and it is an achievement even to do this; perhaps this gesture has some religious or political significance, and he is a brave man who will so defy the gods or the rulers. But with no special background there can be no pride, not because no one could psychologically speaking feel pride in such a case, but because whatever he did feel could not logically be pride. Of course, people can see strange things as achievements, though not just anything, and they can identify themselves with remote ancestors, and relations, and neighbours, and even on occasions with Mankind. I do not wish to deny there are many far-fetched and comic examples of pride.

We could have chosen many other examples of mental attitudes which are internally related to their object in a similar way. For instance, fear is not just trembling, and running, and turning pale; without the thought of some menacing evil no amount of this will add up to fear. Nor could anyone be said to feel dismay about something he did not see as bad; if his thoughts about it were that it was

[1] See L. Wittgenstein, *Philosophical Investigations* (1967), especially sections 243–315.

altogether a good thing, he could not say that (oddly enough) what he felt about it was dismay. 'How odd, I feel dismayed when I ought to be pleased' is the prelude to a hunt for the adverse aspect of the thing, thought of as lurking behind the pleasant façade. But someone may object that pride and fear and dismay are feelings or emotions and therefore not a proper analogy for 'commendation', and there will be an advantage in considering a different kind of example. We could discuss, for instance, the belief that a certain thing is dangerous, and ask whether this could logically be held about anything whatsoever. Like 'this is good', 'this is dangerous' is an assertion, which we should naturally accept or reject by speaking of its truth or falsity; we seem to support such statements with evidence, and moreover there may seem to be a 'warning function' connected with the word 'dangerous' as there is supposed to be a 'commending function' connected with the word 'good'. For suppose that philosophers, puzzled about the property of dangerousness, decided that the word did not stand for a property at all, but was essentially a practical or action-guiding term, used for *warning*. Unless used in an 'inverted comma sense' the word 'dangerous' was used to warn, and this meant that anyone using it in such a sense committed himself to avoiding the things he called dangerous, to preventing other people from going near them, and perhaps to running in the opposite direction. If the conclusion were not obviously ridiculous, it would be easy to infer that a man whose application of the term was different from ours throughout might say that the oddest things were dangerous without fear of disproof; the idea would be that he could still be described as 'thinking them dangerous', or at least as 'warning', because by his attitude and actions he would have fulfilled the conditions for these things. This is nonsense because without its proper object *warning*, like *believing dangerous*, will not be there. It is logically impossible to warn about anything not thought of as threatening evil, and for danger we need a particular kind of serious evil such as injury or death.

There are, however, some differences between thinking a thing dangerous and feeling proud, frightened or dismayed. When a man says that something is dangerous he must support his statement with a special kind of evidence; but when he says that he feels proud or frightened or dismayed the description of the object of his pride or fright or dismay does not have quite this relation to his original statement. If he is shown that the thing he was proud of was not his after all, or was not after all anything very grand, he may have to say that his pride was not justified, but he will not have to take back the statement that he was proud. On the other hand, someone who says that a thing is dangerous, and later sees that he made a mistake in thinking that an injury might result from it, has to go back on his original statement and admit that he was wrong. In neither case, however, is the speaker able to go on as before. A man who discovered that it was not his pumpkin but someone else's which had won the prize could only say that he still felt proud, if he could produce some other ground for pride. It is in this way that even feelings are logically vulnerable to facts.

It will probably be objected against these examples that for part of the way at least they beg the question. It will be said that indeed a man can only be proud of something he thinks a good action, or an achievement, or a sign of noble birth; as he can only feel dismay about something which he sees as bad, frightened at some threatened evil; similarly he can only warn if he is also prepared to speak, for instance, of injury. But this will only limit the range of possible objects of those attitudes and beliefs if the range of these terms is limited in its turn. To meet this objection I shall discuss the meaning of 'injury' because this is the simplest case. Anyone who feels inclined to say that anything could be counted as an achievement, or as the evil of which people were afraid, or about which they felt dismayed, should just try this out. I wish to consider the proposition that anything could be thought of as dangerous, because if it causes injury it is dangerous, and anything could be counted as an injury. I shall consider bodily injury because this is the injury connected with danger; it is not correct to put up a notice by the roadside reading 'Danger!' on account of bushes which might scratch a car. Nor can a substance be labelled 'dangerous' on the ground that it can injure delicate fabrics; although we can speak of the danger that it may do so, that is not the use of the word which I am considering here.

When a body is injured it is changed for the worse in a special way, and we want to know which changes count as injuries. First of all, it matters how an injury comes about; e.g. it cannot be caused by natural decay. Then it seems clear that not just any kind of thing will do, for instance, any unusual mark on the body, however much trouble a man might take to have it removed. By far the most important class of injuries are injuries to a part of the body, counting as injuries because there is interference with the function of that part; injury to a leg, an eye, an ear, a hand, a muscle, the heart, the brain, the spinal cord. An injury to an eye is one that affects, or is likely to affect, its sight; an injury to a hand one which makes it less well able to reach out and grasp, and perform other operations of this kind. A leg can be injured because its movements and supporting power can be affected; a lung because it can become too weak to draw in the proper amount of air. We are most ready to speak of an injury where the function of a part of the body is to perform a characteristic operation, as in these examples. We might hesitate to say that a skull can be injured, and might prefer to speak of damage to it, since although there is indeed a function (a protective function) there is no operation. But thinking of the protective function of the skull we may want to speak of injury here. In so far as the concept of *injury* depends on that of *function* it is narrowly limited, since not even every use to which a part of the body is put will count as its function. Why is it that, even if it is the means by which they earn their living, we would never consider the removal of the dwarf's hump or the bearded lady's beard as a bodily injury? It will be tempting to say that these things are disfigurements, but this is not the point; if we suppose that a man who had some invisible extra muscle made his living as a court jester by waggling his ears, the ear would not have been injured if this were made to disappear. If it were natural to men to communicate by movements of the ear, then ears would have the function of signalling (we have no word for this kind of 'speaking') and an impairment of this function would be an injury; but things are not like this. This court jester would use his ears to make people laugh, but this is not the function of ears.

No doubt many people will feel impatient when such facts are mentioned, because they think that it is quite unimportant that this or that *happens* to be the case, and it seems to them arbitrary that the loss of the beard, the hump, or the ear muscle would not be called an injury. Isn't the loss of that by which one makes one's living a pretty catastrophic loss? Yet it seems quite natural that these are not counted as injuries if one thinks about the conditions of human life, and contrasts the loss of a special ability to make people gape or laugh with the ability to see, hear, walk, or pick things up. The first is only needed for one very special way of living; the other in any foreseeable future for any man. This restriction seems all the more natural when we observe what other threats besides that of injury can constitute danger: of death, for instance, or mental derangement. A shock which could cause mental instability or impairment of memory would be called dangerous, because a man needs such things as intelligence, memory, and concentration as he needs sight or hearing or the use of hands. Here we do not speak of injury unless it is possible to connect the impairment with some physical change, but we speak of danger because there is the same loss of a capacity which any man needs.

There can be injury outside the range we have been considering; for a man may sometimes be said to have received injuries where no part of his body has had its function interfered with. In general, I think that any blow which disarranged the body in such a way that there was lasting pain would inflict an injury, even if no other ill resulted, but I do not know of any other important extension of the concept.

It seems therefore that since the range of things which can be called injuries is quite narrowly restricted, the word 'dangerous' is restricted in so far as it is connected with injury. We have the right to say that a man cannot decide to call just anything dangerous, however much he puts up fences and shakes his head.

So far I have been arguing that such things as pride, fear, dismay, and the thought that something is dangerous have an internal relation to their object, and hope that what I mean is becoming clear. Now we must consider whether those attitudes or beliefs which are the moral philosopher's study are similar, or whether such things as 'evaluation' and 'thinking something good' and 'commendation' could logically be found in combination with any object whatsoever. All I can do here is to give an example which may make this suggestion seem implausible, and to knock away a few of its supports. The example will come from the range of trivial and pointless actions such as we were considering in speaking of the man who clasped his hands three times an hour, and we can point to the oddity of the suggestion that this can be called a good action. We are bound by the terms of our question to refrain from adding any special background, and it should be stated once more that the question is about what can count in favour of the goodness or badness of a man or an action, and not what could be, or be thought, good or bad with a special background. I believe that the view I am attacking often seems plausible only because the special background is surreptitiously introduced.

Someone who said that clasping the hands three times in an hour was a good action would first have to answer the question 'How do you mean?' For the sentence 'this is a good action' is not one which has a clear meaning. Presumably, since our subject is moral philosophy, it does not here mean 'that was a good thing to do' as this might be said of a man who had done something sensible in the course of any enterprise whatever; we are to confine our attention to 'the moral use of "good"'. I am not clear that it makes sense to speak of a 'moral use of "good"', but we can pick out a number of cases which raise moral issues. It is because these are so diverse and because 'this is a good action' does not pick out any one of them, that we must ask 'How do you mean?' For instance, some things that are done fulfil a duty, such as the duty of parents to children or children to parents. I suppose that when philosophers speak of good actions they would include these. Some come under the heading of a virtue such as charity, and they will be included too. Others again are actions which require the virtues of courage or temperance, and here the moral aspect is due to the fact that they are done in spite of fear or the temptation of pleasure; they must indeed be done for the sake of some real or fancied good, but not necessarily what philosophers would want to call a moral good. Courage is not *particularly* concerned with saving other people's lives, or temperance with leaving them their share of the food and drink, and the goodness of *what is done* may here be all kinds of usefulness. It is because there are these very diverse cases included (I suppose) under the expression 'a good action' that we should refuse to consider applying it without asking what is meant, and we should now ask what is intended when someone is supposed to say that 'clasping the hands three times in an hour is a good action'. Is it supposed that this action fulfils a duty? Then in virtue of what does a man have this duty, and to whom does he owe it? We have promised not to slip in a special background, but he cannot possibly have a *duty* to clasp his hands unless such a background exists. Nor could it be an act of charity, for it is not thought to do anyone any good, nor again a gesture of humility unless a special assumption turns it into this. The action could be courageous, but only if it were done both in the face of fear and for the sake of a good; and we are not allowed to put in special circumstances which could make this the case.

I am sure that the following objection will now be raised. 'Of course clasping one's hands three times in an hour cannot be brought under one of the virtues which we recognise, but that is only to say that it is not a good action by our current moral code. It is logically possible that in a quite different moral code quite different virtues should be recognised, for which we have not even got a name.' I cannot answer this objection properly, for that would need a satisfactory account of the concept of a virtue. But anyone who thinks it would be easy to describe a new virtue connected with clasping the hands three times in an hour should just try. I think he will find that he has to cheat, and suppose that in the community concerned the clasping of hands has been given some special significance, or is thought to have some special effect. The difficulty is obviously connected with the fact that without a special background there is no possibility of answering the question 'What's the point?' It is no good saying that here would be a point in doing the action because the action was a morally good action: the question is how it can be given any such description if we cannot first speak about the point. And it is just as crazy to suppose that we can call *anything* the point of doing something without having to say what the point of *that* is. In clasping one's hands one may make a slight sucking noise, but what is the point of that? It is surely clear that moral virtues must be connected with human good and harm, and that it is quite impossible to call anything you like good or harm. Consider, for instance, the suggestion that a man might say he had been harmed because a bucket of water had been taken out of the sea. As usual it would be possible to think up circumstances in which this remark would make sense; for instance, when coupled with a belief in magical influences; but then the harm would consist in what was done by the evil spirits, not in the taking of the water from the sea. It would be just as odd if someone were supposed to say that harm had been done to him because the hairs of his head had been reduced to an even number.[2]

I conclude that assumption (1) is very dubious indeed, and that no one should be allowed to speak as if we can understand 'evaluation', 'commendation' or 'pro-attitude', whatever the actions concerned.

II

I propose now to consider what was called assumption (2), which said that a man might always refuse to accept the conclusion of an argument about values, because what counted as evidence for other people did not count for him. Assumption (2) could be true even if assumption (1) were false, for it might be that once a particular question of values — say a moral question — had been accepted, any disputant was bound to accept particular pieces of evidence as relevant, the same pieces as everyone else, but that he could always

[2] In face of this sort of example many philosophers take refuge in the thicket of aesthetics. It would be interesting to know if they are willing to let their whole case rest on the possibility that there might be aesthetic objections to what was done.

refuse to draw any moral conclusions whatsoever or to discuss any questions which introduced moral terms. Nor do we mean 'he might refuse to draw the conclusion' in the trivial sense in which anyone can perhaps refuse to draw *any* conclusion; the point is that any statement of value always seems to go beyond any statement of fact, so that he might have a reason for accepting the factual premises but refusing to accept the evaluative conclusion. That this is so seems to those who argue in this way to follow from the practical implications of evaluation. When a man uses a word such as 'good' in an 'evaluative' and not an 'inverted comma' sense, he is supposed to commit his will. From this it has seemed to follow inevitably that there is a logical gap between fact and value; for is it not one thing to say that a thing is so, and another to have a particular attitude towards its being so; one thing to see that certain effects will follow from a given action, and another to care? Whatever account was offered of the essential feature of evaluation – whether in terms of feelings, attitudes, the acceptance of imperatives or what not – the fact remained that with an evaluation there was a committal in a new dimension, and that this was not guaranteed by any acceptance of facts.

I shall argue that this view is mistaken; that the practical implication of the use of moral terms has been put in the wrong place, and that if it is described correctly the logical gap between factual premises and moral conclusion disappears.

In this argument it will be useful to have as a pattern the practical or 'action-guiding' force of the word 'injury', which is in some, though not all, ways similar to that of moral terms. It is clear I think that an injury is necessarily something bad and therefore something which as such anyone always has a reason to avoid, and philosophers will therefore be tempted to say that anyone who uses 'injury' in its full 'action-guiding' sense commits himself to avoiding the things he calls injuries. They will then be in the usual difficulties about the man who says he knows he ought to do something but does not intend to do it; perhaps also about weakness of the will. Suppose that instead we look again at the kinds of things which count as injuries, to see if the connection with the will does not start here. As has been shown, a man is injured whenever some part of his body, in being damaged, has become less well able to fulfil its ordinary function. It follows that he suffers a disability, or is liable to do so; with an injured hand he will be less well able to pick things up, hold on to them, tie them together or chop them up, and so on. With defective eyes there will be a thousand other things he is unable to do, and in both cases we should naturally say that he will often be unable to get what he wants to get or avoid what he wants to avoid.

Philosophers will no doubt seize on the word 'want', and say that if we suppose that a man happens to want the things which an injury to his body prevents him from getting, we have slipped in a supposition about a 'pro-attitude' already; and that anyone who does not happen to have these wants can still refuse to use 'injury' in its prescriptive, or 'action-guiding' sense. And so it may seem that the only way to make a *necessary* connection between 'injury' and the things that are to be avoided, is to say that it is only used in an 'action-guiding sense' when applied to something the speaker intends to avoid. But we should look carefully at the crucial move in that argument, and query the suggestion that someone might happen not to want anything for which he would need the use of hands or eyes. Hands and eyes, like ears and legs, play a part in so many operations that a man could only be said not to need them if he had no wants at all. That such people exist, in asylums, is not to the present purpose at all; the proper use of his limbs is something a man has reason to want if he wants anything.

I do not know just what someone who denies this proposition could have in mind. Perhaps he is thinking of changing the facts of human existence, so that merely wishing, or the sound of the voice, will bring the world to heel? More likely he is proposing to rig the circumstances of some individual's existence within the framework of the ordinary world, by supposing for instance that he is a prince whose servants will sow and reap and fetch and carry for him, and so use their hands and eyes in his service that he will not need the use of his. Let us suppose that such a story could be told about a man's life; it is wildly implausible, but let us pretend that it is not. It is clear that in spite of this we could say that any man had a reason to shun injury; for even if at the end of his life it could be said that by a strange set of circumstances he had never needed the use of his eyes, or his hands, this could not possibly be foreseen. Only by once more changing the facts of human existence, and supposing every vicissitude foreseeable, could such a supposition be made.

This is not to say that an injury might not bring more incidental gain than necessary harm; one has only to think of times when the order has gone out that able-bodied men are to be put to the sword. Such a gain might even, in some peculiar circumstances, be reliably foreseen, so that a man would have even better reason for seeking than for avoiding injury. In this respect the word 'injury' differs from terms such as 'injustice'; the practical force of 'injury' means only that anyone has *a* reason to avoid injuries, not that he has an overriding reason to do so.

It will be noticed that this account of the 'action-guiding' force of 'injury' links it with reasons for acting rather than with actually doing something. I do not think, however, that this makes it a less good pattern for the 'action-guiding' force of moral terms. Philosophers who have supposed that actual action was required if 'good' were to be used in a sincere evaluation have got into difficulties over weakness of will, and they should surely agree that enough has been done if we can show that any man has reason to aim at virtue and avoid vice. But is this impossibly difficult if we consider the kinds of things that count as virtue and vice? Consider, for instance, the cardinal virtues, prudence, temperance, courage and justice. Obviously any man needs prudence, but does he not also need to resist the temptation of pleasure when there is harm involved? And how could it be argued that he would never need to face what was fearful for the sake of some good? It is not obvious what someone would mean if he said that temperance or courage were not good qualities, and this not because of the 'praising' sense of these *words*, but because of the things that courage and temperance are.

I should like to use these examples to show the artificiality of the notions of 'commendation' and of 'pro-attitudes' as these are commonly employed. Philosophers who talk about these things will say that after the facts have been accepted – say that X is the kind of man who will climb a dangerous mountain, beard an irascible employer for a rise in pay, and in general face the fearful for the sake of something he thinks worth while – there remains the question of 'commendation' or 'evaluation'. If the word 'courage' is used they will ask whether or not the man who speaks of another as having courage is supposed to have commended him. If we say 'yes' they will insist that the judgement about courage *goes beyond the facts*, and might therefore be rejected by someone who refused to do so; if we say 'no' they will argue that 'courage' is being used in a purely descriptive or 'inverted commas sense', and that we have not got an example of the evaluative use of language which is the moral philosopher's special study. What sense can be made, however, of the question 'does he commend?' What is this extra element which is supposed to be present or absent after the facts have been settled? It is not a matter of liking the man who has courage, or of thinking him altogether good, but of 'commending him for his courage'. How are we supposed to do that? The answer that will be given is that we only commend someone else in speaking of him as courageous if we accept the imperative 'let me be courageous' for ourselves. But this is quite unnecessary. I can speak of someone else as having the virtue of courage, and of course recognise it as a virtue in the proper sense, while knowing that I am a complete coward, and making no resolution to reform. I know that I should be better off if I were courageous, and so have a reason to cultivate courage, but I may also know that I will do nothing of the kind.

If someone were to say that courage was not a virtue he would have to say that it was not a quality by which a man came to act well. Perhaps he would be thinking that someone might be worse off for his courage, which is true, but only because an incidental harm might arise. For instance, the courageous man might have under-estimated a risk, and run into some disaster which a cowardly man would have avoided because he was not prepared to take any risk at all. And his courage, like any other virtue, could be the cause of harm to him because possessing it he fell into some disastrous state of pride.[3] Similarly, those who question the virtue of temperance are probably thinking not of the virtue itself but of men whose temperance has consisted in resisting pleasure for the sake of some illusory good, or those who have made this virtue their pride.

But what, it will be asked, of justice? For while prudence, courage and temperance are qualities which benefit the man who has them, justice seems rather to benefit others, and to work to the disadvantage of the just man himself. Justice as it is treated here, as one of the cardinal virtues, covers all those things owed to other people: it is under injustice that murder, theft and lying come, as well as the withholding of what is owed for instance by parents to children and by children to parents, as well as the dealings which would be called unjust in everyday speech. So the man who avoids injustice will find himself in need of things he has returned to their owner, unable to obtain an advantage by cheating and lying; involved in all those difficulties painted by Thrasymachus in the first book of the Republic, in order to show that injustice is more profitable than justice to a man of strength and wit. We will be asked how, on our theory, justice can be a virtue and injustice a vice, since it will surely be difficult to show that any man whatsoever must need to be just as he needs the use of his hands and eyes, or needs prudence, courage and temperance?

Before answering this question I shall argue that if it cannot be answered, then justice can no longer be recommended as a virtue.

[3] Cf. Aquinas, *Summa Theologica*, I–II, q. 55, Art. 4.

The point of this is not to show that it must be answerable, since justice is a virtue, but rather to suggest that we should at least consider the possibility that justice is not a virtue. This suggestion was taken seriously by Socrates in the Republic, where it was assumed by everyone that if Thrasymachus could establish his premise – that injustice was more profitable than justice – his conclusion would follow: that a man who had the strength to get away with injustice had reason to follow this as the best way of life. It is a striking fact about modern moral philosophy that no one sees any difficulty in accepting Thrasymachus' premise and rejecting his conclusion, and it is because Nietzsche's position is at this point much closer to that of Plato that he is remote from academic moralists of the present day.

In the Republic it is assumed that if justice is not a good to the just man, moralists who recommend it as a virtue are perpetrating a fraud. Agreeing with this, I shall be asked where exactly the fraud comes in; where the untruth that justice is profitable to the individual is supposed to be told? As a preliminary answer we might ask how many people are prepared to say frankly that injustice is more profitable than justice? Leaving aside, as elsewhere in this paper, religious beliefs which might complicate the matter, we will suppose that some tough atheistical character has asked 'Why should I be just?' (Those who believe that this question has something wrong with it can employ their favourite device for sieving out 'evaluating meaning', and suppose that the question is 'Why should I be "just"?') Are we prepared to reply 'As far as you are concerned you will be better off if you are unjust, but it matters to the rest of us that you should be just, so we are trying to get you to be just'? He would be likely to enquire into our methods, and then take care not to be found out, and I do not think that many of those who think that it is not necessary to show that justice is profitable to the just man would easily accept that there was nothing more they could say.

The crucial question is: 'Can we give anyone, strong or weak, a reason why he should be just?' – and it is no help at all to say that since 'just' and 'unjust' are 'action-guiding words' no one can even ask 'Why should I be just?' Confronted with that argument the man who wants to do unjust things has only to be careful to avoid the *word*, and he has not been given a reason why he should not do the things which other people call 'unjust'. Probably it will be argued that he has been given a reason so far as anyone can ever be given a reason for doing or not doing anything, for the chain of reasons must always come to an end somewhere, and it may seem that one man may always reject the reason which another man accepts. But this is a mistake; some answers to the question 'why should I?' bring the series to a close and some do not. Hume showed how *one* answer closed the series in the following passage:

'Ask a man *why he uses exercise*; he will answer, *because he desires to keep his health*. If you then enquire, *why he desires health*, he will readily reply, *because sickness is painful*. If you push your enquiries further, and desire a reason *why he hates pain*, it is impossible he can ever give any. This is an ultimate end, and is never referred to any other object.' (*Enquiries*, appendix I, para. v.) Hume might just as well have ended this series with boredom: sickness often brings boredom, and no one is required to give a reason why he does not want to be bored, any more than he has to give a reason why he does want to pursue what interests him. In general, anyone is given a reason for acting when he is shown the way to something he wants; but for some wants the question 'Why do you want that?' will make sense, and for others it will not.[4] It seems clear that in this division justice falls on the opposite side from pleasure and interest and such things. 'Why shouldn't I do that?' is not answered by the words 'because it is unjust' as it is answered by showing that the action will bring boredom, loneliness, pain, discomfort or certain kinds of incapacity, and this is why it is not true to say that 'it's unjust' gives a reason in so far as any reasons can ever be given. 'It's unjust' gives a reason only if the nature of justice can be shown to be such that it is necessarily connected with what a man wants.

This shows why a great deal hangs on the question of whether justice is or is not a good to the just man, and why those who accept Thrasymachus' premise and reject his conclusion are in a dubious position. They recommend justice to each man, as something he has a reason to follow, but when challenged to show why he should do so they will not always be able to reply. This last assertion does not depend on any 'selfish theory of human nature' in the philosophical sense. It is often possible to give a man a reason for acting by showing him that someone else will suffer if he does not; someone else's good may really be more to him than his own. But the affection which mothers feel for children, and lovers for each other, and friends for friends, will not take us far when we are asked for reasons why a man should be just; partly because it will not extend far enough, and partly because the actions dictated by

4 For an excellent discussion of reasons for action, see G. E. M. Anscombe, *Intention* (Oxford 1957) sections 34–40.

benevolence and justice are not always the same. Suppose that I owe someone money; '... what if he be my enemy, and has given me just cause to hate him? What if he be a vicious man, and deserves the hatred of all mankind? What if he be a miser, and can make no use of what I would deprive him of? What if he be a profligate debauchee, and would rather receive harm than benefit from large possessions?'[5] Even if the general practice of justice could be brought under the motive of universal benevolence – the desire for the greatest happiness of the greatest number – many people certainly do not have any such desire. So that if injustice is only to be recommended on these grounds a thousand tough characters will be able to say that they have been given no reason for practising justice, and many more would say the same if they were not too timid or too stupid to ask questions about the code of behaviour which they have been taught. Thus, given Thrasymachus' premise Thrasymachus' point of view is reasonable; we have no particular reason to admire those who practise justice through timidity or stupidity.

It seems to me, therefore, that if Thrasymachus' thesis is accepted things cannot go on as before; we shall have to admit that the belief on which the status of justice as a virtue was founded is mistaken, and if we still want to get people to be just we must recommend justice to them in a new way. We shall have to admit that injustice is more profitable than justice, at least for the strong, and then do our best to see that hardly anyone can get away with being unjust. We have, of course, the alternative of keeping quiet, hoping that for the most part people will follow convention into a kind of justice, and not ask awkward questions, but this policy might be overtaken by a vague scepticism even on the part of those who do not know just what is lacking; we should also be at the mercy of anyone who was able and willing to expose our fraud.

Is it true, however, to say that justice is not something a man needs in his dealings with his fellows, supposing only that he be strong? Those who think that he can get on perfectly well without being just should be asked to say exactly how such a man is supposed to live. We know that he is to practise injustice whenever the unjust act would bring him advantage; but what is he to say? Does he admit that he does not recognise the rights of other people, or does he pretend? In the first case even those who combine with him will know that on a change of fortune, or a shift of affection, he may turn to plunder them, and he must be as wary of their treachery as they are of his. Presumably the happy unjust man is supposed, as in

[5] Hume, *Treatise*, III. ii. I.

Book II of the *Republic*, to be a very cunning liar and actor, combining complete injustice with the appearance of justice: he is prepared to treat others ruthlessly, but pretends that nothing is further from his mind. Philosophers often speak as if a man could thus hide himself even from those around him, but the supposition is doubtful, and in any case the price in vigilance would be colossal. If he lets even a few people see his true attitude he must guard himself against them; if he lets no one into the secret he must always be careful in case the least spontaneity betray him. Such facts are important because the need a man has for justice in dealings with other men depends on the fact that they are men and not inanimate objects or animals. If a man only needed other men as he needs household objects, and if men could be manipulated like household objects, or beaten into a reliable submission like donkeys, the case would be different. As things are, the supposition that injustice is more profitable than justice is very dubious, although like cowardice and intemperance it might turn out incidentally to be profitable.

The reason why it seems to some people so impossibly difficult to show that justice is more profitable than injustice is that they consider in isolation particular just acts. It is perfectly true that if a man is just it follows that he will be prepared, in the event of very evil circumstances, even to face death rather than to act unjustly – for instance, in getting an innocent man convicted of a crime of which he has been accused. For him it turns out that his justice brings disaster on him, and yet like anyone else he had good reason to be a just and not an unjust man. He could not have it both ways and while possessing the virtue of justice hold himself ready to be unjust should any great advantage accrue. The man who has the virtue of justice is not ready to do certain things, and if he is too easily tempted we shall say that he was ready after all.

XX Goodness and choice
Philippa Foot

It is often said nowadays that the meaning of the word 'good' is to
be explained by talking about some necessary connection between
calling things good and choosing them. This theory is thought to
have the following merits. (1) It seems to distinguish 'good' from
such terms as 'yellow' and 'square' without talking about peculiar
non-natural properties. (2) It seems to show how a value judgement
in general, and a moral judgement in particular, is, as Hume insisted, essentially practical, being supposed 'to influence our passions
and actions, and to go beyond the calm and indolent judgements of
the understanding' (*Treatise*, III. i. i). (3) It seems to solve the problem of how 'good' can have the same meaning when applied to
many diverse things; the relation to choice being offered as the
thread on which these different uses are all strung. Nevertheless, the
subject is full of obscurities and uncertainties, as we can see if we
try to answer questions such as these. (1) Is a connection with the
choices of the speaker ever a *sufficient* condition for the use of the
word 'good', as it would be if a man could ever call certain things
(let us call them *A*'s) good *A*'s merely because these were the *A*'s
which he was thereafter ready to choose? Is there any case in which
he could defend his use of the word 'good' by saying, for instance,
'I committed myself to a choice'? Or, if 'committing himself to
choosing' is not thought quite the right condition, will it do if he fills
in more detail, e.g. about the way he feels if he fails to choose these
A's, and how he encourages others to make the same choice? (2) Is
it even true to say that a connection with the choices of the speaker
is a *necessary* condition of the use of 'good', or of the use of this
word 'in its proper evaluative sense'? Might there not be cases in
which calling an *A* a good *A* does not commit one to anything at all
in the way of choices, perhaps not even to the admission of any
reason for preferring the *A*'s which are good? And where calling an
A a good *A* and choosing it are connected, will they be connected in
just the same way for all the different things that *A* is supposed
to be?

I shall first deal with the question of choice as a sufficient condition. Are facts about the speaker's choices ever a sufficient defence for his calling a certain kind of A a good A, no matter what that kind of A may be? No one, I think, would try to maintain such a view quite generally; it is certain that the expression 'a good A' cannot always be used in this way. Such a theory could not be right, for instance, for the use of 'good' in the expression 'a good knife'; the man who uses these words correctly must use them in conjunction with particular criteria of goodness: those which really are the criteria for the goodness of knives. No matter what he may do in the way of choosing knives which are M he cannot say 'M knives are good knives' unless M is a relevant characteristic, or unless he is prepared to show that M knives are also N knives, and N is a characteristic of the right kind. He could not, for example, say that a good knife was one which rusted quickly, defending his use of the word 'good' by showing that he picked out such knives for his own use. I imagine that almost everyone would agree about this, saying that there are some cases in which the correct use of the expression 'a good A' requires that one set of criteria rather than another should be used for judging the goodness of the things. But many people who would admit this think that in other cases *any* criteria of goodness would be logically possible, so that for some A's the individual calling an A a good A has to decide for himself which characteristics he will take as counting in favour of the goodness of an A. The example which they most often have in mind is that in which 'A' is 'man' or 'action'; for it has seemed to them that moral judgements must be construed in this way. Nevertheless it is supposed that the account given of the use of 'good' in these expressions is one that goes for many other cases as well; indeed the suggestion often seems to be that this is a typical use of 'good', and sometimes other examples are given, as for instance by Hare when he talks about good cacti in the *Language of Morals* (Oxford 1952).[1] A man is described as having imported a cactus, the first cactus, into his own country, and it is implied that he can decide which of the plants he shall count as good cacti, laying down criteria in respect of such things as size and shape. There is no suggestion of any limits to the criteria which can be criteria of goodness in cacti, and Hare obviously thinks that this is quite an ordinary case of the use of the word 'good'. I shall argue that, on the contrary, it is hard to find any genuine example of this kind, so that if Hare's account of the 'good' in 'good man' were correct then this use of the word would seem to be different from all

[1] Pp. 96–7.

other cases in which we speak of a good such-and-such. My thesis is
not, of course, that criteria for the goodness of each and every kind
of thing are determined in the same way as they are determined for
such things as knives, but rather that they are always determined,
and not a matter for decision. (The only qualification to this statement comes from consideration of the range of cases which I shall
call 'complicated examples'.[2])

What is peculiar about a word such as 'knife' is that it names an
object in respect of its function. This is not to say (simply) that it
names an object which has a function, but also that the function is
involved in the meaning of the word, and I shall call such words
functional in the strong sense. That 'knife' is a functional word in
the strong sense is shown by describing another community supposed
to have objects exactly like our knives but never used for cutting.
To save complications let us suppose that never in the history of this
community were knife-shaped objects used as we use knives. These
people have objects which look just like knives, are made of the
same material and so on, but they only use them for some quite
different purpose, such as marking plots of land. If asked whether
they had knives we should not say, 'Yes, but they use them for quite
different purposes from us', but rather, 'No', explaining that they
did as a matter of fact have things just like our knives, but that these
were actually markers. The equivalent of our word 'knife' would
not exist in their language just because they had a word to name
these objects indistinguishable by such things as shape and colour
from our knives. This is not, of course, to deny that given the use of
knives in a particular community one can have things which are, so
to speak, degenerate knives, used only as ornaments, hung upon the
wall, and perhaps manufactured for this purpose; it is another
matter to suppose that in a community which used knife-like objects
only for the purpose of ornaments the word which names them
would be properly translated as 'knife'.

Where a thing has a function the primary (but by no means necessarily the only) criterion for the goodness of that thing will be that it
fulfils its function well. Thus the primary criterion of goodness in a
knife is its ability to cut well. If a man goes into a shop and asks for
a knife, saying that he wants a good knife, he can be understood as
wanting one that cuts well, and since 'knife' is a functional word in
the strong sense 'good knives cut well' must be held to be some kind
of analytic proposition. Moreover, since 'cutting' is the name of an
operation with a particular point, different, for example, from the

activity of producing noises by running steel over wood, no one is at liberty to pick on just any kind of cutting to count as cutting well. We may compare the activity of writing, and its connection with the goodness of pens. The word 'pen' means something used in writing, and writing is making a set of marks designed to be read; so the minimum condition for a good pen is that it writes legibly. One would not know the meaning of the word 'pen' if one did not know that a good pen had to write well, or the meaning of 'writing' without understanding that good writing had to be writing which it was possible to read.[3]

Knives and pens have functions not only because we use them for a central purpose, but also because they are manufactured for a specific use. But it is obvious that there are examples of words which, without naming manufactured things, are functional in the strong sense: 'eye', for instance, and 'lung' are words like this. Moreover words can be functional in the 'strong' sense without naming anything that we ourselves use or need. Any part of a plant or animal may have a function, and often we would refuse to call by the same name something that played no part, or a quite different part, in the life of the living thing. Such things as roots and claws are named in this way.

Are there, in fact, any examples of words naming things which have a function without being functional words in the strong sense? I suppose that this would be the case where the function of some organ was discovered, but it was not renamed. We ask, for instance, 'Has the appendix a function?', and an affirmative answer would surely give us a contingent proposition, at least for a time. A good appendix would thereafter be judged by its ability to perform this function well, but we could not be expected to know what, if anything, had to be done well in knowing the meaning of the word.

It has been common for philosophers to call all words which allow one to derive criteria of goodness from their meaning 'functional words'. This is confusing, for it suggests either a quite improper use of the word 'function' or the denial of clear examples for which the condition stated in the last sentence is fulfilled. This may be seen by considering expressions such as 'good farmer', 'good rider' and

---

[3] Things are not, of course, really as simple as this paragraph might suggest. Some people (hunters, for instance) use their knives as much for stabbing as cutting, and cutting will not be the primary function of their knives. There are also derivative concepts such as 'palette-knife' to be explained. But I do not think that complications of this kind will affect my main point.

'good liar'. Neither 'farmer', 'rider' nor 'liar' picks a man out by reference to a *function*, though of course they name him in respect of something that he does. It would be comic to speak of the function of a rider or a liar, and we can only think of a farmer as having a function if we think of him in some special way as serving the community. In any ordinary context we should be puzzled if asked for the function of a farmer, thinking that the questioner must mean something very odd. But although words such as 'farmer', 'rider' and 'liar' are not functional words, in either the weak or the strong sense, when joined with 'good' they yield criteria of goodness as functional words were seen to do. We say that a man is a good farmer only because of his farming, while what counts as good farming must be e.g. maintaining crops and herds in healthy condition, and obtaining the maximum from the soil. What is good farming will naturally vary somewhat from place to place: a nomadic race could exhaust a piece of land in farming it, though a settled race could not. But within such limits the standards by which farming is judged depend on the meaning of the word, since what counts in farming is only something which has a particular point. If in another community there was an activity (let us call is 'snodding'), and people said that a man snodded well, and was a good snodder, when plants and animals died when in his charge, we should not consider translating 'snodding' as 'farming'; perhaps a snodder would be a black magician or something like that. Similarly, a good liar must tell convincing or artistic untruths, and the minimum condition of good riding is an ability to control a horse.

These examples show that the range of words whose meaning determines criteria of goodness is much wider than that of functional words. And perhaps the range is even greater than these examples suggest. We might consider whether, for instance, 'daughter', 'father' and 'friend' might not be added to the list. It might seem that since 'daughter' simply means 'female offspring' nothing is laid down in the language about the criteria of goodness in daughters, as nothing is laid down about the meaning of 'good female offspring' – if this has a meaning at all. Is it, however, true that a word in another language would be translated by our word 'daughter' whatever the criteria of goodness for those named by this name? Does it make sense to say that they speak of good daughters, but judge daughters on quite different grounds? Of course it will depend on the structure of a particular society – its economic arrangements for instance, and its marriage rules – as to just what is expected of daughters, and to this extent at least what counts as being a good daughter can vary from place to place. But surely it is wrong to suppose that even anything expected of a female offspring could be part of what counted when the goodness of a daughter was being weighed. If it were expected, as in Nazi Germany, that a daughter (like a son) should denounce disloyal parents to the police, this still could not be part of being a good *daughter*; a word which combined with 'good' to give this result would be closer to our word 'citizen' or 'patriot'. Only in the context of a belief that denunciation would lead to regeneration could this be seen as one of the things by which the goodness of a daughter could be judged.

'Father' seems to be another word of roughly the same kind; for a man can only be said to be a good father if he looks after his children as best he can. Being a good *father* must have something to do with bringing up children, and more specifically caring for them. While opinions may differ as to what is best for children, and while more or less of the children's care may be assigned to parents in different communities, it is only within such limits that the criteria of a good father will differ from place to place. If, in a certain community, a man were said to be a good *A* in so far as he offered his children up for sacrifice, '*A*' could not be translated by our word 'father', but would be like 'citizen' again, or 'provider of children for the state'. Similarly, a good *friend* must be one who is well disposed towards the man whose friend he is; it makes no sense to say that he would be a good friend in so far as he cheated the other, or left him in the lurch. One interesting point about being a good father, daughter, or friend is that it seems to depend on one's intentions, rather than on such things as cleverness and strength. No one could be counted a bad father because he failed to make a living, though he tried as hard as he could. Similarly, the best of daughters might lack the capacity to provide for aged parents, while good friends are those who want to help us rather than those who actually have the capacity to succeed. That is not to deny that in such a context much may be held against people besides the things they *intended* to do, and that it is hard to know where to draw the line, but if for instance someone were said to be a bad friend on grounds of tactless or obtuse behaviour, it would be a fault of character and not mere lack of cleverness which was involved. On investigation we might decide that 'father', 'daughter' and 'friend' should be called moral terms, especially if we thought that a wholly good man could not be bad in any of these respects.

We have now described two classes of words whose meaning determines criteria of goodness for the things they name: functional words such as 'knife', 'pen', eye' and 'root', and non-functional words such as 'farmer', liar' and 'father'. This is not, however, the only way in which criteria of goodness are fixed; they can be just as determinate, leaving the individual as little scope for decision, in cases where it would be impossible to get them from the meaning of a word. We have mentioned one example of this kind in speaking of things that have a function, but are not named in respect of their function, and there will be many more. Take, for instance, the word 'coal'. The question is 'What could be counted as good coal?' and the answer seems to be that depends on what coal happens to be used for. 'Happens to be used for' is the right expression here, though it would not have been had we still been talking about knives or pens. For it makes sense to suppose that in some other community coal – the same stuff – was mined as we mine it but used quite differently, for some magical or ornamental purpose perhaps. Because of these different purposes, what counts as good coal here might count as bad coal there, though within either community prospectors and coal merchants must take these purposes into account in promising their customers good coal. Within each society the goodness of coal is settled by the purposes for which coal is used, while outside such a context it is not clear how anyone could talk about coal as good or bad at all.

There will obviously be many cases of this sort, where the criteria of goodness are fixed by the use to which the thing is usually put; but there is another range of examples rather like this where it would be better to speak of the interest we have in something, and what we expect from it, than the use to which it is put. We do not, for instance, *use* works of literature, or not normally, and could not say that it is by their use that the criteria for their goodness are determined. On the other hand, the interest which we have in books and pictures determines the grounds on which their excellence is judged. Just as we cannot consider the question 'Is this a good piece of coal?' without taking into account the use which we have for coal, so we cannot consider the criteria of goodness in books and pictures without noticing the part which literature and art play in a civilisation such as ours. First of all, we treat works of art very seriously, and while we may expect to enjoy reading a good novel or looking at a good picture, we are prepared to take trouble about them. We study pictures, and may learn new languages to read works of literature, all of which depends on the fact that we expect a lot from such things. We expect them to interest us profoundly, and this must have something to do with the fact that we are not allowed to give as support for a judgement of aesthetic merit the mere fact that a book passes the time easily, or makes us cry, or cheers us up. That when we speak about a good book or picture we do very often mean to judge it as a work of art depends on the role which these things have, though perhaps only in the lives of a minority whose word has become law. Obviously it would be possible to imagine a society in which things would be quite different, where, for instance, pictures though hung on the walls were never looked at with concentration except by chance. Pictures might in fact be treated rather as we usually treat wall-paper, as a cheerful background decoration which should not demand full attention for itself. There are thus some similarities between 'a good picture' and 'a good piece of coal', and in neither case can someone seize on anything he likes as the criteria of goodness and badness, justifying his use of the word 'good' by pointing to his own choices. He might resolve to read only novels which would soon send him to sleep, and might choose them only for this reason, but he could not say that for him this was the characteristic which made a novel a good novel.

This is not, however, to deny that sometimes a particular man's interests determine what is good and bad. For it is always possible to speak of an *A* as being 'a good *A* for *X*'s purposes', when the criteria of goodness may be quite different from those by which the goodness of *A*'s is judged. But since it is one thing to speak of 'a good *A*' and another to speak of 'a good *A* for so-and-so's purposes' this cannot be used to show anything about the use of the former expression. Nor does it give us a case in which criteria of goodness have to be *decided upon* by the man who uses the word 'good'. He can choose what he will try to do, which games he will play, and so on; but given his purposes, and in general his interests, it is a plain matter of fact that particular *A*'s will be good *for his purposes*, or *from his point of view*. In such a context he will be able to attach the word 'good' even to such things as pebbles or twigs, implying 'for my purposes' or 'for someone playing this game'. But even here it is not by his readiness to pick up the pebbles that he legitimises his words.

Where then are the cases to be found in which someone can simply decide to take anything he likes as criteria of goodness for a certain kind of thing? A perfect example might seem to be that of the show dog pronounced by the judge to be 'better' than others of his breed because of some fancy quality such as length of ears. Here the standard may be simply conventional; it is decided, in some more or less deliberate way, that a twist in the tail or an extra inch

on the ears shall be a criterion of goodness in a particular breed.
There is usually no point in picking on these characteristics; it is
not a matter of beauty or strength in the animal, but simply what
we have decided to call 'good'. This case belongs with a number of
others which we might call 'competition examples', belonging to the
game of 'Let's see who can do this'. Suppose, for instance, that
people decide, for a joke, to see who can produce something – say
the longest sentence containing only Anglo-Saxon words, or the
musical instrument which will produce the lowest note. Then,
although there may be no point in having such instruments or such
sentences, there is a point in producing one once the competition
has been set, and it is by its ability to serve as a good entry in the
competition that the sentence or instrument is then judged good.
That long ears can be one of the criteria of goodness in a spaniel
depends entirely on the competition element in the breeding of
show dogs. If we take away this background, and suppose that someone says 'Good spaniels have long ears', it will not be clear what he
means. It is true that in such cases a man who is in a special position
can lay down standards quite arbitrarily, but he must be in the
position of setting the competition, so that when he says 'This is to
be the mark of a good *X*' he means 'This is the target you are to try
to hit'. In one sense the man who is allowed to choose the target
decides 'what shall be the criterion of a good shot', but in another
sense he does not; the criterion of a good shot is that it should hit
the target, and he merely chooses what the target shall be.

What has just been said may be applied to the discussion of statements about good cacti in Hare's *Language of Morals*.[4] Hare sup-
poses that someone has just imported the first cactus into the country,
and that since no one has ever seen them before no one has yet
called one cactus good and another bad. But other people bring
them in too, and eventually someone claims that his is a good cactus;
he sets up standards for cacti, and people may set up rival standards
of their own. This is all quite possible, but what Hare does not give
us is the necessary background, and as he describes it, it is not clear
how the criteria could be criteria of *goodness* at all. There is no
reference to the fact that a cactus is a living organism, which can
therefore be called healthy or unhealthy, and a good or bad speci-
men of its kind. But in that case we must be told what the role of
the cacti is to be. If they are to be used as ornaments, then good cacti
must possess the kind of shape and colour that we find pleasing or
curious, and the criteria of goodness are determined by the interest

[4] Pp. 96–7.

which we have in the things, and not by any standard set up by the importer. If, on the other hand, cacti are to be collected and grown for cactus shows, standards may be *set*, but only by those who are in some special position of authority. In this case we have 'a competition example', and this will hardly seem suitable as a model for the use of 'good' in moral contexts.

The reason why it seems as if choice alone, or some condition connected with choice, might be a sufficient condition for the use of the word 'good' probably lies in certain facts about the concept of choice. First, choosing is not just pointing at something; for while even pointing is not simply extending one's hand in the direction of a certain object, given our institution of pointing I can say, 'Point to one of the windows in this room' without giving any idea of what if anything is to happen next. Whereas if I said 'Choose one of the windows in this room' the question would be 'For what?' It would hardly count as choosing if people made pointing gestures, or touched particular objects, and nothing followed, or was meant to follow. It may look as if choosing could be just distinguishing, or marking, or separating out, because we are used to games in which people are told for instance to choose a card, and they do not necessarily know what they are choosing it for. But there are two points to notice about this example:

(1) The context of a card trick does tell us roughly the role which the chosen card will play, and children who were used to choosing sweets and toys, not knowing about card tricks, might be puzzled when asked to choose a card.

(2) Choosing for a role which is kept secret is itself a kind of game. But then the whole point is that X knows the role but is keeping it from Y; it is not a case of choosing but not for anything, but rather of choosing 'for whatever X has in mind'.

So when one chooses one chooses for a role. One chooses something to have, or to throw away, to sit on, or to put in the mantelpiece; a road to drive down or to have closed. But now the question arises – will anything that happens as the intended consequence of the distinguishing gesture do as the role for which one is choosing the thing? Suppose, for instance, that someone said 'Choose a window pane for me to put my finger on' or 'Choose a pebble to have a handkerchief waved at it.' Could these things be the object of choice? One is inclined to say that choosing is rather the kind of picking out for a role, which has a ground; we choose one thing rather than another because it has some advantage in the context, as a flat pebble is best for playing ducks and drakes, and a heavy stone to stop a car from running downhill. There are, indeed, what we might call peripheral cases of choosing, when we 'just pick' a card from the pack for instance, or take any one of a number of objects which would serve equally well. But a word which applies *only* to such activities would not properly be translated by our word 'choice', and we are inclined to say in such cases that 'there was nothing to choose' between the alternatives. In any case these are certainly not the examples which we have in mind when we think that there is a very close connection between choosing something and calling it good. For in so far as the choosing was supposed to be choosing of this kind it is not guaranteed that the word 'good' will be given an application by the connection with choice. However strictly a man might set himself to choose a card in a certain position in the pack when told to 'choose a card' by someone showing a card trick, we should not be able to describe him as thinking cards in this position the best cards or the best cards to take unless he were prepared to *justify* his choice. And he could only do that by asserting, for instance, that this was the best card to take in order to beat the trick. He could never say, 'Those just are, to my mind, the best ones to take.'

In the beginning we raised two questions about the relation between choosing something and calling it good, asking whether some connection with choice (1) could give a sufficient condition, and (2) was a necessary condition for the application of the word. The rest of this paper will be about question (2).

It is very often said that the use of 'good' in its 'proper evaluative sense' commits a man to choosing the things he calls good in preference to others, or at least that 'other things being equal' this is what he must do. Such statements are quite misleading in so far as they suggest that a man is only at liberty to call an *A* a good *A* if he thinks that such *A*'s are *A*'s he has reason to choose. Consider, for example, someone who is choosing a pen. Since a good pen is one which will write well, he will have reason to choose a good pen if he wants to write with it and to write well. But what if his purposes are different? Suppose that he wishes to cover a piece of paper with blots? Perhaps we might say that he is not choosing a pen to write with, and so not as a pen, hoping to keep the connection between good pens and the pens which a man should choose (other things being equal) if he is choosing a pen as a pen. But there is also the case of the man who wants a pen to write with, but has some reason for wanting to write untidily or illegibly, or to whom it does not matter either way. We could hardly say that he was not choosing a pen as a pen, and he would have no reason to choose a good pen, perhaps rather the reverse. That most men must have a reason to choose good pens depends on the purposes which we take for granted in talking about good and bad pens at all: we cannot suppose that the standard case is that of wanting pens for the creation of blots, or undecipherable marks without dissociating pens from writing, and changing the concept *pen*. The necessary connection lies here, and not in some convention about what the individual speaker must be ready to choose if he uses the word 'good'.

There seems to be an exact parallel in the case where 'good' is used with a word such as 'rider', naming a man in respect of some activity with a characteristic point. (It is only where the activity has a point that we can speak of a good -er or a bad; there are no good foot-wagglers, or tree-touchers, because nothing counts as doing these things well.) Since the point of riding is pleasure, exercise, or locomotion, riders are judged good or bad by their ability to do such things as staying in the saddle and controlling the horse, with additional requirements of elegance and style. Anyone who shares the typical purposes of the rider has a reason to ride well rather than badly, and will want to be a good rider rather than a bad. But it is quite possible for someone to be riding with different purposes in view; perhaps he wants to play the fool and make people laugh. It is tempting to say that anyone must be called a good rider if he is achieving what he wants, but on reflection one sees that this is not 'the language of mankind'. Good riding is the kind of riding likely to achieve the characteristic purposes of the rider, not those which a particular individual may happen to have.

In such cases the point of the activity lies in something commonly wanted by the man who engages in it, but there are other things normally done for hire. Then the one who hires is the one who has a direct interest in what is done, and will normally want it done well. For instance, someone going to a tailor, or engaging a teacher, will usually have reason to choose a good one, though here again we cannot say that there is a necessary connection between calling an *A* a good *A* and having reasons for choice. For someone may choose a teacher, and even choose him as a teacher – that is with an interest in his teaching – without wanting the teaching to be done well. A wicked uncle choosing a tutor for his nephew would be a case in point.

If this is a correct account of the connection that there is between calling an *A* a good *A* and chosing it where an *A* is something that we use, or where '*A*' is the name of a man who does something that he or others want done, it is not surprising that the word 'good' can sometimes be used without any implications for choice. For where there is no connection with anything that we use, or need, or want doing, the *A* that is called good may be one that *no one* has reason to choose. We say, in a straightforward way, that a tree has good roots, meaning by this that they are well suited to the performance of their function, serving the plant by anchoring it and drawing moisture out of the soil. Our interests are not involved, and only someone in the grip of a theory would insist that when we speak of a good root we commit ourselves in some way to choosing a root like that. Nor do we need to look for such a connection in order to find 'what is common' to the different cases where we apply the word 'good'. Because the root plays a part in the life of the organism we can say 'it has a function', relating what it does to the welfare of the plant. And good roots are like good eyes, good pens, and many other things that are good, in being of the kind to perform their function well.

If someone should say that in the expression 'a good root' 'good' is not used 'evaluatively' this would only increase the artificiality of the notion of 'evaluation' as used in moral philosophy, and it would raise a number of awkward problems as well. For if the 'good' in 'good roots' is said to lack 'evaluative meaning' because good roots are not things that we should have any reason to choose, then presumably 'good claws' and 'good fangs' are expressions which must be treated in the same way. But then we shall be in difficulties over examples such as 'good eyes', 'good muscles' and 'good stomachs'. We could hardly say that the meaning of 'good' changes when the word is applied to those parts of organisms which can belong to our bodies; it would seem therefore that if 'good roots' and 'good claws' are non-evaluative expressions, 'good eyes' must be the same.

Nor is it easy to see how a distinction between 'evaluative' and 'non-evaluative' uses of 'good' would be applied in cases such as that of the good pen. I suppose it would be said that one who, wanting to write illegibly, rejected the pen he called a good pen, must use the word in its 'non-evaluative sense'. This case might seem easy to decide, but what of a man discussing the merits of something like a pen or a motor car in the abstract, as people often do? What criteria would we introduce for deciding whether he was using 'good' evaluatively or not? Should we take into account his last choice, or his next choice, or the choices he made in the majority of cases, or what he thought he would choose if he were to choose just now? If he himself had no use for the kind of thing under discussion the last clause would lack a definite sense. And in any case it seems entirely arbitrary, and unimportant, that any particular decision should be made. The man who calls roots good roots uses 'good' in a straightforward sense, which has nothing to do with the irony or reported speech marked by the use of inverted commas. So too does the man who calls a pen a good pen, and says that being a good one it is not one that he has any reason to choose.

The conclusion seems to be that a connection with the choices of the speaker is not a necessary condition of the use of the word 'good' in its ordinary sense. If a man who calls an *A* a good *A* has reason, other things being equal, to prefer it to other *A*'s, this is because of the kind of thing that an *A* is, and its connection with his wants and needs. It is clear that most people will have reason to choose good pens and good knives if they are choosing pens and knives, and that they will have reason to try to ride well if they are riding, and to tell good lies if they are going in for lying. But this is because the word 'good' is here joined to the name of objects or activities which are characteristically chosen with given ends in view. It is not nearly so easy to see just when someone will have reason for choosing to be, or to have, a good *A* where '*A*' is e.g. 'parent' or 'daughter' or 'friend'. Since the most basic needs and desires are involved here it is not at all surprising that the word 'good' should have an application in cases like these; but while there will often be obvious reason to be given for choosing to be, or to have, a good *A*, when '*A*' is a word in this range, it is impossible to say offhand how far these reasons will extend. Anyone may properly ask why he should choose to have, or to be, the kind of *A* he has called a good *A*, and we may or may not be able to give him a reply.

XXI On morality's having a point

D. Z. Phillips and H. O. Mounce

In 1958, moral philosophers were given rather startling advice. They were told that their subject was not worth pursuing further until they possessed an adequate philosophy of psychology.[1] What is needed, they were told, is an enquiry into what type of characteristic a virtue is, and, furthermore, it was suggested that this question could be resolved in part by exploring the connection between what a man ought to do and what he *needs*: perhaps man needs certain things in order to flourish, just as a plant needs water; and perhaps what men need are the virtues, courage, honesty, loyalty, etc. Thus, in telling a man that he ought to be honest, we should not be using any special (moral) sense of ought: a man ought to be honest just as a plant ought to be watered. The 'ought' is the same: it tells us what a man needs.

Those who agree with the above advice must be pleased at the way things have gone since. Its implications have been worked out in some detail by Philippa Foot in a number of influential papers.[2] The attack on the naturalistic fallacy which it involves has been welcomed by a contemporary defender of Utilitarianism.[3] Strong support for a deductive argument from facts to values has come from a leading American philosopher,[4] while agreement with this general approach in ethics can be found in the work of a recent Gifford lecturer, who, amid all the varieties of goodness, cannot find a peculiar *moral* sense of 'good'.[5] Also, contemporary philosophers have been prompted to explore the connections between morality

[1] Paper XVIII.
[2] See Papers XIX and XX and 'Moral Arguments' in *Mind*, LXVII (1958).
[3] See Mary Warnock's Introduction to *Utilitarianism*, Fontana ed. (1962) p. 31.
[4] Paper X.
[5] G. H. von Wright, *The Varieties of Goodness* (Routledge 1963).

and prudence,[6] and even to express the hope that past masters will have a salutary influence on the future relationship between philosophy and psychology.[7] It seems fair to say that the advice of 1958 has produced a climate of opinion, a way of doing moral philosophy. For this reason, it is all the more important to expose the radical misunderstanding involved in it.

I

It has come to be thought important once again in ethics to ask for the point of morality. Why does it matter whether one does one thing rather than another? Surely, it is argued, if one wants to show someone why it is his duty to do something, one must be prepared to point out the importance of the proposed action, the harm involved in failing to do it, and the advantage involved in performing it. Such considerations simply cannot be put aside. On the contrary, the point of moral conduct must be elucidated in terms of the reasons for performing it. Such reasons separate moral arguments from persuasion and coercion, and moral judgements from likes and dislikes; they indicate what constitutes human good and harm.

If we take note of the role of reasons in morality, we shall see that not anything can count as a moral belief. After all, why does one regard some rules as moral principles, and yet never regard others as such? Certainly, we *can* see the point of some rules as moral principles, but in the case of other rules we cannot. How is the point seen? There is much in the suggestion that it is to be appreciated in terms of the backgrounds which attend moral beliefs and principles.[8] When rules which claim to be moral rules are devoid of these backgrounds we are puzzled. We do not know what is being said when someone claims that the given rule is a moral rule.

Normally, we do not speak of these backgrounds when we express and discuss moral opinions. It is only when we are asked to imagine their absence that we see how central they must be in any account we try to give of morality. Consider the rules, 'Never walk on the lines of a pavement', and 'Clap your hands every two hours'. If we

⁶ See R. S. Peters and A. S. Phillips Griffiths: 'The Autonomy of Prudence', in *Mind*, LXXI (1962).

⁷ See Richard Wollheim's Introduction to Bradley's *Ethical Studies*, O.U.P. paperback ed. (1962), p. xvi.

⁸ See Mrs Foot's excellent paper, 'When Is A Principle A Moral Principle?', in *Proceedings of the Aristotelian Society*, supp. vol. XXVIII (1954).

saw people letting such rules govern their lives in certain ways, taking great care to observe them, feeling upset whenever they or other people infringe the rules, and so on, we should be hard put to understand what they were doing. We fail to see any point in it. On the other hand, if backgrounds are supplied for such rules, if further descriptions of the context in which they operate are given, sometimes, they can begin to look like moral principles. Given the background of a religious community, one can begin to see how the rule, 'Never walk on the lines of a pavement', could have moral significance. Think of, 'Take off thy shoes for thou art on holy ground', and its connections with the notions of reverence and disrespect. It is more difficult, though we do not say it is impossible, to think of a context in which the rule, 'Clap your hands every two hours', could have moral significance. Our first example shows how we can be brought to some understanding of a moral view when it is brought under a concept with which we are familiar. By linking disapproval of walking on the lines of a pavement with lack of reverence and disrespect, even those not familiar with the religious tradition in question may see that a *moral* view is being expressed. Such concepts as sincerity, honesty, courage, loyalty, respect, and, of course, a host of others, provide the kind of background necessary in order to make sense of rules as moral principles. It does not follow that all the possible features of such backgrounds need be present in every case. The important point to stress is that unless the given rule has *some* relation to such backgrounds, we would not know what is meant by calling it a moral principle.

The above conclusion follows from a more extensive one, namely, that commendation is internally related to its object. Mrs Foot, for example, suggests that there is an analogy between commendation on the one hand, and mental attitudes such as pride and beliefs such as 'This is dangerous' on the other. One cannot feel proud of *anything*, any more than one can say that *anything* is dangerous. Similarly in the case of commendation: how can one say that clapping one's hands every two hours is a good action? The answer is that one cannot, unless the context in which the action is performed, for example, recovery from paralysis, makes its point apparent.

Certainly, those who have insisted on the necessity of a certain conceptual background in order to make sense of moral beliefs and moral judgements have done philosophy a service. They have revealed the artificiality of locating what is characteristically moral in a mental attitude such as a pro-attitude, or in a mental activity such as commending. They have shown the impossibility of making sense of something called 'evaluative meaning' which is thought of as being externally or contingently related to its objects. One could have a pro-attitude towards clapping one's hands every two hours, and one could commend one's never walking on the lines of a pavement, but neither pro-attitude nor commendation would, in themselves, give a point to such activities.

If the point of virtues is not to be expressed in terms of pro-attitudes or commendations, how is it to be brought out? It has been suggested that this could be done by showing the connection between virtues and human good and harm. But this is where the trouble starts, for if we are not careful, we may, in our eagerness to exorcise the spirit of evaluative meaning, fall under the spell of the concept of human good and harm, which is an equally dangerous idea. Unfortunately, this has already happened, and much of the current talk about human good and harm is as artificial as the talk about 'attitudes' in moral philosophy which it set out to criticise.

The point of calling an action (morally) good, it is suggested, is that it leads to human good and avoids harm. Further, what is to count as human good and harm is said to be a *factual* matter. Thus, one must try to show that there is a logical connection between statements of fact and statements of value, and that the logical gap supposed to exist between them can be closed. Men cannot pick and choose which facts are relevant to a moral conclusion, any more than they can pick and choose which facts are relevant in determining a physical ailment. Admittedly, the notion of a fact is a complex one, but this makes it all the more important to exercise care in the use of it. Let us try to appreciate this complexity in terms of an example.

Someone might think that pushing someone roughly is rude, and that anyone who denies this is simply refusing to face the facts. But this example, as it stands, is worthless, since it tells one nothing of the context in which the pushing took place. The reference to the context is all important in giving an account of the action, since not any kind of pushing can count as rudeness. Consider the following examples:

(a) One man pushing another person violently in order to save his life.

(b) A doctor pushing his way through a football-match crowd in response to an urgent appeal.

(c) The general pushing which takes place in a game of rugby.

(d) A violent push as a customary form of greeting between close friends.

In all these cases, pushing someone else is not rude. If someone took offence at being pushed, he might well see in the light of the situation that no offence had been caused. But what of situations where there is general agreement that an offence *has* been caused? Is the offence a fact from which a moral conclusion can be deduced? Clearly not, since what this suggestion ignores is the fact that *standards already prevail* in the context in which the offence is recognised. If one wants to call the offence a fact, one must recognise that it is a fact which already has moral import. The notion of 'offence' is parasitic on the notion of a standard or norm, although these need not be formulated. The person who wishes to say that the offence is a 'pure fact' from which a moral conclusion can be deduced is simply confused. What are the 'pure facts' relating to the pushing and the injury it is supposed to cause? A physiological account of the pushing (which might be regarded as pure enough) would not enable one to say what was going on, any more than a physiological account of the injury would tell us anything about what moral action (if any) is called for as a result. It makes all the difference morally whether the grazed ankle is caused by barging in the line-out or by barging in the bus queue. Any attempt to characterise the fact that an offence has been caused as a non-evaluative fact from which a moral conclusion can be deduced begs the question, since in asserting that a *kind of offence* has been caused, a specific background and the standards inherent in it have already been invoked.

But our opponent is still not beaten. He might give way on the confusion involved in the talk about deducing moral conclusions from 'pure facts', and agree that 'pushing' does not constitute rudeness in all contexts. Nevertheless, he might argue, where the circumstances *are* appropriate, it is possible to determine the rudeness of an action in a way which will settle any disagreement. But, again, this is clearly not the case. Whenever anyone says, 'That action is rude', there is no logical contradiction involved in denying the assertion, since although two people may share a moral concept such as rudeness, they may still differ strongly in its application. This is possible because views about rudeness do not exist *in vacuo*, but are often influenced by *other* moral beliefs. A good example of disagreement over the application of the concept of rudeness can be found in Malcolm's Memoir of Wittgenstein. Wittgenstein had lost his temper in a philosophical discussion with Moore, and would not allow Moore sufficient time to make his point. Moore thought that Wittgenstein's behaviour was rude, holding that good manners should always prevail, even in philosophical discussion. Wittgenstein, on the other hand, thought Moore's view of the matter absurd: philosophy is a serious business, important enough to justify a loss of temper; to think this rudeness is simply to misapply the judgement. Here, one can see how standards of rudeness have been influenced by wider beliefs; in other words, how the judgement, 'That is rude', is not entailed by the facts.

The position we have arrived at does not satisfy a great many contemporary moral philosophers. They are not prepared to recognise the possibility of permanent radical moral disagreement. They want to press on towards ultimate agreement, moral finality, call it what you will. They propose to do this by considering certain non-moral concepts of goodness in the belief that they will throw light on the notion of human good and harm. The non-moral example, 'good knife', has been popular in this respect. The word 'knife' names an object in respect of its function. Furthermore, the function is involved in the meaning of the word, so that if we came across a people who possessed objects which looked exactly like knives, but who never used these objects as we use them, we should refuse to say that they had the concept of a knife. Now when a thing has a function, the main criterion for its goodness will be that it serves that function well. Clearly, then, not anything can count as a good knife. But how does this help our understanding of moral goodness? Moral concepts are not functional. One can see what is to count as a good knife by asking what a knife is *for*, but can one see the point of generosity in the same way? To ask what generosity is *for* is simply to vulgarise the concept; it is like thinking that 'It is more blessed to give than to receive' is some kind of policy!

Yet, although moral concepts are not functional words, they are supposed to resemble them in important respects. The interesting thing, apparently, about many non-functional words, is that when they are linked with 'good' they yield criteria of goodness in much the same way as 'good knife' and other functional words do. For example, it seems as if 'good farmer' might yield criteria of goodness in this way. After all, farming is an activity which has a certain point. To call someone a good farmer will be to indicate that he has fulfilled the point of that activity. What 'the point' amounts to can be spelled out in terms of healthy crops and herds, and a good yield from the soil. The philosophical importance of these examples is that they show that the range of words whose meaning provides criteria of goodness extends beyond that of functional words. But what if the range is even wider than these examples suggest? It is

clear what the philosophers who ask this question have in mind:
what if the meaning of moral concepts could yield criteria of goodness
in the same way? If this were possible, one need not rest content
with expounding 'good knife' or 'good farmer'; 'good man' awaits
elucidation. The goal is to find out what constitutes human flourishing. Furthermore, once these greater aims are achieved, all moral
disputes would be, in principle at least, resolvable. Anyone claiming
to have a good moral argument would have to justify it by showing
its point in terms of human good and harm. And, once again, not
anything could count as human good and harm.

The programme is nothing if not ambitious. Unfortunately, it will
not work. The reason why is no minor defect: the whole enterprise
is misconceived almost from the start. As far as land farming is
concerned, the confusion could have been avoided had one asked
why 'farming' yields criteria when joined with 'good'. To say that
this type of farming is an activity which has a point, that farming
serves some end, and that to call someone a good farmer is to say
that he achieves this end, is only to tell part of the story. The most
important part is left out, namely, *that the end in question is not in
dispute*. That is why it makes sense to talk of experts in farming, and
why problems in farming can be solved by technical or scientific
means. For example, farmers might disagree over which is the best
method of growing good wheat, but there is no disagreement over
what is to count as good wheat. On the other hand, the situation is
different where animal farming is concerned. Suppose it were established that the milk yield was not affected by keeping the cattle
indoors in confined quarters, and by cutting their food supply.[9]
Many people would say that no good farmer would be prepared to
do this, despite the economic factors involved. Others may disagree
and see nothing wrong in treating animals in this way. The point to
note is that here one has a *moral* dispute. We recognise it as such
because of the issues of cruelty, care, and expediency involved in it.
The dispute cannot be settled by reference to the point of farming
in this instance, since it is agreed that whichever side one takes, the
milk yield remains the same. One must recognise that there are
different conceptions of what constitutes good farming. Similarly,
we shall find that there is no common agreement on what constitutes
human good and harm. We shall argue presently that human good is
not independent of the moral beliefs people hold, but is determined
by them. In short, what must be recognised is that there are different
conceptions of human good and harm.

[9] We owe this example to Dr H. S. Price.

II

The above argument would not satisfy the philosophers we have in mind. For them, moral views are founded on facts, the facts concerning human good and harm. We shall argue, on the other hand, that moral viewpoints determine what is and what is not to count as a relevant fact in reaching a moral decision. This philosophical disagreement has important consequences, for if we believe that moral values can be justified by appeal to *the* facts, it is hard to see how one man can reject another man's reasons for his moral beliefs, since these reasons too, presumably, refer to the facts. If, on the other hand, we hold that the notion of factual relevance is parasitic on moral beliefs, it is clear that deadlock in ethics will be a common occurrence, simply because of what some philosophers have unwisely regarded as contingent reasons, namely, the different moral views people hold.

Many philosophers are not convinced that there need be a breakdown in moral argument. It is tempting to think that anyone who has heard *all* the arguments in favour of a moral opinion cannot still ask why he ought to endorse it, any more than anyone who has heard all there is to say about the earth's shape can still ask why he ought to believe that the earth is round. Anyone who has heard *all* the reasons for a moral opinion has, it seems, heard all the facts. Sometimes the facts are difficult to discern, but there is in principle no reason why moral disagreement should persist. Therefore, it is difficult to see how 'x is good' can be a well-founded moral argument when 'x is bad' is said to be equally well founded. So runs the argument.

Certainly, it is difficult for philosophers who argue in this way to account for moral disagreement, since for them, moral judgements are founded on the facts of human good and harm, and the facts are incontrovertible. It is not surprising to find Bentham being praised in this context, since he too alleged that there is a common coinage into which 'rival' moral views could be cashed. The rivalry is only apparent, since the felicific calculus soon discovers the faulty reasoning. On this view, moral opinions are hypotheses whose validity is tested by reference to some common factor which is the sole reason for holding them. Bentham said the common factor was pleasure; nowadays it is called human good and harm. Whether one's moral views are 'valid' depends on whether they lead to human good and

harm. But how does one arrive at these facts? One is said to do so
by asking the question, 'What is the point?' often enough.

Philosophers are led to argue in this way by misconstruing the
implications of the truth that a certain conceptual background is
necessary in order for beliefs to have moral significance. Instead of
being content to locate the point of such beliefs in their moral goodness, they insist on asking further what the point of *that* is. If one
does not give up questioning too soon, one will arrive at the incontrovertible facts of human good and harm which do not invite any
further requests for justification. Injury seems to be thought of as
one such final halting place. To ask what is the point of calling
injury a bad thing is to show that one has not grasped the concept of
injury. To say that an action leads to injury is to give *a* reason for
avoiding it. Injury may not be an overriding reason for avoiding the
action which leads to it, as injustice is, but its being *a* reason is
justified because injury is necessarily a bad thing. Even if we grant
the distinction between reasons and overriding reasons, which is
difficult enough if one asks who is to say which are which, is it clear
that injury is always a reason for avoiding the action which leads
to it?

The badness of injury, it is argued, is made explicit if one considers what an injury to hands, eyes, or ears, prevents a man from
doing and getting; the badness is founded on what all men want.
Mrs Foot, for example, expounds the argument as follows,

> ... the proper use of his limbs is something a man has reason to
> want if he wants anything.
> I do not know just what someone who denies this proposition
> could have in mind. Perhaps he is thinking of changing the facts
> of human existence, so that merely wishing, or the sound of the
> voice, will bring the world to heel? More likely he is proposing to
> rig the circumstances of some individual's existence within the
> framework of the ordinary world, by supposing for instance that
> he is a prince whose servants will sow and reap and fetch and
> carry for him, and so use their hands and eyes in his service that
> he will not need the use of his.[10]

But, Mrs Foot argues, not even this supposition will do, since the
prince cannot foresee that his circumstances will not change. He still
has good reason to avoid injury to his hands and eyes, since he may
need them some day. But there was no need to have thought up such
an extravagant example to find objections to the view that injury is
necessarily bad. There are more familiar ones close at hand which

[10] Above, p. 207.

are far more difficult to deal with than the case of the fortunate prince. For example, consider the following advice,

> And if thine eye offend thee, pluck it out, and cast it from thee: it is better to enter into life with one eye, rather than having two eyes to be cast into hell fire. (Matt. xviii. 9.)

Or again, consider how Saint Paul does not think 'the thorn in the flesh' from which he suffered to be a bad thing. At first, he does so regard it, and prays that it be taken away. Later, however, he thanks God for his disability, since it was a constant reminder to him that he was not sufficient unto himself. Another example is worth quoting.[11] Brentano was blind at the end of his life. When friends commiserated with him over the harm that had befallen him, he denied that his loss of sight was a bad thing. He explained that one of his weaknesses had been a tendency to cultivate and concentrate on too many diverse interests. Now, in his blindness, he was able to concentrate on his philosophy in a way which had been impossible for him before. We may not want to argue like Saint Paul or Brentano, but is it true that we have no idea what they have in mind?

A readiness to admit that injury might result in incidental gain will not do as an answer to the above argument. True, there would be a gain in being injured if an order went out to put all able-bodied men to the sword, but are we to regard the examples of Saint Paul and Brentano as being in this category? In some peculiar circumstances where this gain could be foreseen, we might even imagine a person seeking injury rather than trying to avoid it. But is this the way we should account for saints who prayed to be partakers in the sufferings of Christ? Obviously not. It is clear that Paul himself does not regard his ailment as something which happens to be useful in certain circumstances. But in any case, why speak of *incidental* gain in any of these contexts, and why speak of the contexts themselves as *peculiar*? In doing so, is not the thesis that injury is necessarily bad being defended by calling any examples which count against it incidental or peculiar? In so far as moral philosophers argue in this way, they lay themselves open to the serious charge which Sorel has made against them:

> The philosophers always have a certain amount of difficulty in seeing clearly into these ethical problems, because they feel the impossibility of harmonising the ideas which are current at a given time in a class, and yet imagine it to be their duty to reduce everything to a unity. To conceal from themselves the fundamental heterogeneity of all this civilised morality, they have recourse

[11] We owe it to Mr Rush Rhees.

to a great number of subterfuges, sometimes relegating to the rank of exceptions, importations, or survivals, everything which embarrasses them. . . .[12]

Is it not the case that we cannot understand Brentano's attitude to his blindness unless we understand the kind of dedication to intellectual enquiry of which he was an example, and the virtues which such dedication demands in the enquirer? Again, we cannot understand Saint Paul's attitude to his ailment unless we understand something of the Hebrew-Christian conception of man's relationship to God, and the notions of insufficiency, dependence, and divine succour, involved in it. These views of personal injury or physical harm cannot be cashed in terms of what all men want. On the contrary, it is the specific contexts concerned, namely, dedication to enquiry and dedication to God, which determine what is to constitute goodness and badness. We can deny this only by elevating one concept of harm as being paradigmatic in much the same way as Bentham elevated one of the internal sentiments. We can say that injury is necessarily bad at the price of favouring one idea of badness.

In so far as philosophers construct a paradigm in their search for 'the unity of the facts of human good and harm', they are not far removed from the so-called scientific rationalists and their talk of proper functions, primary purpose, etc. One of these, in an argument with a Roman Catholic housewife over birth control, stressed the harm which could result from having too many children. He obviously thought that the reference to physical harm clinched the matter. The housewife, on the other hand, stressed the honour a mother has in bringing children into the world. It seems more likely that the scientific rationalist was blind to what the housewife meant by honour, than that she was blind to what he meant by harm. Are we for that reason to call the honour incidental gain?

How would the scientific rationalist and the housewife reach the agreement which some philosophers seem to think inevitable if all the facts were known? It is hard to see how they could without renouncing what they believe in. Certainly, one cannot regard their respective moral opinions as hypotheses which the facts will either confirm or refute, for what would the evidence be? For the rationalist, the possibility of the mother's death or injury, the economic situation of the family, the provision of good facilities for the children, and so on, would be extremely important. The housewife too agrees about providing the good things of life for children, but believes that

[12] Georges Sorel, *Reflections On Violence*, trans. T. E. Hulme (Collier-Macmillan, 1961) pp. 229–30.

one ought to begin by allowing them to enter the world. For her, submission to the will of God, the honour of motherhood, the creation of a new life, and so on, are of the greatest importance. But there is no settling of the issue in terms of some supposed common evidence called human good and harm, since what they differ over is precisely the question of what constitutes human good and harm. The same is true of all fundamental moral disagreements, for example, the disagreement between a pacifist and a militarist. The argument is unlikely to proceed very far before deadlock is reached.

Deadlock in ethics, despite philosophical misgivings which have been voiced, does not entail liberty to argue as one chooses. The rationalist, the housewife, the pacifist, or the militarist, cannot say what they like. Their arguments are rooted in different moral traditions within which there are rules for what can and what cannot be said. Because philosophers believe that moral opinions rest on common evidence, they are forced to locate the cause of moral disagreement in the evidence's complexity: often, experience and imagination are necessary in assessing it. One can imagine someone versed in the views we have been attacking, and sympathetic with them, saying to an opponent in a moral argument, 'If only you could see how wrong you are. If only you had the experience and the imagination to appreciate the evidence for the goodness of the view I am advocating, evidence, which, unfortunately, is too complex for you to master, you would see that what I want is good for you too, since really, all men want it'. Such appeals to 'the common good' or to 'what all men want' are based on conscious or unconscious deception. It may be admitted that the majority of mothers nowadays want to plan the birth of their children, to fit in with the Budget if possible, and regard the rearing of their children as a pause in their careers. But this will not make the slightest difference to the housewife of our previous example. She believes that what the majority wants is a sign of moral decadence, and wants different things. But she does not believe because she wants; she wants because she believes.

The view that there are ways of demonstrating goodness by appeal to evidence which operate *independently* of the various moral opinions people hold is radically mistaken. Sometimes, philosophers seem to suggest that despite the moral differences which separate men, they are really pursuing the same end, namely, what all men want. The notion of what all men want is as artificial as the common evidence which is supposed to support it. There are no theories of goodness.

XXII Descriptivism
R. M. Hare

I

The term 'Descriptivism' was first suggested to me by a phrase of the late Professor Austin's. He refers in two places to what he calls the 'descriptive fallacy' of supposing that some utterance is descriptive when it is not;[1] and, although I agree with him that the word might mislead, it will serve. 'Descriptivism', then, can perhaps be used as a generic name for philosophical theories which fall into this fallacy. I shall, however, be discussing, not descriptivism in general, but the particular variety of it which is at present fashionable in ethics; and I shall not attempt to discuss all forms even of ethical descriptivism, nor, even, all the arguments of those descriptivists whom I shall consider. A sample will be all that there is time for. I cannot claim that my own arguments are original – I am in particularly heavy debt to Mr Urmson and Professor Nowell-Smith; but if old mistakes are resuscitated, it is often impossible to do more than restate, in as clear a way as possible, the old arguments against them. Philosophical mistakes are like dandelions in the garden; however carefully one eradicates them there are sure to be some more next year, and it is difficult to think of novel ways of getting rid of their familiar faces. 'Naturalistas expellas furca, tamen usque recurrent.' But in fact the best implement is still the old fork invented by Hume.

An essential condition for the use of this tool is that there should be a distinction between description and evaluation; and, since the more sophisticated of modern descriptivists sometimes seek to impugn this distinction, I must start by establishing its existence, though I shall not have time to add to what I have said elsewhere about its nature.[2] This problem is very like that concerning the dis-

[1] *Philosophical Papers* (Oxford 1961) p. 71; cf. *How to Do Things with Words* (Oxford 1962) p. 3.
[2] *Language of Morals* (*LM*) (Oxford 1952), esp. ch. 7; *Freedom and Reason* (*FR*) Oxford 1963) pp. 22–7, 51, 56.

tinction between analytic and synthetic (indeed, it is an offshoot of that problem). Both distinctions are useful – indeed essential – tools of the philosopher, and it is no bar to their use that we have not yet achieved a completely clear formal elucidation of their nature.

The fundamental distinction is not that between descriptive and evaluative *terms*, but that between the descriptive and evaluative meaning which a single term may have in a certain context. In order to establish that there is a distinction between descriptive and evaluative meaning, it is not necessary to deny the existence of cases in which it is difficult to say whether a term is being used evaluatively or not. There is a clear distinction between a heap of corn and no corn at all, even though it is hard to say just when the corn that I am piling up has become a heap.[3] The descriptive and evaluative meaning of a term in a given context may be tied to it with varying degrees of tightness (we may be more, or less, sure that one or other of them would or would not get detached if we were faced with varying instances of its use: for example, if the cause to which a man was contributing large sums of money were one which I considered not good but pernicious, would I still say that he was generous?). But for all that, the distinction between descriptive and evaluative meaning may be a perfectly sustainable one.

II

We can show that such a distinction exists, at any rate, if we can isolate one of these two sorts of meaning in a given context, and show that it does not exhaust the meaning of the term in that context. Suppose, for example, that we can show that in a certain context a term has descriptive meaning; and suppose that we can isolate this descriptive meaning by producing another term which could be used in the same context with the same descriptive meaning, but such that the two terms differ in that one has evaluative meaning and the other not; then we shall have established that there can be these two different components in a term's meaning.

Let us suppose that somebody says that a certain wine (let us call it 'Colombey-les-deux-églises 1972') is a good wine. I think it will be obvious that he says that it is a good wine *because* it has a certain taste, bouquet, body, strength, etc. (I shall say 'taste' for

[3] See Cicero, *Lucullus*, 16; Sextus Empiricus, *Adv. Math.* i. 69, 80 and *Hyp. Pyrrh.* ii. 253.

short). But it is equally clear that we do not have a name for precisely the taste which this wine has. A descriptivist might therefore argue as follows (thereby committing the fashionable fallacy of *nullum nomen nullum nominandum*): there is nothing more we can say about this wine, by way of telling somebody what is good about it, or what makes us call it good (which would be to give the descriptive meaning of 'good' in this context); we can only repeat that it is good. It is good because it tastes as it does, admittedly; but this is like saying that a thing is red because it looks as it does. How else could we describe the way it tastes than by saying that it is good? Therefore the description cannot be detached from the evaluation, and the distinction is rendered ineffective.

In this instance, such an argument would not carry conviction. If a descriptivist tried to show, by this means, that the descriptive meaning of 'good' in this context could not be isolated, we should no doubt answer that the difficulty lies only in the non-existence of a *word* for the quality that we are seeking to isolate. But this does not matter, provided that it is possible to coin a word and give it a meaning. This I shall now show how to do. I may point out in passing that, if we did not have the words 'sweet', 'juicy', 'red', 'large', and a few more, it would be impossible, without inventing words, to isolate the descriptive meaning of 'good' in the phrase 'good strawberry'; but this would not stop us saying that the phrase has a descriptive meaning distinct from its evaluative meaning. We should just have to coin a word meaning 'like this strawberry in respect of taste, texture, size, etc.'; and this is what I am now going to do in the 'wine' case.

Let us invent a word, 'ϕ', to stand for that quality of the wine which makes us call it a good wine. The quality is, as I have explained, a complex one. Will you allow me to suppose, also, that (as is not improbable) by the time 1972 wines of this sort begin to be good, the science of aromatics (if that is the right name) will have advanced enough to put the wine-snobs out of business; that is to say, that it will have become possible to manufacture by chemical means additives which, put into cheap wines, will give to them tastes indistinguishable by any human palate from those of expensive wines. We should then have a chemical recipe for producing liquid tasting ϕ. This would make it easy (though even without such scientific advance it would be perfectly possible) to teach somebody to recognise the ϕ taste by lining up samples of liquids tasting ϕ, and others having different tastes, and getting him to taste them, telling him in each case whether the sample tasted ϕ or not. It is worth noticing that I could do this whether or not he was himself disposed to think that these liquids tasted good, or that, if they were wines, they were good wines. He could, that is to say, learn the meaning of 'ϕ' quite independently of his own estimation of the merit of wines having that taste.

It is possible, indeed, that, if he did think that wines having that taste were good wines, he might mistake my meaning; he might think that 'ϕ wine' (the expression whose meaning I was trying to explain to him) meant the same as 'good wine'. It is always possible to make mistakes when a person is trying to explain to one the meaning of a word. But the mistake could be guarded against. I might say to him, 'I want you to understand that, in calling a wine ϕ, I am not thereby commending it or praising it in any way, any more than it is commending it or praising it to say that it is produced by this chemical recipe; I am indeed (for such is my preference) disposed to commend wines which have this taste; but in simply saying that a wine is ϕ I am not thereby commending it any more than I should be if I said that it tasted like vinegar or like water. If my preference (and for that matter everybody else's) changed in such a way that a wine tasting like this was no longer thought any good, and we could do nothing with it but pour it down the drain, we could still go on describing it as ϕ.'

Now it seems to me that the descriptive argument which we are considering depends on what I have just said being quite unintelligible. If a man can understand the explanation of the meaning of 'ϕ', he must reject the descriptivist argument. For if the explanation works, then it is possible to explain the meaning of 'ϕ' ostensively as a descriptive expression; and when this has been done, we can separate out the descriptive from the evaluative meaning of the expression 'good wine' in the sentence 'Colombey 1972 is a good wine'. For it will be possible for two people to agree that Colombey 1972 tastes ϕ, but disagree about whether it is a good wine; and this shows (which is all that I am trying to show) that there is more to the statement that Colombey 1972 is a good wine than to the statement that Colombey 1972 is a wine which tastes ϕ. The more is, of course, the commendation; but I shall not in this lecture try to explain what this is, since I have done my best elsewhere.

This answer to the descriptivist argument is not, as might be thought at first hearing, circular. It is true that I introduced into it the distinction between commendation and description, which was what I was trying to establish; but I did not merely assume it as a premise in my argument – I produced a clear example in which we could not do without it. What I did was to ask, 'Was it possible to understand what I was saying when I explained to the man that to call a thing ϕ is not thereby to commend or praise it, any more than it is praise or commendation to say that it tastes like the product of a certain chemical recipe, or that it tastes like vinegar or water?' And the premiss which I put into the argument was that this was perfectly intelligible. A determined descriptivist might at this point protest 'It isn't intelligible to me'; but I can only ask you whether, if he said this, he would not be professing to find unintelligible a distinction which we all know perfectly well how to operate (a familiar habit of philosophers). The distinction has, indeed, to be elucidated, and this is the task of moral philosophy; but it exists.

III

This 'wine' case is one where the difficulty arises because there is no word available having the descriptive meaning of 'good' in a certain context without its evaluative meaning. But a very similar difficulty arises when, as in most moral and aesthetic cases, there is no *one* word which has just the descriptive meaning that we want, but a multitude of possible ways of describing, in greater or less detail, the sort of thing that we have in mind. Here what is required is not ostensive definition (though that may help) but a long story. It is, for example, very hard to say what it is about a particular picture which makes us call it a good one; but nevertheless what makes us call it a good one is a series of describable characteristics combined in just this way. We can see this quite clearly if we think of the painter himself building up the picture – putting in features and then perhaps painting them out again and trying something else. There is no doubt whatever that what makes him satisfied or dissatisfied is something there on the canvas which is certainly describable in neutral terms (e.g. he has a lot of things round the edge of the picture which draw the eye, but no feature in the middle which does so). Or, to take a simpler example, let us suppose that the painter is somebody like Kandinsky, and that the only thing that dissatisfies him about the picture is the precise colour of one of the exactly-drawn circular patches near the top right-hand corner. Suppose then that the painter is suddenly and incurably paralysed, but wants to finish the picture; can he not get a pupil to alter the colour for him, telling him, in neutral descriptive terms, just what paints to mix in what proportions and where to put the resulting mixture in order to make it a better picture? The paralysed painter would not have to say 'Make the picture better' or 'Make the circular patch in the top right-hand corner a better colour'; he could tell the pupil just how to do these things.

If, instead of asking what makes a man call *this* picture a good one, we ask what in general makes him call pictures (or wines or men) good ones, the position becomes even more complicated. But in principle it remains true that the descriptive meaning which the man attaches to the expression 'good picture' could be elicited, as a very complex conjunction and disjunction of characteristics, by questioning him sufficiently closely about a sufficiently large number of pictures.[4] For to have a settled taste in pictures is to be disposed to think pictures good which have certain characteristics. That such a process would reveal a good deal about his taste to the man himself does not affect the argument; the process of rendering articulate the grounds of evaluation is always a revealing one. If his evaluations have been made on vague or uncertain grounds, as will be the case with a man whose taste is not well developed, the process of trying to explain the grounds may well cause the evaluations themselves to change in the course of being made articulate. This again is irrelevant to the argument; for nobody wants to maintain that the descriptive meaning attached to people's evaluations is in all cases precise or cut-and-dried.

Lest you should think that I have been talking about pictures simply in order to make a logical point about value-judgements, I should like to say that there seems to me to be a lesson, in all this, about how to improve one's appreciation of works of art. In so far as I have attained to any articulate appreciation of any sorts of works of art – or of anything else which has aesthetic merit – it has been by trying to formulate to myself what I find good or bad about particular works, or about the works of a particular style or period. This is, of course, no substitute for the completely inarticulate absorption in a work – say a piece of music – which alone makes art worth while; but analysis does undoubtedly help. I have derived much more profit from looking at pictures and buildings, listening to music, etc., and asking myself what it is about them that I find worth while, than I have from reading the works of critics; and

---

[4] Though not competent to judge of such matters, I do not find the experiments described by Prof. H. J. Eysenck, *Sense and Nonsense in Psychology*, ch. 8, at all incredible, though I do not agree with his interpretation of them.

when critics have helped me, it has been by doing the same sort of thing, i.e. drawing attention to and characterising particular features of works of art which contribute to their excellence. I think that many descriptivists would agree with me about this. But unless what I have said is true (viz. that the descriptive meaning of 'good' in a given context can always in principle be given) critics would be unable to tell us why they think certain works of art good; they would just have to go on repeating that they are good.

IV

Morality is in these respects quite like aesthetics. There are certain ways of behaving, describable in perfectly neutral terms, which make us commend people as, for example, courageous. Citations for medals do not simply say that the recipient behaved courageously; they give descriptive details; and though these, for reasons of brevity, often themselves contain evaluative terms, this need not be the case, and in a good citation it is the neutral descriptions which impress. They impress us because we already have the standards of values according to which to do *that* sort of thing is to display outstanding merit.

A descriptivist might object to this argument that in some of my examples, although it is perfectly easy to say what the *descriptive* meaning of the term in question is, there is no separately discernible *evaluative* meaning. For example, it might be claimed that if we have said that the man has done what he has done, then we have said, implicitly, that he has been courageous; and if 'courageous' is a term of commendation, we have commended him. The commendation is simply the description. This I think to be false. With the standards of values that we have, and which it is natural for us to have in our historical circumstances (or perhaps in any likely historical circumstances), we shall all be disposed to commend such a man. But the commendation is a further step which we are not logically compelled to take. A man who said that such behaviour did not make a man any better would be morally eccentric, but not logically at fault. I have argued this point elsewhere.[5]

It follows that it is possible for two people without logical absurdity to agree about the description but disagree about the evaluation

[5] *FR*, pp. 187–9.

– though it would not affect my argument if nobody ever actually disagreed. And therefore the distinction between evaluative and descriptive meanings is not impugned.

V

I have sought to establish that there is this distinction, because I shall need it later. I shall now go on to deal with some particular descriptive arguments. Most of the arguments which I shall be discussing have a feature in common: namely that the descriptivism which they seek to establish is of a very minimal kind. That is to say, they seek to establish only that there are *some* logical restrictions upon what we can call good, right, etc. They fall far short of attempting to prove anything that could be helpful to us when faced with any serious moral problem, as will be at once apparent to anyone who tries to use the types of reasoning proposed in any actual moral perplexity. But in this lecture I shall address myself mainly to arguments for these very weak forms of descriptivism, because they might seem more difficult to refute.

Consider the following argument. It is not possible, it might be said, to think *anything* good, or good of its kind, just as it is not possible to want *anything*; it is possible to want or to think good only such things as are thought to be either the subjects of what have been called 'desirability characterisations', or else means to attaining them. This expression 'desirability characterisations' comes from Miss Anscombe's book *Intention* (1957), pp. 66 ff.; but I hesitate to ascribe the argument itself to her, because, as I shall show, the expression admits of at least two quite different interpretations, and I am not sure in which sense, if either, she was using the term; and therefore I am not sure which of two possible versions of the argument, if either, she would support. Since, however, although both versions are perfectly valid, neither proves anything from which I wish to dissent, I shall not try to do more than clear up the ambiguity – an ambiguity which has, I think, led some people to suppose that the argument does prove something with which a prescriptivist like myself would have to disagree.

The first way of taking the expression 'desirability characterisation' is to take it as meaning 'a description of that about the object which makes it an object of desire'. If I may be allowed to revert to my previous example: suppose that I want some Colombey 1972, or think it a good wine, because it tastes ϕ; then to say that it tastes ϕ is to give the required desirability characterisation. If this is how the phrase is to be taken, then the argument shows that whenever we think something good, we do so because of something about it. Since I have often maintained the same position myself, nobody will expect me to demur.[6] It shows further that the 'something about it' must be something thought desirable, or thought to be a means to something desirable. I do not think that I want to object to this either, provided that 'desire' and 'desirable' are taken in fairly wide senses, as translations of the Aristotelian *orexis* and *orekton*. So interpreted, the argument shows that, whenever we think something good, it must be, or be thought by us to be a means to, something to 'try to get'[7] which (in actual or hypothetical circumstances) we have at least some disposition. This conclusion, which has, it may be noticed, marked non-descriptivist undertones, is one I can agree with. The crucial thing to notice, however, is that the argument does nothing to show what may or may not be the subject of a desirability characterisation. It could, so far as this way of taking the argument goes, be anything you please. Thus, if our desires concerning wines were different, which they logically could be, 'tasting ϕ' might be an '*un*desirability characterisation'; and we should not be in the least put out if we found a man who wanted *not* to drink Colombey 1972 because it tasted like that.

The second way of taking the expression 'desirability characterisation' is as follows: we give a desirability characterisation of an object if we say something about it which is *logically* tied in some way (weak or strong) to desiring. An example of this would be to say that something would be fun; others would be to call it pleasant, or interesting, or delightful. Notice that, in this sense of 'desirability characterisation', to say that the wine tasted ϕ would *not* be to give a desirability characterisation of it; for there is no logical connection between thinking that a thing tastes ϕ and desiring it. As I have said, a man might without logical fault say that he wanted *not* to drink Colombey 1972 because it tasted ϕ; and he might also say something less committal, namely that the fact that it tasted ϕ did not make him either want to drink it or want not to drink it – in short that he was indifferent to its tasting ϕ. But it would be logically odd for somebody to say that the fact that something would be pleasant, or fun, or interesting, or delightful, did not make him – to the smallest

[6] *FR*, p. 71; *LM*, p. 133.
[7] See Anscombe, *Intention*, p. 67; *FR*, p. 70.

degree – disposed to do it (though of course he might not be disposed to do it when he considered the whole situation, including its consequences and the alternatives).

It may be that there is also a connection in the reverse direction between being fun, etc., and being desired or thought good; though, if so, the nature of the connection is obscure and tenuous. It may be, that is to say, that if we have said that we want something, or that we think it good, it is natural for us, if asked why, to say that it would be fun, or pleasant, or to give it some other characterisation falling within an ill-defined class which includes these. It may even be true that it is logically compulsory, on pain of making ourselves incomprehensible, that we should be prepared to give such an explanation.

The difficulty with this suggestion is that it is not possible to rule out, *a priori*, additions to the list of desirability characterisations in this second sense. And it is a somewhat vacuous claim that an explanation falling within a certain class must be forthcoming, if the class itself is so easily expansible. 'Exciting' is a desirability characterisation – and in at least some uses a desirability characterisation in the second of my two senses. Let us suppose, then, that there is a race of men who have not, up till now, valued the experience of danger (perhaps because their conditions of life have been such as to give them altogether too much of it), and have therefore not had the favourable characterisation 'exciting' in their vocabulary, but only such unfavourable characterisations as 'frightening' and 'terrifying'. Then, when their life becomes less exposed to terrors, they begin to know what it is to be bored, and so come to value excitement for its own sake. There then comes to be a need for the favourable characterisation 'exciting', and they duly invent it. This is an example of what I mean by an addition to the list of desirability characterisations in the second sense.

One reason why it is easy to be confused by these two possible senses of the phrase 'desirability characterisation' is that words which are very commonly used as desirability characterisations in the first sense often end up by becoming desirability characterisations in the second sense. That is to say, they acquire a logical, as opposed to a merely contingent, connection with being desired. The Latin word *virtus* underwent such a shift, owing to the contingent fact that the properties which are typical of the male sex are properties which the Romans desired people to have. Thus in particular cases it is sometimes hard to say whether a word is being used as a desirability characterisation in the second sense. But this will not cause concern to anybody unless he is a victim of the 'heap' fallacy to which I referred earlier.

A confusion between the two senses of 'desirability characterisation' might lead a careless descriptivist to suppose that descriptivism could be established in the following way. We should first establish that anything that is thought good must also be thought to be the subject of some desirability characterisation, or a means to such (and here it does not matter for the argument in which sense the phrase is used; let us allow for the sake of argument that this premise is true in both senses). We should then point out (correctly) that only some *words* can be desirability characterisations (sense two). Then we should assume that this proved that only some *things* can be the subjects of desirability characterisations (sense one). And so we should think that we had proved that only some things can be thought good. But the two connected fallacies in this argument should by now be obvious. The first is the equivocation on the phrase 'desirability characterisation'. The second is the assumption that by proving that there are certain words that cannot be or that must be used in conjunction with the statement that something is good, we have proved that certain things cannot be thought good.

It must always be possible to want, or to think good, *new* sorts of things (for example, new experiences); and therefore it can never be nonsense to *say* that we want them, or that they are good, provided that we are careful not to describe them in a way which is logically inconsistent with this. It is said that under the influence of mescaline people say things like 'How simply marvellous that at the corner of the room three planes meet at a point!' So perhaps they might, on occasion, say (to use Miss Anscombe's example) 'How simply marvellous to have this saucer of mud!' And if somebody asks what is marvellous about it, why should they not reply, with respectable precedent, 'We can't tell you; you have to have the experience before any word for it would mean anything to you:

> Nec lingua valet dicere,
> Nec litera exprimere;
> Expertus potest credere'?

It may readily be admitted that whenever we desire something, it must be because of something about it; but if pressed to say what this something is, we may be tempted, since most of my opponents on this question are of the opposite sex, to rejoin with Wilbye's madrigal:

> Love me not for comely grace,
> For my pleasing eye or face,
> Nor for any outward part;
> No, nor for my constant heart;
> For those may fail or turn to ill,
> So thou and I shall sever.
> Keep therefore a true woman's eye,
> And love me still, but know not why,
> So hast thou the same reason still
> To dote upon me ever.

Note that the poet does not here say that there is *no* reason for a woman's loving, but that she does not have to know (in the sense of 'know how to say') what it is.

That logic cannot determine what we are going to be attracted by or averse from was well known to Shakespeare. He makes Shylock say, when challenged as to his motives for demanding the pound of flesh,

> Some men there are love not a gaping pig;
> Some, that are mad if they behold a cat;
> And others, when the bag-pipe sings i' th' nose,
> Cannot contain their urine; for affection,
> Mistress of passion, sways it to the mood
> Of what it likes or loaths.
>
> > (*M. of V.*, IV. i)

And he knew about love-potions, of one of which he says,

> The juice of it, on sleeping eyelids laid,
> Will make or man or woman madly dote
> Upon the next live creature that it sees...
> The next thing then she waking looks upon,
> (Be it on lion, bear, or wolf, or bull,
> On meddling monkey, or on busy ape,)
> She shall pursue it with the soul of love.
>
> > (*M.N.D.*, II. i)

There are no logical limits (at least none relevant to the present issue)[8] to what such potions could make even a descriptivist philosopher desire; and therefore, if an argument about what can (logically) be thought good is based upon what can (logically) be desired, it is bound to fail. Logic tells us, indeed, that, if a man claims to desire a certain thing, there are certain *words* which he must not apply to

---

[8] For some restrictions which, though interesting, do not affect the present argument, see Anscombe, *Intention*, p. 66 and A. Kenny, *Action, Emotion and Will* (1963) p. 112. Since states of affairs can be desired for their own sakes, the restriction that what is desired must be desired *for* something is a vacuous one.

it, and perhaps also that there are certain other words, some of which at least he must be prepared to apply to it. But the latter half of this logical restriction is rather indefinite and elusive, and I leave it to those who have a stake in it to make it more determinate than it is so far. The trouble is that, as Miss Anscombe rightly says, *Bonum est multiplex*; and I can see no way of putting a logical limit to its multiplicity.

VI

The point that I have been making – or a closely related point – can be put in the following way. We can perhaps distinguish between objective properties of objects – i.e. those which they have, however a person is disposed towards them – and subjective properties, which an object has only if a person is disposed towards it in a certain way. I must confess that I do not like these words, because they have been used in too many different senses; but perhaps, as so defined, they will serve our present purposes. In a similar way, we might distinguish between objective conditions which have to be satisfied before we can use a certain word of an object, and subjective conditions. The former consist in the possession by the object of objective properties; the latter in a person's being disposed in a certain way towards it. Now descriptivists often seem to be wanting to demonstrate to us that there are certain objective conditions for the use of words like 'good'. But the most that arguments like the foregoing can show is that there are certain subjective conditions.

Here, moreover, we must guard against another, related, ambiguity in the expression 'conditions for the use of a word'. It might mean 'conditions for a word being said to be used correctly to express what the speaker who calls a thing "good" (for example) is wishing to convey'; or it might mean 'conditions for a thing's being said to be good'. This ambiguity is well illustrated on the first page of an article by Mrs Foot.[9] In outlining a position which she is going to attack, she asks: 'Is a connection with the choices of the speaker ever a *sufficient* condition for the use of the word 'good', as it would be if a man could ever call certain things (let us call them *A*'s) good *A*'s simply because these were the *A*'s which he was thereafter ready to choose?' She goes on to argue that it is neither a sufficient nor a necessary condition; in this she deviates from Miss

[9] Paper XX, p. 214.

Anscombe, who thinks that if we call a thing good, we must attribute to it some desirability characteristic, and that 'the primitive sign of wanting is trying to get'.[10]

Now if here 'a sufficient condition for the use of the word "good"' meant 'a sufficient condition for a thing's being said to be good', then it is, I think, quite plain that a connection with choices is not a sufficient condition. At any rate, I have never thought that it was; indeed, though the view has sometimes been attributed to me that 'So and so is a good *x*' means the same as 'So and so is the *x* (or kind of *x*) that I would choose', this is a position which I have explicitly argued against.[11] Now there are indications in the article which might lead one to suppose that Mrs Foot was taking the words 'sufficient condition for the use of the word "good"' to mean 'sufficient condition for a thing's being said to be good'. The chief indication is that few if any of her arguments are even plausible unless this were what she was trying to disprove. Also, her words in several places naturally bear this sense. For example, she says (referring to an example of a person playing a game with pebbles) 'it is not by his readiness to pick up the pebbles that he *legitimises his words*' (my italics); and she has just said that, on the contrary, 'it is a plain matter of fact that the particular *A*'s [in this example pebbles] *will be* good for his purposes, or from his point of view' (see above, p. 221; my italics). A similar kind of expression occurs earlier (see p. 215), where she says, of a man talking about knives, 'He could not . . . say that a good knife was one which rusted quickly, *defending his use* of the word "good" by showing that he picked out such knives for his own use' (my italics). It certainly looks, at first sight, as if in both these instances, by 'legitimise his words' and 'defend his use' she means, not 'show that he really does think that sort of knife or pebble good, and is therefore expressing correctly what he thinks', but rather 'show that the knives or pebbles which he calls good *are* good'. So it looked to me, when I first read the article, as if, when she was constructing these arguments, she had the purpose of attacking a position which I, at any rate, have never defended, and with which, therefore, I need not concern myself.

However, we must consider the other possible interpretation, in view of the fact that, unless my memory is deceiving me, and my notes incorrect (and I am not confident on either point), this was the interpretation which she authorised at the meeting at which her paper was discussed, after I had pointed out to her that on the first

[10] *Intention*, p. 67; see above, p. 248.
[11] *LM*, p. 107.

interpretation she was attacking a position which was not mine. If this second interpretation were what she meant, then in the 'pebble' example she would be maintaining that, if a man were ready to pick up a certain kind of pebble for playing a game, and habitually did so, to point this out would not be a way of showing that those were the pebbles that he thought good for his purposes or from his point of view, and thus 'legitimising' the use of the word 'good' by showing that it correctly expressed his thought (however preposterous the thought). But if so, she was maintaining something that is not very plausible. For if a man consistently and deliberately chose a certain kind of pebble, we *should* infer that he thought that kind of pebble good for his purposes or from his point of view; if we had doubts, they would be about what on earth the purposes or the point of view could be. I conclude that either she was attacking a position which I have never held, or else she was attacking one which I might, with certain explanations, accept, but attacking it in a way which could carry conviction only to somebody who confused the two possible interpretations of the phrase 'condition for'.

VII

This seems to be the best point at which to deal with another common descriptivist manœuvre. The manœuvre is rendered attractive by the following fact, which I think we can all admit. There are some things which, if wanted or thought good by somebody, seem to call for no explanation (for example, food, a certain degree of warmth, etc.). Other things, if wanted or thought good, require explanation. The explanation can perhaps be given: a man who wants a flat pebble may want it to play ducks and drakes with, and think it good for this purpose; but, as we progress to more and more bizarre examples, the explanation gets harder and harder to give. It therefore seems to be open to the descriptivist to take a very extraordinary imaginary example, and ask rhetorical questions about it, such as 'Suppose that a man says that somebody is a good man because he clasps and unclasps his hands, and never turns NNE after turning SSW; could we understand him?'[12] It is implied that an anti-descriptivist has to claim that he can understand such an absurd statement, and this is treated as a *reductio ad absurdum* of his position.

[12] The example comes from Mrs Foot's paper, above, p. 197.

This type of argument rests on a confusion between, on the one hand, logical absurdity and its various weaker analogues, and, on the other, various sorts of contingent improbability. That is why I said earlier that the problem about the distinction between descriptive and evaluative is an offshoot of the problem about the distinction between analytic and synthetic. It is contingently extremely unlikely, to say the least, that I should become able to lift a ton weight with my bare hands; but it is not logically impossible for this to happen, nor is it logically absurd, in any weaker way, to claim that it has happened. By this I mean that if a man claimed to be able to do this, there would be no ultimate obstacle to our understanding him. Admittedly, we might well think at first that we had misunderstood him; it is so improbable that anybody should even think that it had happened, that, if a person claimed that it had happened, we should think at first that he could not be meaning the words in their literal senses. We might think that he meant, for instance, that the weight in question was counterbalanced, so that he could put his hands underneath it and lift, and make it go up. That is to say, when a man says something which is sufficiently improbable (as we think the universe to be constituted), we tend to assume that he cannot mean it literally, and that therefore we have to search for some non-literal meaning if we are going to understand him. But for all that, what he says has in its literal sense nothing *logically* wrong with it. It follows that no conclusions whatever are to be drawn concerning the meanings or uses of words from the oddity of such a remark; what is odd is not the use of words, but that anybody should think such a thing.

The case before us is much the same. If a man said that somebody was a good man because he clasped and unclasped his hands, we should, indeed, at first find ourselves wondering whether we had understood him. But the reason is that, although what has been said is perfectly *comprehensible* in its literal sense, it is very odd indeed for anybody to think it. We should therefore look around for non-literal senses or contrived explanations, and should be baffled if we failed to find any. Why would it be odd for anybody to think this? For a reason which can, indeed, be gathered from the writings of descriptivists, who have given a tolerably correct account of it, vitiated only by their assumption that it can teach us anything about the uses or meanings of words, and that therefore it can support, or discredit, logical theses. The reason is that very few of us, if any, have the necessary 'pro-attitude' to people who clasp and unclasp their hands; and the reason for this is that the pro-attitudes which we have do not just occur at random, but have explanations, albeit not (as the descriptivists whom I am discussing seem to think) explanations which logic alone could provide. To think something good of its kind is, let us say, to have at least some disposition to choose it when, or if, choosing things of that kind, in actual or hypothetical circumstances. After what I have said earlier, you will not, I know, confuse this thesis with the thesis that for something to *be* good is for us to have a disposition to choose it. Now we do not have, most of us, any disposition to choose, or to choose to be, men who clasp and unclasp their hands. We do not, accordingly, think that men who do this are good.

The explanation of our not thinking this is that such choices would hardly contribute to our survival, growth, procreation, etc.; if there have been any races of men or animals who have made the clasping and unclasping of hands a prime object of their pro-attitudes, to the exclusion of other more survival-promoting activities, they have gone under in the struggle for existence. I am, I know, being rather crude; but in general, to cut the matter short, we have the pro-attitudes that we have, and therefore call the things good which we do call good, because of their relevance to certain ends which are sometimes called 'fundamental human needs'.

To call them this, however, is already to make a *logical* connection between them and what it is good for a man to have. This, indeed, is why descriptivists have fallen into the trap of supposing that, because the word 'good' is logically tied in certain contexts to the *word* 'needs', it is therefore logically tied to certain concrete *things* which are generally thought to be needs. But since this mistake is the same mistake as I discussed at length in connection with desires, it need not detain us. The two words 'desires' and 'needs' have both misled descriptivists in the same way – and that because there is an intimate logical relation between what is needed and what is desired, so that in many contexts we could say that for a thing to be needed is for it to be a necessary condition for satisfying a desire. It follows that if 'things desired' do not form a closed class, 'things needed' will not either. If, as I said, logic does not prevent us from coming to desire new things, or ceasing to desire old ones, it cannot, either, determine what we do or do not need.

A man who used the word 'good' of things which were unrelated to those ends which most of us call 'needs' might, nevertheless, be using it, quite correctly, to express the thought which he had; but this might be (if a sufficiently crazy example were taken) a very extraordinary thought for a man to have, because most of us have a high regard for our survival, and for such other things as I mentioned, and our pro-attitudes are fairly consistently related to these. It is not, indeed, logically necessary that they should be. Those of some people are not. And it would not affect my argument (though it would obviously affect gravely that of the opposite party) if there were some things which some people just do, unaccountably, have a high regard for, like the music of Beethoven.

In short, our disposition to call only a certain range of things good (and to choose and desire them) can be explained – in so far as it can be explained – without bringing in logic; and therefore the explanation contributes nothing to logic either, and, specifically, tells us nothing about the meanings or uses of the evaluative words, except that they have certain common *descriptive* meanings.

VIII

I shall end this lecture with an attempt to clear up a quite simple confusion about the word 'because' – a confusion which seems to me to lie at the root of a great many things which descriptivists say. If I am choosing between an ordinary mushroom and a poisonous toadstool to put in the dish that I am making for myself, I naturally choose, and prefer, and think it best to choose and that I ought to choose, the mushroom and not the toadstool; and I think this *because* the latter is poisonous (i.e. such as to cause death if eaten). That the toadstool is poisonous is my *reason* for rejecting it. Now it might be thought that, if I reject it *because* it is poisonous, there must be some logical connection between the statement 'It is poisonous' and the statements 'It ought not to be chosen to eat' or 'It is not good to eat'; or between my thought that it is poisonous and my disposition not to eat it. By 'logical connection' I mean that the *meanings* of the expressions are somehow linked (the precise nature of the link need not concern us; some descriptivists would make it a firmer one than others). Now to say this is to confuse logical entailment, together with its many weaker analogues, on the one hand, with the relation between choice and reasons for choice on the other. The relation between choice and reasons for choice is not a logical relation. There is no logical compulsion on me, or even any weaker logical constraint, to refrain from eating what I know will kill me. I refrain from eating it *because* I know it will kill me; but if I did the opposite, and *ate* it because I knew it would kill me, I should not be offending against any logical rule regulating the uses of words, however fashionably tenuous the rule is supposed to be.

There is, indeed, a logical inference that can be elicited from this situation. Given that the toadstool would kill me, I can infer that I ought not to eat it, if I also accept a further premise that I ought not to eat what would kill me. To accept this other premise is to have one of a class of things which I shall call, in Professor Braithwaite's phrase, 'springs of action'.[13] Desires belong to this class, as do convictions that something is better than something else. In fact anything belongs to it which can, as it were, turn a descriptive statement into a reason for doing something; or, more formally, the expression of which in language (though not, of course, its *description* in language), together with some descriptive statement, logically entails some prescription. But there is no logical link between the descriptive premiss, *by itself*, and the prescriptive conclusion.

A parallel from a quite distinct field of discourse, which has nothing to do with prescriptions, will perhaps make this point clear. There is a valid logical inference from the statement that cyanide is a poison, together with the statement that this dish contains cyanide, to the conclusion that this dish contains poison. But there is no logical connection which can justify the inference from the statement, by itself, that the dish contains cyanide, to the conclusion that it contains poison. This is because the other premise, that cyanide is a poison, is synthetic. Nevertheless, the dish is poisonous *because* it contains cyanide.

Now if anybody thinks that one can never say 'q because p' unless there is a logical connection between 'p' and 'q', he is likely to attempt to place opponents of descriptivism in the following dilemma. Either we have to admit that there is a logical connection between statements of fact, taken by themselves, and evaluative conclusions (which is to surrender to at any rate a weak form of descriptivism); or else we must hold that evaluative judgements are never made *because of* anything – i.e. that they are quite irrational. It is to be hoped that if descriptivists reflect upon the falsity of this dilemma, they will abandon at least some of their arguments.

This lecture has been polemical. I felt it necessary to discuss certain mistaken views (as I think them to be); for it seems to me that, if we could put them behind us, we might liberate the subject for a real advance. In this sense my lecture has had a constructive purpose.

[13] *Proceedings of the Aristotelian Society*, supp. vol. xx (1946), 9. Aristotle's *orexeis* and Kenny's 'volitions' (*Action, Emotion and Will*, p. 214) play similar roles.

Appendix

Professor Searle's reply to his critics

EDITOR'S NOTE

In his book *Speech Acts: An Essay in Philosophy of Language*, published by Cambridge University Press in 1969, Professor J. R. Searle has a chapter on 'Deriving "ought" from "is"' (op. cit. pp. 175–198). In section 8.1 of this chapter he restates his derivation substantially as it appears above in Paper XII, which is reprinted here from *The Philosophical Review* of 1964. There are, however, one or two alterations of some importance which seem to me to be in line with my own attempted defence of Searle against certain criticisms in Paper XVII above.

Searle, in his 1969 derivation, drops the *ceteris paribus* considerations between steps (3) and (4) and steps (4) and (5) which appeared in his 1964 derivation. His grounds for doing so are his belief that these were 'a standing invitation to various kinds of irrelevant objections' (op. cit. p. 180) and that he can, in fact, get from 'is' to 'ought' without bringing in such *ceteris paribus* clauses. All that needs to be recognised, at the points where he brought them in, is, he says: 'that the existence of the obligation is at the time of the undertaking of the obligation and the "ought" is relative to the existence of the obligation' (op. cit. p. 182). I will try to show rather more fully what he means.

Between premises (3) and (4), in the 1969 version, he has only the tautological premise:

> (3a) All those who place themselves under an obligation are (*at the time when they so place themselves*) under an obligation (italics mine).

And he comments: 'In order to get a straightforward entailment between 3 and 4 we need only construe 4 in such a way as *to exclude any time gap* between the point of the completion of the act in which the obligation is undertaken, 3, and the point at which it is claimed the agent is under an obligation, 4. So construed, 3 entails 4 straight off. Formalists may wish to preface each of 1–5 with the phrase ' "at time *t*" . . .' (op. cit. p. 179, italics mine).

Between premises (4) and (5), in the 1969 derivation, Searle has only the tautological premise:

> (4a) If one is under an obligation to do something, then *as regards that obligation* one ought to do what one is under an obligation to do (italics mine).

He points out that (5) – i.e. 'Jones ought to pay Smith five dollars' – may be interpreted in either of two ways as follows:

> (5′) *As regards his obligation* to pay Smith five dollars, Jones ought to pay Smith five dollars (italics mine).
> (5″) *All things considered*, Jones ought to pay Smith five dollars (italics mine).

Searle comments: 'Now clearly if we interpret 5 as 5″ we cannot derive it from 4 without additional premises. But equally clearly if we interpret it as equivalent to 5′, which is perhaps the more plausible interpretation given its occurrence in the discourse, we can derive it from 4. And regardless of whether we wish to interpret 5 as 5′, we can simply derive 5′ from 4, which is quite sufficient for our present purposes.' – i.e. for getting 'ought' from 'is' (op. cit. p. 181). Searle claims that, when (5) is interpreted as (5′), the 'ought' in (5′) is categorical, not hypothetical. He obviously has in mind the objection, brought against his 1964 derivation by Professor and Mrs Thompson in Paper XVI above, that, if a *ceteris paribus* clause is embodied in the conclusion (5) of his derivation, then the 'ought' in that conclusion cannot be, as he says in the 1964 version that it is, categorical. A similar objection, Searle is arguing, cannot be brought against 5′. He says: '5′ does not say that Jones ought to pay *if he wants such and such*. It says he ought, as regards his obligation, to pay up.' (op. cit. p. 181.)

In a footnote on p. 180 of his 1969 derivation, Searle, in effect, contends that (5) would follow from (4) even though Jones were involved in a conflict of obligations. The footnote runs: 'It is perhaps important to emphasise that the fact that an obligation might be outweighed by another obligation or the fact that an obligation might be discharged or excused does not even qualify the obligation, let alone deny its existence. There has to be an obligation in the first place to be countervailed or excused. I may be in a conflict as to which of two conflicting obligations I ought to carry out, which of the two I should perform and which I should breach. I may be justified in not doing what I ought to do as regards a particular obligation. My breach may even be excused, sanctioned, or even encouraged. To all this the fact that I ought to do what I have undertaken an obligation to do is logically anterior.'

What follows this present note is the concluding section of Searle's chapter on the derivation of 'ought' from 'is' (op. cit. pp. 188–98). It contains his summary of the objections brought against his 1964 derivation and his replies to these criticisms.

W. D. HUDSON

Deriving 'ought' from 'is': objections and replies

J. R. Searle

The reader unfamiliar with the philosophical controversy surrounding this problem may well feel that the claims made in section 8.1 (see p. 259 – Ed.) are harmless and obvious enough. Yet there is no contention in this book that will arouse and has aroused as much controversy as the derivation in that section. Published criticisms of the derivation tend to fall into two categories – those which attacked the *ceteris paribus* clause and those which attacked the alleged logical connection between promising, obligation, and 'ought'. The first set I have sidestepped by excluding from consideration within the proof the various kinds of consideration that the *ceteris paribus* clause is designed to deal with. The second set goes to the heart of the matter at issue and deserves consideration in more detail. These objections to the derivation are very revealing of many problems, both in the philosophy of language and elsewhere. In what follows I shall present and answer in dialogue form what I take to be the most sincere objections made against the proof.

FIRST OBJECTION: There is a kind of conservatism implicit in the whole account. You seem to be saying that it is logically inconsistent for anyone to think that one ought never to keep promises, or that the whole institution of promising is evil.

REPLY: This objection really is a misunderstanding of the whole proof and, in fact, a misunderstanding of the whole book. It is perfectly consistent with my account for someone to argue 'One ought never to keep promises'. Suppose, for example, a nihilistic anarchist argues that one ought never to keep promises because, for example, an unseemly concern with obligation impedes self-fulfilment. Such an argument may be silly, but it is not, as far as my account is concerned, logically absurd. To understand this point, we need to make a distinction between what is external and what is internal to the institution of promising. It is internal to the concept of promising that in promising one undertakes an obligation to do something. But whether the entire institution of promising is good or evil, and whether the obligations undertaken in promising are overridden by other outside considerations are questions which are external to the institution itself. The nihilist argument considered above is simply an external attack on the institution of promising. In effect, it says that the obligation to keep a promise is always overridden because of the alleged evil character of the institution. But it does not deny the point that promises obligate, it only insists that the obligations ought not to be fulfilled because of the external consideration of 'self-fulfilment'.

Nothing in my account commits one to the conservative view that institutions are logically unassailable or to the view that one ought to approve or disapprove this or that institution. The point is merely that when one enters an institutional activity by invoking the rules of the institution one necessarily commits oneself in such and such ways, regardless of whether one approves or disapproves of the institution. In the case of linguistic institutions, like promising (or statement making), the serious utterances of the words commit one in ways which are determined by the meaning of the words. In certain first-person utterances, the utterance is the undertaking of an obligation. In certain third-person utterances, the utterance is a report of an obligation undertaken.

SECOND OBJECTION: The answer to the first objection suggests the following *reductio ad absurdum*. On this account, any institution could arbitrarily obligate anyone depending only on how one arbitrarily decides to set up the institution.

REPLY: This objection is based on an incorrect conception of obligations which is not implied by the account given here. The notion of an obligation is closely tied to the notion of accepting, acknowledging, recognising, undertaking, etc., obligations in such a way as to render the notion of an obligation essentially a contractual notion.[1] Suppose a group of people in Australia completely unknown to me sets up a 'rule' whereby I am 'obligated' to pay them $100 a week. Unless I am somehow involved in the original agreement, their claims are unintelligible. Not just any arbitrary decision by X can place Y under an obligation.

THIRD OBJECTION: But now it begins to emerge that the original evaluative decision is the decision to accept or reject the institution of promising. On your account as soon as someone uses the word 'promise' seriously he is committed in such and such ways, which only shows that the evaluative premise is 1*a*. It shows that 1*a* is really a substantial moral principle. (For 1a see above p. 121 – Ed.)

REPLY: This objection begins to approach the heart of the matter. 1*a* is indeed a crucial premise, for it is the one which gets us from the brute to the institutional level, the level that contains obligations. But its 'acceptance' is quite unlike the decision to accept a certain moral principle. 1*a* states a fact about the meaning of a descriptive word, 'promise'. Furthermore, anyone who uses that word in serious literal speech is committed to its logical consequences involving obligations. And there is nothing special in this respect about promises; similar rules are built into statements, warnings, advice, reports, perhaps even commands. I am here challenging a certain model of describing linguistic facts. According to that model, once you have described the facts in any situation, the question of any 'evaluations' is still left absolutely open. What I am here arguing is that, in the case of certain institutional facts, the evaluations involving obligations, commitments, and responsibilities are no longer left completely open because the statement of the institutional facts involves these notions.

It is a matter of immense fascination to me that authors who are 'anti-naturalists' when they think about it, tacitly accept the derivations of evaluative from descriptive when they are just doing philosophy and disregarding their ideology. Consider the following passages from R. M. Hare:[2] 'If a person says that a thing is red, he is *committed* [my italics] to the view that anything which was like it

[1] Cf. E. J. Lemmon, 'Moral Dilemmas', *Philosophical Review* (1962).
[2] R. M. Hare, *Freedom and Reason* (Oxford 1963) p. 11.

in the relevant respects would likewise be red.' Hare also says[3] that he is committed '*to calling it red*' [my italics]; and this is purely in virtue of the meaning of the relevant words. Leaving aside the question of whether what Hare says is true,[4] it is of the same form as my argument. I say if a person promises he is committed to doing the thing promised, and this is purely in virtue of the meaning of 'promise'.

The only important difference between the two theses is that the commitment in Hare's example is to future linguistic behaviour. The commitment in mine is not restricted to linguistic behaviour. In structure, they are identical. But let us suppose someone can show they are not the same; very well, then I should simply conduct my derivation on this example. 'He called it red' is a straightforward statement of fact (like, for example, 'he promised'). 'He is committed to perform a certain act' is evaluative since commitment (though wider than) is a member of the same family as obligation. Hence it is the very thesis of Hare's example that evaluative statements follow from descriptive statements. Hare is disturbed by what he takes to be the claim that tautologies generate obligations.[5] But what he appears to overlook is that the tautologies are hypothetical and hence do not by themselves generate any obligations. What they say is, for example, 'If he calls it red, he is committed.' So we need the empirical premise, 'He called it red' to get the conclusion: 'He is committed.' No one is claiming that tautologies 'prescribe' behaviour categorically but only conditionally on some institutional fact (as Hare's example illustrates).

In reply to this point, it might be said that all he meant by 'committed' is that a speaker who did not observe these commitments would be contradicting himself. Thus, commitments are construed 'descriptively'. But this only forces the question back a step. Why should a speaker concern himself at all if his statements are self-contradictory? And the answer is clearly that it is internal to the notion of a statement (descriptive word) that a self-contradiction (descriptive word) is a defect (evaluative word). That is, he who states is committed (*ceteris paribus*) to avoiding self-contradictions. One does not first decide to make statements and then make a separate evaluative decision that they would be better if they were not self-contradictory. So we are still left with commitments being essentially involved in facts.

[3] Ibid. p. 15.
[4] It can't be quite true in its stronger version on p. 15. A man may call one object red and not say anything at all about the next red object he sees.
[5] 'The promising game', Paper XIV above.

FOURTH OBJECTION: The answer to the third objection really misses the point. All you have shown in your derivation is that 'promise' (and no doubt 'state', 'describe' and certain others) are really evaluative words. It may be useful to point out that notions we once thought descriptive are really evaluative, but that in no way gets over the descriptive–evaluative gap. Having shown that 2 is evaluative, all that really follows is that 1*a* must be evaluative since the descriptive premises 1 and 1*b* are insufficient to entail 2 by themselves. (For 1 and 2, see above p. 121; and for 1*b*, p. 122 – Ed.)

REPLY: There is no independent motivation for calling 2 evaluative, other than the fact that it entails an evaluative statement 3 (p. 121 – Ed.). So now the thesis that descriptions cannot entail evaluations is becoming trivial, for the criterion of whether or not a statement is descriptive will be whether or not it entails something evaluative. But unless there are independently identifiable classes of descriptive and evaluative statements about which we can then further discover that members of the former do or do not entail members of the latter, our definition of descriptive will include 'does not entail any evaluative statements', and that will render our thesis trivial. 2 is intuitively a straightforward statement of fact. If our linguistic theory forces us to deny that, and to assert that it is a subjective evaluation, then there is something wrong with the theory.

FIFTH OBJECTION: The fourth objection needs merely to be restated. The point about words like 'promise' is that they have both an evaluative and a descriptive sense. In the descriptive sense (sense 1) 'promise' means simply *uttering certain words*. In the evaluative sense (sense 2) 'promise' means *undertaking an obligation*. Now, if 1*a* really is descriptive, then all your move from 1 to 2 proves is that Jones made a promise in sense 1, but in order to get from 2 to 3 you would have to prove he made a promise in sense 2 and that would require an extra evaluative premise.

In short, there is a simple fallacy of equivocation over 'promise'. You prove that Jones made a promise in sense 1 and then assume that you have proved he made a promise in sense 2 by assuming incorrectly that these two senses are the same. The difference between sense 2 and sense 1 is the difference between a committed participant and a neutral observer. It is both necessary and decisive to make this distinction between the committed participant and the neutral observer, for it is only the neutral observer who is making genuine factual or descriptive statements. As soon as you interpret the word 'promise' from the point of view of the committed par-

ticipant you have tacitly slipped in an evaluation but, until you
have done that, the proof will not work. You really should not suppose that every word comes already marked as evaluative or descriptive. Some apparently descriptive words can have an evaluative
sense, as in sense 2 of 'promise', as well as a descriptive sense. It is
only in sense 1 of 'promise' that it is purely descriptive.

REPLY: There is no sense 1. That is, there is no literal meaning
of 'promise' in which all it means is uttering certain words. Rather
'promise' denotes speech acts characteristically performed in the
utterance of certain words. But 'promise' is not lexically ambiguous
as between uttering words and undertaking obligations. The objection above tries to offer a sense of promise in which the statement
'He made a promise' would state a brute fact and not an institutional
fact, but there is no such sense. The reasoning in this objection is
the same as in objection 4. It consists of the invocation of the classical model, but it is precisely the classical model that is here being
challenged.

I shall try to spell this out a bit more. Linguistic facts as stated
in linguistic characterisations provide the constraints on any linguistic theory. At a minimum, the theory must be consistent with
the facts; an acceptable theory would also have to account for or
explain the facts. Now in the present instance the following linguistic characterisations state certain facts:

1. A statement of the form 'X made a promise' states an objective
fact and, except for borderline cases, is not subjective or a matter of
opinion.

2. By definition, promising is undertaking an obligation or commitment, etc., to do something.

3. A sentence of the form 'X made a promise' is not lexically
ambiguous as between 'X said some words' and 'X really promised'.
'Promise' is not thus homonymous.

4. Promising is characteristically performed by uttering certain
sorts of expressions in certain contexts and with certain intentions.

5. A statement of the form 'X undertook an obligation' is 'evaluative', since it is a statement predicating the so-called evaluative
notion, obligation.

Consistency with these facts is a condition of adequacy on any
linguistic theory purporting to deal with this area. Objection 4 is
inconsistent with statement 1. Objection 5 patches up that point
by being inconsistent with statement 3. Both of these manœuvres
are motivated by the failure of the classical model to account for 1

and 2 together, given 5. Nearly all of the objections to the proof consist of efforts to deny one or more of these linguistic characterisations.

The objection you just made (5) is an attempt to introduce a sense of 'promise' in which a promise is not an undertaking, but is completely defined in terms of statement 4. But there is no such literal sense. You are motivated to that manœuvre because your theory cannot accommodate both the fact that promises obligate and the fact that it *is* a matter of fact that someone has made a promise.

SIXTH OBJECTION: Well, I am still not convinced so let me try again. It seems to me you do not adequately appreciate my distinction between the committed participant and the neutral observer. Now I can agree with you that as soon as we literally and unreservedly use the word 'promise', an evaluative element enters in, for by literally and unreservedly using that word we are committing ourselves to the institution of promising. But that involves an evaluation, so as soon as you specify which of the early uses is a literal and committed use we can see that it is really evaluative.

REPLY: In a way, you are here stating my argument as if it were an objection against me. When we do use a word literally and unreservedly we are indeed committing ourselves to the logical properties of that word. In the case of promise, when we assert 'He made a promise' we commit ourself to the proposition that he undertook an obligation. In exactly the same way, when we use the word 'triangle' we commit ourselves to its logical properties. So that when we say, for example, 'X is a triangle' we commit ourselves to the proposition that X has three sides. And the fact that the commitment in the first case involves the notion of obligation shows that we are able to derive from it an 'evaluative' conclusion, but it does not show that there is anything subjective (matter of opinion, not a matter of fact, or a matter of moral decision) in the statement 'He made a promise', any more than the fact that the statement 'X is a triangle' has logical consequences, shows that there is a moral decision involved in the committed use of the word 'triangle'.

I think the reason you are confused here is simply this. There are two radically different ways of taking the phrase 'commit oneself to (accept) the institution of promising'. In one way it means something like (*a*) 'undertake to use the word "promise" in accordance with its literal meaning, which literal meaning is determined by the internal constitutive rules of the institution'. A quite different way to take the phrase is to take it as meaning (*b*) 'endorse the institution as a good or acceptable institution'. Now, when I do assert literally that he made a promise I do indeed commit myself to the institution in the sense of (*a*); indeed, it is precisely because the literal meaning involves me in this commitment that the derivation goes through. But I do not commit myself in the sense of (*b*). It is perfectly possible for someone who loathes the institution of promising to say quite literally, 'Jones made a promise', thus committing himself to the view that Jones undertook an obligation. Sense (*b*) of commitment really is a matter of opinion (at least as far as the present discussion is concerned) but there is nothing subjective about the statements made involving commitments in the sense of interpretation (*a*). To make this clear, note that exactly the same distinction holds for geometry. Someone who thinks the whole study and subject of geometry is evil still commits himself to the logical consequences of '*X* is a triangle' when he asserts '*X* is a triangle'. In neither case is there anything evaluative – in the sense of subjectiveness – about the commitment. Both 'He made a promise' and '*X* is a triangle' are statements of fact. (Of course it is logically possible for people to try to sabotage promising – or geometry – by using words in incoherent ways, but that is irrelevant to the validity of the derivations in both cases.)

Now, when you say that the evaluative element enters in when we literally and unreservedly characterise something as a promise, that can mean one of two things, either:

1. The statement 'He made a promise' made literally and unreservedly entails the evaluative statement 'He undertook an obligation'; or

2. The statement 'He made a promise' is always subjective or a matter of opinion because to make it involves thinking that the institution of promising is a good thing.

Now in the first case, what you say is quite true and indeed is the crux of my argument and rests on interpretation (*a*) above. But if what you mean is expressed by the second claim, which is based on interpretation (*b*), then it is obviously false. It is obviously false both that 'He made a promise' is subjective or a matter of opinion and false that in order to say unreservedly, 'He made a promise' one needs to think the institution of promising a good thing.

In the classical theory of 'evaluative' statements, there are two elements, one, the recognition of a class of statements intuitively felt to be evaluative (unfortunately it turns out that this is a very heterogeneous class indeed) and secondly, the theory that all such statements must be subjective or a matter of opinion. I am not challenging the first half of this; I think there are certain paradigms at least of evaluative utterances, and I am willing to go along with the orthodox theorists that 'He is under an obligation' is one of them. But what I am challenging is the second half, the theory that every member of this class must be subjective and that no factual or objective statement can entail any member of this class.

SEVENTH OBJECTION: I am still unconvinced. Why can't I speak in a detached anthropological sense? It seems obvious to me that one can say 'He made a promise', meaning something like 'He made what they, the people of this Anglo-Saxon tribe, call a promise'. And that is a purely descriptive sense of promise which involves no commitment to evaluative statements at all. Now it is this anthropological point of view that I am trying to express when I make my distinction between the committed participant and the neutral observer.

REPLY: Of course, you can speak in *oratio obliqua*, and thus avoid the commitments of speaking straight out. You can even employ the forms of speech for speaking normally and still be speaking in disguised *oratio obliqua*, or what you called the detached anthropological sense. But notice that this is really quite irrelevant and does not show that there are different senses of the words involved, or that the original statement was a concealed evaluation. For notice that one can do exactly the same thing with any word you like. One can adopt a detached anthropological attitude towards geometry, and indeed a sceptical anthropologist from another planet might adopt just such an attitude.[6] When he says '*X* is a triangle' he might mean no more than '*X* is what they, the Anglo-Saxons, call a triangle', but that doesn't show that there are two senses of 'triangle', a committed or evaluative sense and a detached or descriptive sense. Nor does it show that Euclid was a disguised moralist because his proofs require a 'committed' use of the terms involved. The fact that one can adopt a detached attitude towards anything at all is irrelevant to the validity of deductive arguments involving the committed use of the words involved. If it

[6] Notice incidentally that anthropologists do in fact talk about religions in this way: for example, 'there are two gods, of whom the rain god is the more important for it is he who produces rain'. This does not show that there are different meanings to any words involved, it merely shows that it is possible in certain contexts to speak in *oratio obliqua* without employing the forms of *oratio obliqua*.

were really a valid objection to the derivation in section 8.1 (see p. 259 – Ed.) to say that by reinterpreting the words in a detached anthropological sense we can produce an invalid argument, then the same objection would refute every possible deductive argument, because every valid argument depends on the committed occurrence of the terms crucial to the derivation. All the objection says is that for any deductive argument whatever you can construct a parallel argument in *oratio obliqua* from which the conclusion of the original cannot be validly derived. But so what? Such a fact could never affect the validity of any of the original arguments. What my argument requires, like any valid argument, is a serious, literal, non-*oratio obliqua* occurrence of the crucial words it contains. The fact that there are other possible non-serious occurrences of these words is quite irrelevant.

Of all the arguments used against the original proof, the argument from anthropology is both the most common[7] and the weakest. It has the following structure: Take any valid derivation of a conclusion from premises. Then take any crucial word W in the premises, be it 'promise', 'triangle', 'red', any word you like which is crucial to the argument. Reinterpret W so it doesn't mean W but means, for example, 'what somebody else calls W'. Now rewrite the derivation with W so reinterpreted and see if it is still valid. Chances are it is not; but, if it is, keep repeating the same procedure with other words until you get a version where it is not. Conclusion: the derivation was invalid all along.

The fact that the critics of the derivation repeatedly advance an argument which, if it were valid, would threaten all valid derivations is illustrative of the irony I cited at the beginning of this chapter. The urge to read the metaphysical distinction between Fact and Value back into language as a thesis about valid entailment relations must inevitably run up against counter-examples, because speaking a language is everywhere permeated with the facts of commitments undertaken, obligations assumed, cogent arguments presented, and so on. In the face of these counter-examples the temptation becomes overwhelming to reconstrue the terminology of the counter-examples in a 'descriptive' vein, to adopt the 'detached anthropological standpoint'. But the price of doing that is that words no longer mean what they mean and the price of a really consistent application of the 'detached anthropological standpoint' would be an end to all validity and entailment. The attempt to

[7] In spite of the fact that it was considered and answered in the original presentation. Cf. J. R. Searle, Paper XII above.

elude the counter-examples and repair the inconsistency by re-treating from the committed use of the words is motivated by the desire to cling to the thesis, come what may. But the retreat from the committed use of words ultimately must involve a retreat from language itself, for speaking a language – as has been the main theme of this book – consists of performing speech acts according to rules, and there is no separating those speech acts from the commitments which form essential parts of them.